Diversity, Equality, and Inclusion in Caribbean Organisations and Society

Jacqueline H. Stephenson · Natalie Persadie ·
Ann Marie Bissessar · Talia Esnard

Diversity, Equality, and Inclusion in Caribbean Organisations and Society

An Exploration of Work, Employment, Education, and the Law

Jacqueline H. Stephenson
University of the West Indies
St. Augustine, Trinidad and Tobago

Ann Marie Bissessar
University of the West Indies
St. Augustine, Trinidad and Tobago

Natalie Persadie
The University of Trinidad
and Tobago
Point Lisas, Trinidad and Tobago

Talia Esnard
University of the West Indies
St. Augustine, Trinidad and Tobago

ISBN 978-3-030-47613-7   ISBN 978-3-030-47614-4   (eBook)
https://doi.org/10.1007/978-3-030-47614-4

This Palgrave Macmillan imprint is published by the registered company Springer Nature
Switzerland AG
The registered company address is: Gewerbestrasse 11, 6330 Cham, Switzerland

FOREWORD

This book will focus on equality, inclusion and discrimination within the English-speaking Caribbean region, specifically as it relates to employment, education, society and the law. Within extant literature, discrimination has been examined primarily from the perspective of industrialised nations. This book is the first of its kind to comprehensively assess equality and inclusion within the Caribbean region.

One of the primary reasons for a lack of diversity and inclusion within contemporary organisations is the perpetuation of discrimination within society. This can be explained (in part) through the framework of the theory of social categorisation, where individuals categorise others into groups with the objective of identifying those who are similar to and/or different from themselves (Wenzel 2004) and hence those with whom they anticipate successful work and other relationships (Kurzban, Tooby and Cosmides 2001).

Discrimination (which is the treatment of one person less favourably than another) has been referred to as the behavioural manifestation of stigma (Thornicroft, Rose, Kassam and Sartorius 2007; Thornicroft, Brohan, Kassam and Lewis-Holmes 2008). The application of disparate treatment to organisational members as a consequence of fear, ignorance or acceptance of prejudicial stereotypes, could lead to the exclusion of suitable candidates for employment, promotion, training or retention within workplaces (Kirton and Greene 2000). This approach to the supervision or management of human resources invariably leads to workers of similar backgrounds being considered homogenous rather than as individuals with varying levels of skills and competence (Duncan 2003; Taylor and Walker 1998). It has been suggested (Woodhams, Lupton and Cowling 2015), that continuous use of discriminatory practices could have a multiplier effect in many areas of the economy and by extension the wider society. This in turn could be manifested through lack of economic growth, reduced tax revenues and increases in public expenditure—for example in relation to increased income support required (McGuire and Roberson 2007; Neumark 2009).

Across the Commonwealth Caribbean, the Constitution provides for an entitlement to equal treatment for all citizens. More specifically, within the region, there are three island states which have enacted legislation with the explicit purpose of prohibiting discrimination on the basis of specified grounds and promoting equality. These islands are Guyana (Prevention of Discrimination Act 1999), St. Lucia (Equality of Opportunity and Treatment in Employment and Occupation Act 2000) and Trinidad and Tobago (Equal Opportunity Act 2000). While the specific grounds of discrimination prohibited by these Acts vary, the commonly covered areas are: sex, race, religion, ethnic origin, marital status and disability. Notably, within the Caribbean region, sexual orientation has been excluded from the enacted equality legislation.

The current iteration of the equality discourse, is focused on the concept of managing diversity, where organisations are encouraged to strengthen their workforce and competitive advantage by employing people who are different from the status quo. Further, it advocates inclusivity and embracing the skills and talents of different types of employees (Thomas 1990), which may involve changing workplace policies and practices such that there are no exclusions (intentional or unintentional), by reason of an employee's immutable characteristics (for example, age, sex, race). It has been argued that even though the language used in relation to equality is continuously updated, the changes are variations in emphasis, rather than paradigm shifts (Oswick et al. 2010). This is to say that the underlying premise remains unchanged, i.e. the achievement of equity and fairness in employment (Liff 1999).

Though anti-discrimination law has been enacted in the Caribbean, this, in and of itself, neither translates to societal changes nor changes within the organisational context. Within the context of society and related organisations and institutions, the directive of the law is only one factor which contributes to the facilitation of change. Some of the leading drivers for organisational diversity and inclusion have been identified as legal pressures, the need to recruit and retain the best talent, social responsibility, potential business benefits, moral arguments and the pursuit of social justice (CIPD 2007). Moreover, the realisation of desired changes may necessitate challenging the veracity of accepted stereotypes by showing that they are flawed, and as such people should be treated fairly, irrespective of their membership in a minority group. In addition, it has been suggested (Hornstein 2001) that the efficacy of anti-discrimination legislation, in other jurisdictions, has been assisted by simultaneously promoting equal rights and enhancing the education of both employers and employees in relation to their rights and obligations as well as rigorous enforcement of the law. It may be argued that within society, change will only occur where there is a clear and obvious reason; where political and societal leaders embrace the proposed changes and norms are updated which are congruent with the changing dynamics of the society.

Where discrimination has been institutionalised in a society or an organisation, prejudicial patterns of employment practice may be followed without question, as a result of expectations within the workplace (Renskin 2000). Indeed the existence of widespread discrimination within society (Banaji 1999) may make it more challenging for changes to be made to attitudes and practices within the organisational context or other social institutions.

In this text the authors will examine:

i) Race Relations in the Caribbean: The Myth of Representative Bureaucracy

ii) Equality and Discrimination on the Basis of Sex

iii) Sexual Orientation and Inclusivity in the Caribbean Region

iv) Disability: Disparate Treatment or Inclusion in Caribbean Organisations

v) Politics and Inclusivity in the Caribbean

vi) Equality and the Law: A Caribbean Perspective

vii) Equality Laws Compared: The Caribbean, the UK and the USA

viii) Liberalisation of Higher Education in the Caribbean: Situating Matters of Access, Diversity and Equity

ix) The Challenge of Equity, Diversity and Inclusion Within Educational Reform: The Case of Trinidad and Tobago

John LaGuerre
Professor Emeritus
University of the West Indies
St. Augustine, Trinidad and Tobago

REFERENCES

Banaji, M. R. (1999). *The roots of prejudice*. Greensboro, NC: Kendon Smith Lectures, University of North Carolina.

CIPD. (2007). *Diversity in business—A focus for progress, survey report March 2007*. London: Chartered Institute of Personnel and Development (CIPD).

Duncan, C. (2003). Assessing Anti-Ageism Routes to older worker re-engagement. *Work, Employment and Society, 17*(1), 101–120.

Equal Opportunity Act. (2000). Trinidad & Tobago.

Equality of Opportunity and Treatment in Employment and Occupation Act, 2000—St. Lucia.

Hornstein, Z. (Ed.). (2001). *Outlawing age discrimination: Foreign lessons, UK choices*. Bristol: Policy Press.

Kirton, G., & Greene, A. M. (2000). *The dynamics of managing diversity*. Oxford: Butterworth Heinemann.

Kurzban, R., Tooby, J., & Cosmides, L. (2001). Can race be erased? Coalitional computation and social categorization. *Proceedings of the National Academy of Sciences, 98*(26), 15387–15392.

Liff, S. (1999). Diversity and equal opportunities: Room for a constructive compromise? *Human Resource Management Journal, 9*(1), 65–75.

McGuire, S., & Roberson, M. (2007). Assessing the potential impact of the introduction of age discrimination legislation in UK firms from an HRM and JKM perspective. In *Proceedings of Organizational Learning, Knowledge and Capabilities Conference (OLKC), 2007—Learning Fusion*.

Neumark, D. (2009). The age discrimination in employment act and the challenge of population aging. *Research on Aging, 31*(1), 41–68.

Oswick, C., Grant, D., Marshak, R. J., & Wolfram Cox, J. (2010). Organizational discourse and change: Positions, perspectives, progress and prospects. *Journal of Applied Behavioral Science, 46*(1), 8–15.

Prevention of Discrimination Act. (1999). Guyana.

Renskin, B. F. (2000). The proximate causes of employment discrimination. *Contemporary Sociology, 29*, 319–328.

Taylor, P., & Walker, A. (1998). Policies and practices towards older workers: A framework for comparative research. *Human Resource Management Journal, 8*(3), 61–76.

Thomas, R. R. (1990). From affirmative action to affirming diversity. *Harvard Business Review*. March–April, 107–117.

Thornicroft, G., Brohan, E., Kassam, A., & Lewis-Holmes, E. (2008). Reducing stigma and discrimination: Candidate interventions. *International Journal of Mental Health Systems, 2*(1), 3.

Thornicroft, G., Rose, D., Kassam, A., & Sartorius, N. (2007). Stigma: Ignorance, prejudice or discrimination? *The British Journal of Psychiatry, 190*(3), 192–193.

Wenzel, M. (2004). A social categorisation approach to distributive justice. *European Review of Social Psychology, 15*(1), 219–257.

Woodhams, C., Lupton, B., & Cowling, M. (2015). The presence of ethnic minority and disabled men in feminised work: Intersectionality, vertical segregation and the glass escalator. *Sex Roles, 72*(7–8), 277–293.

CONTENTS

LIST OF TABLES

CHAPTER 1

Introduction

The Anglophone Caribbean is an archipelago of former colonies of the United Kingdom (UK), which gained independence during the 1960s and 1970s. These islands include Antigua and Barbuda, the Bahamas, Barbados, Belize, Dominica, Grenada, Jamaica, St. Kitts and Nevis, St. Lucia, St. Vincent and the Grenadines, and Trinidad and Tobago. These populations vary in size from 52,441 (St. Kitts and Nevis) to 2,890,299 (Jamaica), according to the most recent census data (i.e. 2000–2001). The economies in the Caribbean region rely largely on tourism, oil and gas, manufacturing, agriculture, financial services and, in the main, are stable. These island states are considered variously as the third world or developing countries but are generally economies managed by qualified individuals with stable political governance and limited political unrest.

Despite being a collection of individual islands, governed by separate independent governments, the Caribbean region is often regarded as homogeneous, however, although the English-speaking islands are collectively referred to as the Commonwealth Caribbean, there is a widespread diversity across the island chain. Diversity may be broadly categorised as either surface- or deep-level diversity. Surface-level diversity refers to observable personal attributes such as sex, age, race *inter alia*, while deep-level diversity refers to less observable characteristics including one's beliefs, values, attitudes and culture *inter alia* (Barak 2016; Phillips and Loyd 2006; Roberson 2019). Within these groups there are several points of departure particularly with respect to differences

© The Author(s) 2020
J. H. Stephenson et al., *Diversity, Equality,
and Inclusion in Caribbean Organisations and Society*,
https://doi.org/10.1007/978-3-030-47614-4_1

in age, sex, race, culture, socialisation and education, which are evident globally and by extension in the Caribbean region. Currently, there is a paucity of literature in relation to equality, diversity and inclusion with a focus on the English-speaking Caribbean (see Stephenson and Persadie 2019), hence the objective of this book is to critically assess whether, and the extent to which, these issues are practically and theoretically relevant, in respect of work, education, employment and society. *To wit*, this text examines diversity, discrimination, inclusion and exclusion, on the basis of sex, race, sexual orientation and disability, in relation to employment, education, politics and applicable legal and societal systems, in the Caribbean.

The debate concerning equal opportunities and non-discrimination is said to have evolved over time, from simply considering equality from a radical or liberal perspective (Jewson and Mason 1986), to enveloping new concepts, namely managing diversity accepting differences and inclusion (Kirton and Greene 2006). The three primary categories of equality are: equality of results, treatment/opportunity and consistency (Jewson and Mason 1986). It has been suggested that pursuing equality, with a view of treating everyone the same could be an "*oversimplification of the problem*". This is because treating everyone the same could result in disadvantage, where for example within the organisational context, all employees are given access to the same printed employee manual. Although this may appear, *prima facie*, as an attempt to treat everyone the same, employees who are visually impaired would be unable to access the information in the manual, unless it is converted into braille or they are permitted to use specially designed software in order to access it. Such occurrences are observed in the workplace daily and this contributes to the failure of some equal opportunity initiatives (Liff and Wajcman 1996). Moreover, there is an absence of irrefutable evidence to support any assertion that equal treatment approaches have resulted only in benefits in relation to equality; in part, this is because acceptance of stereotypes appear to create some difficulty for organisational managers to conceptualise job requirements in neutral terms (Collinson et al. 1990; Curran 1988). An alternative approach to equality of treatment is to find a way to value and utilise employee differences. This is the *managing diversity* approach where organisations are encouraged to strengthen their workforce and competitive advantage by employing different people from those already in the workforce. This approach challenges the equal treatment model suggesting that people do not necessarily wish to be treated the same in every aspect of their working life but, by offering different working arrangements or benefits, employers facilitating the diversity approach may realise greater benefits within their workplaces, relative to those pursuing equality (Liff and Wajcman 1996). Managing diversity encourages a focus on inclusivity and embracing the skills and talents of different types of employees (Thomas 1990), which may involve changing workplace policies and practices such that there are no exclusions (intentional or unintentional) based on an employee's immutable characteristics (i.e. age, sex, race, etc.). It has been argued that even though the language being used in relation to equality is continuously being updated, the changes are variations in emphasis, rather than paradigm shifts (Oswick et al. 2010). Otherwise stated, the underlying premise remains unchanged, i.e. the achievement of equity and fairness (Liff 1999).

One of the prevailing objectives in this ongoing discourse is the reduction and/or elimination of discrimination. Discrimination is said to occur when one person is treated less favorably than another, typically on the basis of immutable characteristics (Dipboye and Colella 2013). Discrimination in the Caribbean is prevalent primarily on the grounds of race, sexual orientation, sex and disability. As it relates to *race*, given the history of enslavement and indentured servitude within the region, there remains some latent hostilities among racial groups which comprise the populace (Bissessar 2002; Chadee 2003), which in turn gives rise on occasion, to discrimination on the basis of race, particularly between racial groups (primarily persons of African and Indian descent). Moreover, with buggery laws still in place in many Caribbean islands, a remnant of colonial rule, discrimination is rife against persons with an other than heterosexual *orientation*, i.e. members of the Lesbian, Gay, Bisexual, Transgender and Queer (LGBTQ) community. This is further reinforced by the extent to which deterrent punitive measures are embedded in relevant legislation, prevailing cultural norms, and religious beliefs, which dictate expected and accepted sexual behavior, such that any deviation is opposed and rejected without due consideration (CADRES 2013a, b, c). Further, discrimination on the grounds of *sex* is manifested within society with men and women expected to perform certain roles in the home, workplace and society more broadly. For women, disparate treatment can have an adverse effect on their ability to obtain and retain desirable full employment, their remuneration, development and career progression (Bissessar 2014; Esnard et al. 2015; Mahabir and Ramrattan 2015). Within the Caribbean region, for persons of working age, having a disability may prove challenging when trying to secure employment; this is in part due to the acceptance of stereotypes by employers as it relates to persons with disabilities (PWD) and their capabilities. Such disparate treatment is also evident within wider society as persons with disabilities experience less inclusion, and social satisfaction as a result of their treatment and perception by the populace, as a homogeneous group with significant limitations which prohibit their involvement and potential contribution. Moreover, when compared with other grounds of discrimination such as age, race, sex, members of these marginalised groups have been associated with advantages to society and employment unlike persons with disabilities (Woodhams and Danieli 2000).

One of the primary reasons for discrimination, a lack of diversity and inclusion within contemporary societies is the acceptance of stereotypes, particularly as it relates to groups of persons with whom individuals are not familiar. Further, it has been argued that stereotypes are used as heuristics, when individuals are unable (and/or unwilling) to apply more comprehensive and analytical methods (Chiu et al. 2001; McGregor and Gray 2002). In the workplace context, willingness by employers to accept negative stereotypes can affect the ability of a worker to find and retain gainful employment (Renskin 2000), which may impact the extent to which they are able to be actively engaged in the labor force. Nonetheless, the discussion above should not be taken to mean that stereotypes are the only reason for the perpetuation of discrimination; indeed, discrimination may also be based on animus, lack of knowledge about the target group; divergent perceptions, the adoption of a prejudicial pattern of practice which is followed without question; and as a result of cultural expectations (Kirton and Greene 2006; Renskin 2000). Discrimination can also occur as a rational outcome of economic analyses made about the potential contribution and productivity of workers based on their characteristics (Gandy 2010; Harcourt et al. 2005; Smith and Moore 2010).

Traditionally, jurisdictions may take action to address inequality and discrimination by enacting equality legislation, establishing diversity policies, promoting diversity initiatives, facilitating cultural change, pursuing moral suasion or pursuing a combination of these measures. Globally, these approaches have had varying degrees of success, as it relates to eliminating or reducing existing exclusionary and/or discriminatory policies and practices. This is evident in developed countries including (*but not limited to*) the UK, Canada and the USA, where, although equality and anti-discrimination legislation and non-legislative measures have been established since the 1960s and 1970s, marginalised groups continue to experience inequality and disparate treatment (though their reported incidence has declined). Notwithstanding this, such measures are vital, as legislation, for example, provides guidance by outlining legal prohibitions and raising the profile of the ethical and moral problems of discrimination and exclusion, and contributes to the reduction in targeted and unfavorable attitudes and behavior against marginalised societal groups (Bennington and Wein 2000).

It may be argued that the limited impact of these legal measures may be attributed to the comparatively non-litigious nature of the Caribbean region, relative to that of developed countries; lack of awareness by the Caribbean populace of their legal rights; unwillingness by them to make complaints and/or file claims; perceived length of the process; and lack of support for actions which may be necessary to see the process through to its logical conclusion. In enacting legislation to outlaw discrimination, where change is desired beyond that which is superficial, it is important for legislators to acknowledge the role of attitudes and the influence and complex nature of societal culture. Failure to do so could mean that the response to established legal measures intended to eliminate discriminatory practices is likely to be sluggish (Dickens 2005; Loretto and White 2006). However, where there is fear of the imposition of punitive measures, legislative compliance appears to be more readily observed (Dickens 1999; Taylor and Walker 1998). Further, legal protection offered by anti-discrimination legislation, may have an unintended discriminatory effect in respect of employment, education and the provision of goods and services, such that individuals are not hired; offered places within educational institutions; or allowed access to goods and services, because of fears on the part of relevant institutions, that any action taken (in relation to members of marginalised groups), could result in legal action, if perceived to be discriminatory, even where it is not. For example, where a person with a disability is justifiably terminated due to insubordination, misconduct, unacceptable behaviour which violate the workplace's policies and/or subpar performance, organisations may fear that although the reasons for termination are legitimate and unrelated to the employee's disability, that this may be used to support their claim of discrimination or wrongful dismissal, thus adversely affecting the organisation and its reputation, even where the organisation is ultimately found by the courts and/or employment tribunals to be justified in their action. Organisations are one of the key stakeholders in the economies of the region, hence, where discrimination is widespread, this could result in unemployment or underemployment, which could mean that displaced individuals will rely on state payments which in turn could have an adverse effect on the sustainability of the islands' economies.

Where the extant culture is such that stereotypes are accepted, there is no evidence to suggest that anti-discrimination legislation has been effective in resulting in immediate, in-depth and sustained changes towards inclusion or non-discrimination. In fact, prevailing societal and organisational culture has often developed over time and has become institutionalised, thus change requires the commitment of relevant stakeholders but, even with this, change cannot be expected to occur immediately and without resistance. The passage of this type of legislation is likely to result in the diminution of blatant discriminatory practices and policies, however, those policies and practices which represent indirect discrimination, and as such are more latent are likely to continue to be perpetuated. In short, change, where it is required by legislation is likely to be incremental.

Turning to other influential change drivers, where organisations are motivated by the objective of being as fair as possible to all employees (Dickens 1999; Kirton and Greene 2006), the pursuit of *social justice* could be influential in the policies and changes within the workplace (CIPD 2007). Finally, a desire to follow the *business case* approach may lead to changes in employment practice where employers are motivated to make changes to practice, which would be beneficial to their workplace, *as for example*, where it results in increased productivity or increased profitability (CIPD 2007, 2018; Dickens 1994). These potential change drivers are not mutually exclusive and may be most effective when applied together. Indeed, Dickens (2007) advanced the notion of a three-pronged approach where the elements of the business case, legal regulation and social regulation are most likely to effectively address issues of discrimination.

As it relates to the organisational context, the business case benefits of inclusion and non-discrimination may include: increased profitability, offsetting labour and skill shortages (since a diverse workforce reflects the composition in society and consequently the goods and/or services produced by the workplace are likely to have greater appeal to a wider cross-section of society); a diverse workplace could mean a greater level of innovation and ideas (Kochan et al. 2003; Subeliani and Tsogas 2005). Moreover, it has been contended that discrimination is largely irrational thus, when workplaces realise this they will cease to discriminate and abandon their exclusionary practices, in favour of non-discrimination and the potential for business benefits (Gandy 2010; Rubenstein 1987). However, this simplistic and somewhat idealistic view has been challenged and its legitimacy is the subject of debate (Bendick et al. 1991; Hayles and Mendez 1997), not least because of the absence of tangible evidence to support such an assertion. It has been further suggested that the point of departure as to whether workplaces are likely to realise benefits is dependent on the environment in which the workplace functions (Herring 2009; Kochan et al. 2003). This may consist of the culture of the workplace, the commitment of management to non-discrimination, the way in which non-discriminatory practices are implemented and the composition of the workforce, as well as external influences which may include the competitive nature of the sector in which the workplace functions.

Across the islands of the Commonwealth Caribbean, the Constitutions of each jurisdiction provides for an entitlement to equal treatment for all citizens. More specifically, within the region, there are three island states which have enacted legislation with the explicit purpose of promoting equality and prohibiting discrimination on the basis of specified grounds. These islands are *Guyana* (Prevention of Discrimination Act 1999), *St. Lucia* (Equality of Opportunity and Treatment in Employment and Occupation Act 2000) and *Trinidad and Tobago* (Equal Opportunity Act 2000). Moreover, several Caribbean island states are signatories to international equality conventions, including the International Labour Organisation's (ILO) C111—Discrimination (Employment and Occupation) Convention, 1958 (No. 111); the ILO's Equal Remuneration Convention, 1951 (No. 100); the United Nations Convention on the Elimination of All Forms of Discrimination against Women, 1979; and the United Nations Convention on the rights of Persons with Disabilities, 2006. While the specific grounds of discrimination prohibited by the indicated Acts vary, the commonly covered areas are: sex, race, religion, ethnic origin, marital status, origin and disability. Notably, within the Caribbean region, sexual orientation has been excluded from enacted equality legislation and, in many island states, most notably (to date) with the exception of Belize and the Bahamas, same-sex sexual conduct is illegal.

Notwithstanding the limited passage of non-discrimination legislation, inequalities and disparate treatment continue to prevail within
the Caribbean region. There is no legislative obligation to treat members of marginalised groups more favourably, with the intent of improving their outcomes, as this would necessitate *positive discrimination*,
which is not permitted within the Caribbean region's legislative model.
Moreover, a legislative obligation of non-discrimination simply means
the imposition of an obligation on the populace (and relevant societal
stakeholders) not to discriminate, but this has not been extended to a
requirement to treat each individual fairly, such that there is equality
of opportunity and equality of outcome, across the board. This would
arguably require (particularly where there is cause for concern) more
rigorous and comprehensive attention to policy, changes to practice and
monitoring and enforcement of the workplace to ensure that the principles of equality continue to be upheld. Nevertheless, the enactment of
anti-discrimination legislation in the region is important to ensure: (i) an
awareness of discriminatory practices which are considered unacceptable;
and (ii) the establishment of a legal framework to offer recourse to any-
one against whom acts of discrimination have been perpetrated.

This book is important at this time because there is a paucity of literature on issues of discrimination, inclusion and diversity in the Caribbean
region and, where such publications exist, they give only cursory consideration to theoretical applications. Further, due to the recent and
limited enactment of anti-discrimination legislation in the Caribbean,
there is limited extant literature which assesses the way in which the law
has been applied to filed discrimination cases, and the extent to which
it has been effective in addressing disparate treatment for those groups
specifically protected therein. This book also establishes a benchmark for
future researchers, who may explore further the issues of discrimination
and its effect on the populace. Legislators and policy makers may wish
to consider the analysis within this text in making legislative amendments or enacting new laws, with a view to broaden the range of persons protected as it relates particularly to sexual orientation. In addition,
organisational practitioners may find these discussions useful, where current policies and/or practices are shown to be unlikely to further their
organisation objective vis-à-vis productivity and sustainability. This discussion is important as there is limited available literature as it relates to
discrimination, diversity, inclusion and equality in the Caribbean region
and, much of what is accepted as representative of reality, is based on

anecdotal evidence. Insights may be gleaned from the experiences and outcomes of international jurisdictions where anti-discrimination legislation has been enacted for significant periods of time. As an existing issue within the Caribbean region, this text offers a timely catalyst through which these important issues may be discussed and understood. It also facilitates opportunities to consider amendments and policy directives and expands the extant literature on these significant issues. This book may therefore be a useful reference text for undergraduate and postgraduate students, organisational practitioners, societal groups, political and community leaders. It offers empirical data and rigorously reviewed literature and critical analyses of the issues of equality, diversity and inclusion in the Caribbean.

The chapters in this volume are as follows: This first chapter introduced the concepts of equality, discrimination and diversity, and offered an overview of the relevant practices in the Caribbean region in key areas within society. In Chapter 2, relationships between members of those racial groups represented in the region are evaluated, as it relates to effectively managing racial segregation in Guyana and Trinidad and Tobago. This is followed by Chapter 3 where equality and discrimination on the basis of sex in the Caribbean is assessed, specifically as it relates to employment, salient issues such as pay equality, opportunities for promotion and development and recruitment are primarily considered. Chapter 4, which follows, critically analyses the history and current status of sexual orientation and inclusivity in the Commonwealth Caribbean. Included here is an analysis of the type of discrimination faced by members of the LGBTQ community, the legal protections to which members of the group have access and the consequences on this community and society more broadly as a result of their exclusion. Chapter 5 then discusses persons with disabilities and their experiences within Caribbean organisations, their access to gainful employment, the prevailing stereotypes with respect to persons with disabilities and accommodations made for persons with disabilities in organisations. Chapter 6 examines the extent to which the political structure and systems in Trinidad and Tobago and Guyana facilitate inclusion of different societal groups. This is followed by Chapter 7, which presents an overview of the equality laws that exist in this region, based on existing statute that provides for equality in a broad manner as well as statutory provisions that address equality or non-discrimination for employment purposes. This is complemented by a review of applicable case law which illustrates how the law has been applied. Chapter 8 then facilitates a comparison of the equality laws in the region with legislation from selected developed countries as it relates to their overarching and key principles and offers some insight to legislators, practitioners and government officials as to how equality laws in the Caribbean may be improved to make them more effective. After this, Chapter 9 critically discusses the meanings/constructions, policy leanings or strategies, and challenges associated with advancing inclusive agendas within the education system of Trinidad and Tobago. This chapter also analyses global educational trends, the associated challenges and nuanced ways in which these complicate and influence equity and diversity within the Caribbean region. Following this is Chapter 10 which critically analyses changing educational landscapes, and how these collide and intensify contextual concerns, and complicate the call for promoting equity, diversity and social inclusion within the Caribbean region. The final Chapter 11 concludes the text by evaluating key findings from each of the preceding chapters as it relates to diversity, equality, discrimination and inclusion in the island states of the Caribbean region.

REFERENCES

Barak, M. E. M. (2016). *Managing diversity: Toward a globally inclusive workplace*. Thousand Oaks, CA: Sage.

Bendick, M., Jackson, C. W., Reinoso, V. A., & Hodges, L. A. (1991). Discrimination against Latino job applicants: A controlled experiment. *Human Resource Management, 30*(4), 469–484.

Bennington, L., & Wein, R. (2000). Anti-discrimination legislation in Australia: Fair, effective, efficient or irrelevant? *International Journal of Manpower, 21*(1), 21–33.

Bissessar, A. M. (2002). Addressing ethnic imbalances in the public services of plural societies: The case of Guyana and Trinidad and Tobago. *International Journal of Public Sector Management, 15*(1), 55–68.

Bissessar, A. M. (2014). Challenges to women's leadership in ex-colonial societies. *International Journal of Gender and Women's Studies, 2*(3), 13–35.

Caribbean Development Research Services (CADRES). (2013a). *Attitudes towards homosexuals in Barbados (2013)*. Barbados: Caribbean Development Research Services.

Caribbean Development Research Services (CADRES). (2013b). *Attitudes towards homosexuals in Guyana (2013)*. Barbados: Caribbean Development Research Services.

Caribbean Development Research Services (CADRES). (2013c). *Attitudes towards homosexuals in Trinidad and Tobago (2013)*. Barbados: Caribbean Development Research Services.

Chadee, D. (2003). Fear of crime and risk of victimization: An ethnic comparison. *Social and economic studies, 52*, 73–97.

Chiu, W. C. K., Chan, W., Snape, E., & Redman, T. (2001). Age stereotypes and discriminatory attitudes towards older Workers: An East-West comparison. *Human Relations, 54*(5), 629–661.

CIPD. (2007, March). *Diversity in business—A focus for progress* (Survey Report). Chartered Institute of Personnel and Development (CIPD).

CIPD. (2018, June). *Diversity and inclusion at work—Facing up to the business case* (Survey Report). Chartered Institute of Personnel and Development (CIPD).

Collinson, D. L., Knights, D., & Collinson, M. (1990). *Managing to discriminate*. London: Routledge.

Curran, M. (1988). Gender and recruitment: People and places in the labour market. *Work, Employment & Society, 2*(3), 335–351.

Dickens, L. (1994). The business case for women's equality: Is the carrot better than the stick? *Employee Relations, 16*(8), 5–18.

Dickens, L. (1999). Beyond the business case: A three-pronged approach to equality action. *Human Resource Management Journal, 9*(1), 9–19.

Dickens, L. (2005). Walking the talk? Equality and diversity in employment. In S. Bach (Ed.), *Managing human resources: Personnel management in transition* (4th ed., pp. 179–208). London: Blackwell.

Dickens, L. (2007). The road is long: Thirty years of equality legislation in Britain. *British Journal of Industrial Relations, 45*(3), 463–494.

Dipboye, R. L., & Colella, A. (Eds.). (2013). *Discrimination at work: The psychological and organizational bases*. New York: Psychology Press.

Equal Opportunity Act, 2000—Trinidad and Tobago.

Equality of Opportunity and Treatment in Employment and Occupation Act, 2000—St. Lucia.

Esnard, T., Cobb-Roberts, D., Agosto, V., Karanxha, Z., Beck, M., Wu, K., et al. (2015). Productive tensions in a cross-cultural peer mentoring women's network: A social capital perspective. *Mentoring & Tutoring: Partnership in Learning, 23*(1), 19–36.

Gandy, O. H. (2010). Engaging rational discrimination: Exploring reasons for placing regulatory constraints on decision support systems. *Ethics and Information Technology, 12*(1), 29–42.

Harcourt, M., Lam, H., & Harcourt, S. (2005). Discriminatory practices in hiring: Institutional and rational economic perspectives. *The International Journal of Human Resource Management, 16*(11), 2113–2132.

Hayles, R., & Mendez, R. A. (1997). *The diversity directive*. New York: McGraw Hill.

Herring, C. (2009). Does diversity pay?: Race, gender, and the business case for diversity. *American Sociological Review, 74*(2), 208–224.

Jewson, N., & Mason, D. (1986). The theory and practice of equal opportunities policies: Liberal and radical approaches. *The Sociological Review, 34*(2), 307–334.

Kirton, G., & Greene, A. M. (2006). The discourse of diversity in unionised contexts: Views from trade union equality officers. *Personnel Review, 35,* 431–448.

Kochan, T., Bezrukova, K., Ely, R., Jackson, S., Joshi, A., Jehn, K., et al. (2003). The effects of diversity on business performance: Report of the diversity research network. *Human Resource Management, 42,* 3–21.

Liff, S. (1999). Diversity and equal opportunities: Room for a constructive compromise? *Human Resource Management Journal, 9*(1), 65–75.

Liff, S., & Wajcman, J. (1996). Sameness and difference revisited—Which way forward for equal opportunity initiatives. *Journal of Management Studies, 33*(1), 79–94.

Loretto, W., & White, P. (2006). Employers' attitudes, practices and policies towards older workers. *Human Resource Management Journal, 16*(3), 313–330.

Mahabir, R., & Ramrattan, D. (2015). Influences on the gender wage gap of Trinidad and Tobago: An economic concept or a social construct? *World Journal of Entrepreneurship, Management and Sustainable Development, 11*(2), 140–151.

McGregor, J., & Gray, L. (2002). Stereotypes and older workers: The New Zealand experience. *Social Policy Journal of New Zealand, 18,* 163–177.

Oswick, C., Grant, D., Marshak, R. J., & Wolfram Cox, J. (2010). Organizational discourse and change: Positions, perspectives, progress and prospects. *Journal of Applied Behavioral Science, 46*(1), 8–15.

Phillips, K. W., & Loyd, D. L. (2006). When surface and deep-level diversity collide: The effects on dissenting group members. *Organizational Behavior and Human Decision Processes, 99*(2), 143–160.

Prevention of Discrimination Act, 1999—Guyana.

Renskin, B. F. (2000). The proximate causes of employment discrimination. *Contemporary Sociology, 29,* 319–328.

Roberson, Q. M. (2019). Diversity in the workplace: A review, synthesis, and future research agenda. *Annual Review of Organizational Psychology and Organizational Behavior, 6,* 69–88.

Rubenstein, M. (1987). Modern myths and misconceptions. *Equal Opportunities Review, 16*(Nov/Dec), 48.

Smith, V. K., & Moore, E. M. (2010). Behavioral economics and benefit cost analysis. *Environmental & Resource Economics, 46*(2), 217–234.

Stephenson, J., & Persadie, N. (2019). Anti-discrimination legislation in the Caribbean: Is everyone protected? *Equality, Diversity and Inclusion: an International Journal, 38*(7), 779–792.

Subeliani, D., & Tsogas, G. (2005). Managing diversity in the Netherlands: A case study of Rabobank. *The International Journal of Human Resource Management, 16*(5), 831–851.

Taylor, P., & Walker, A. (1998). Employers and older workers: Attitudes and employment practices. *Ageing & Society, 18*(6), 641–658.

Thomas, R. R. (1990, March–April). From affirmative action to affirming diversity. *Harvard Business Review, 68,* 107–117.

Woodhams, C., & Danieli, A. (2000). Disability and diversity-a difference too far? *Personnel Review, 29*(3), 402–417.

Race Relations in the Caribbean: The Myth of Representative Bureaucracy

INTRODUCTION

Trinidad and Tobago, a twin-island Republic is often classified as a model of a plural society. According to Furnival (1948), in a plural society each group maintained its own religion, culture and language, their own ideas and ways and met in the *market place*.[1] He argued that the dominance of one group by the other was the essential precondition for the maintenance of social and political order. In the case of Trinidad and Tobago, the two majority groups were East Indian and African descended populations who were imported to work on the plantations. Unlike a *true* plural society the two groups have adopted a common language (English); many to a large extent share religious beliefs,[2] and their children attend common schools both at the elementary, secondary and tertiary levels.[3] While there has been some measure of assimilation, yet,

---

[1] J. S. Furnival. *Netherland Indies.* London: Cambridge University Press.

[2] According to the 2011 Census, 33.4% of the population was Protestant (including 12.0% Pentecostal, 5.7% Anglican, 4.1% Seventh-day Adventist, 3.0% Presbyterian or Congregational, 1.2% Baptist and 0.1% Methodist), 21.5% was Roman Catholic, 14.1% was Hindu and 8% were Muslim. A small number of individuals subscribed to traditional Caribbean religions with African roots, such as the Spiritual Baptists (sometimes called Shouter Baptists) (5.7%); and the Orisha (0.1%). The smaller groups were Jehovah's Witnesses (1.5%) and unaffiliated (2.2%).

[3] There are of course denominational schools at these levels as well.

© The Author(s) 2020
J. H. Stephenson et al., *Diversity, Equality, and Inclusion in Caribbean Organisations and Society,*
https://doi.org/10.1007/978-3-030-47614-4_2

what the data seems to suggest is that ethnic considerations have led to polarisation at the political sphere and during the period 1962–1992 was also visible at the upper echelons of the public sector.[4] During the period 1992–2015, therefore, based on allegations of discrimination by groups, a number of mechanisms to allow for appeal and investigation was introduced via various Acts of Parliament. The extent to which these mechanisms allowed for greater inclusion will be accordingly examined.

Trinidad and Tobago is just one of a number of countries in the Commonwealth Caribbean which has been classified, because of ethnic variations among groups in these societies, as *plural societies*. While M. G. Smith (1965)[5] and R. T. Smith (1971)[6] focused on Jamaica and Burma and Java, respectively, later on theorist such as Despres (1964)[7] and La Guerre (1974)[8] expanded the discussion to include countries such as Suriname, Guyana and Trinidad in which two groups, namely Africans and East Indians were numerically represented. Indeed, the description of Furnivall's medley of ethnic groups which he met in Burma and Java, was also applicable in the context of these ex-colonial countries as well. R. T. Smith noted (in the case of Burma and Java):

> …. *They mix but they do not combine. Each group holds its own religion, its own culture and language, its own ideas and ways. As individuals they meet, but only in the market place, in buying and selling.*[9]

---

[4]Centre for Ethnic Studies. 1992. *Ethnicity and employment practices in Trinidad and Tobago*. Centre for Ethnic Studies: The University of the West Indies, St Augustine, Trinidad. In this report, the data revealed that the top positions in the public sector was mainly held by persons of African descent. After this report, further data re ethnic groups employed in the public sector have been forthcoming.

[5]Michael Garfield Smith. 1965. *The plural society in the British West Indies*. Berkeley: University of California Press.

[6]Raymond T. Smith. 1971. "Race and political conflict in Guyana." *Race and Class*, Vol. 12, No. 4: 415–427.

[7]Leo Despres. 1964 October. "The implications of nationalist politics in British Guiana for the development of cultural theory." *American Anthropologist*, Vol. 66, No. 5: 1051–1077.

[8]John Gaffar La Guerre. 1974. *Calcutta to Caroni: The East Indians of Trinidad*. School of Continuing Studies, Trinidad and Tobago, St Augustine.

[9]R. T. Smith (1971, p. 415).

To these theorists, the plural society was therefore an unstable society in which ethnic conflicts could erupt. Indeed, it should be recalled that ethnic conflicts are frequent occurrences in the developed as well as the developing countries. Regions such as Afghanistan, Angola, Armenia, India, Indonesia, Sri Lanka, Sudan, Bangladesh, Belgium, Northern Ireland and Rwanda have all been the focus of media attention because the breadth and depth of the ethnic conflicts that have occurred in these countries. Even in the more advanced countries such as the USA, the UK and Canada, however, it is found that increasing ethnic conflicts are replacing what was formerly classified as class struggles.

Because of the nature and depths of ethnic conflicts which have emerged, policymakers have increasingly sought mechanisms to allay such conflicts and a number of techniques have been introduced. These include ethnic reconciliation, ethnic separation and ethnic re-engineering. While these mechanisms were introduced to aid with a broader assimilation process or the attempt to encourage nationalism, it was understood that while government had power to redistribute resources, as well as to re-stratify a society, politics involves a complex interaction between groups, institutions, ideologies and values. One of the more critical institutions in this interaction, of course, was the public sector. Accordingly, given the importance of this institution, a number of administrative "solutions" were also required as well. These included the use of quota systems and affirmative action programmes to allow for a more "representative" bureaucracy. This paper will accordingly focus on the mechanisms to allow for inclusiveness of the various groups in the public sector of a small island state, Trinidad and Tobago. It will attempt to evaluate these mechanisms.

Summary Overview of the Theory of Representative Bureaucracy

The concept of a more representative-type bureaucracy, it should be noted, is an old debate commencing with the work of Donald Kingsley (1944).[10] He suggested that civil service should be represented according to economic class, region and religion. Later theorists

---

[10]Donald Kingsley. 1944. *Representative bureaucracy.* Yellow Springs, OH: Antioch Press.

elaborated on this concept (Van Riper 1958; Kelsall 1955; Long 1952; Subramaniam 1967; Dauda 1990).[11] Essentially the concept of a more representative-type of bureaucracy suggests that if a public service mirrors the social demographics of the entire population it would lead as Agyapong (2018)[12] observed to active representation where bureaucrats press the interest of groups with whom they share similar identities. The fundamental assumption was that individuals who shared similar social origins or demographics would also share similar socialisation experiences. These experiences could then lead to the formation of similar values/attitudes that could influence bureaucratic behaviour. As Evans (1974)[13] had to point out, however, the arguments concerning representation were best viewed as arguments which related to purpose, function and effectiveness of the representative body, not the composition.

Yet, even in its early initiation, it was clear that Kingsley's (1944) argument for representation did not translate into a representation in the bureaucracy of the wider groups of the society. Rather he asserted that if an administration is to be responsive to changes in the political climate, it must represent the dominant class in the society. He argued that a bureaucracy may be "responsible" when it broadly reflects society but that it is "representative" when leaders of the governing party and senior bureaucrats share similar backgrounds and values (Kingsley 1944, p. 185). According to Kim (1994),[14] Kingsley's emphasis was on the

[11] P. Van Riper. 1958. *History of the United States Civil Service.* Evanston, IL: Row Peterson. R. K. Kelsall. 1955. *Higher Civil servants in Britain.* London: Routledge and Keagan Paul. N. E. Long. 1958. "Implementing equal opportunities in the 1980s: An overview" *Public Administration*, Vol. 67: 7–18. V. Subramaniam. 1967. "Representative bureaucracy: A reassessment." *The American Political Science Review*, Vol. LXI, No. 4: 1010–1019. Bhola Dauda. 1990. "Fallacies and dilemmas: The theory of representative bureaucracy with a particular reference to the Nigerian Public Service 1950–1986." *International Review of Administrative Sciences*, Vol. 56: 467–495.

[12] Elijah Agyapong. 2018. Critical assessment of representative bureaucracy: Toward a more expanded theory. https://patimes.org/a-critical-assessment-of-representative-bureaucracy-toward-a-more-expanded-theory/.

[13] Defining Representative Bureaucracy Author(s): James W. Evans Source: *Public Administration Review*, Vol. 34, No. 6 (November–December, 1974), pp. 628–631. Published by: Wiley on behalf of the American Society for Public Administration Stable URL: https://www.jstor.org/stable/974367. Accessed: 21 March 2019, 14:27 UTC.

[14] Pan S. Kim. 1994. "A theoretical overview of representative bureaucracy: Synthesis." *International Review of Administrative Sciences*, Vol. 60: 385–397, 386.

representation of dominant upper middle-class of British society rather than of the society as a whole. In other words, Kingsley's argument was not that the public bureaucracy should be a microcosm of the wider society but rather that the bureaucracy would reflect the "ideals" and translate those into policy that would be beneficial for the nation's elites.

The concept of "representation" was further expanded by Long in 1952.[15] Contrary to Kingley's argument, Long (1952), in the case of the USA felt that the federal bureaucracy was more diverse demographically and therefore was more representative of the people. This was further supported by Van Riper (1958).[16] He contended that a "genuinely" representative bureaucracy must be:

i. A reasonable cross-section of the body politic in terms of occupation, class, geography and the like;
ii. Be in tune to the ethos and attitudes of the society of which it is a part (Van Riper 1958, p. 552). According to Van Riper, a representative bureaucracy was one in which there was a minimal distinction between the bureaucracy as a group and their administrative behaviour on the one hand and the community or societal membership and its administrative behaviour of government on the other (Kim, p. 386).

Following on this, Mosher (1968),[17] deepened the argument suggesting that bureaucratic decisions are influenced by the orientations and values of administrators. In turn, the values held by the administrator are, in turn, determined by his or her social background, training, education and current associations. He noted:

A public service and more specifically the leadership personnel of a public service which is broadly representative of all categories of the population in these respects, may be thought of as satisfying Lincoln's prescription of government 'by the people' in the limited sense. (Mosher 1968, pp. 12–13)

[15] Norton Long, 1952. "Bureaucracy and constitutionalism." *American Political Science Review*, Vol. 46: 808–818.

[16] Paul P. Van Riper. 1958. *History of the United States Civil Service*. Evanston, IL: Row Peterson.

[17] Frederick C. Mosher. 1968. *Democracy and the public service*. New York: Oxford University Press.

Emerging out of the analysis of the arguments for representative bureau-cracy, Kim (1994) suggested that this could be summed up as a relation-ship between passive and active approaches to representation. Essentially, the passive approach is largely based on demography and its goal is a bureaucracy that mirrors society as a whole with proportional numbers of members from each economic class, region and ethnic group. On the other hand, the active approach places emphasis on legislation or policy on behalf of social groups regardless of the backgrounds of individual civil servants.

In many countries around the world the challenge to introduce greater representation of groups in the workplace have led to a number of introductions, which to a large extent seem to lean on the "active" approach to representation. These mechanisms range from affirmative action policies or the establishment of quota systems. In some countries, also, legal measures were introduced such as instruments allowing for the establishment of an Equal Opportunity Commission and an Equal Opportunity Tribunal.

In the case of Trinidad and Tobago, the latter mechanism was intro-duced. The discussion which follows will accordingly present a historical overview of the challenges of ethnic under-representation in the public sector of the twin-island republic and later discuss as well as assess the mechanisms which were introduced to allow for equal distribution of groups in this sector.

ADDRESSING ETHNIC IMBALANCES IN THE PUBLIC SECTOR OF TRINIDAD AND TOBAGO AND THE SEARCH FOR MECHANISMS

Trinidad and Tobago is a small country with a population of approxi-mately 1.3 million persons. The two majority groups within the coun-try are descendants of East Indian indentured labourers who were brought from India and an African descended population whose forbears were slaves who were imported to work on the plantations. It has been contended that the seeds of discord among the two eth-nic groups were partly sown by the British, who with their politics of divide and rule, pitted these groups against each other (Hitzen 1994[18];

---

[18] Percy Hitzen. 1994. "The colonial foundations of race relations and Ethno-politics in Guyana." *Guyana History Gazzette*, No. 65.

Brown 1999[19]). In addition, factors including the historically developed complex of rules, routines and institutional arrangements were also influential in creating what over time became a "clash of culture" among the two majority groups. The East Indians who were an essentially agrarian group settled in the rural areas while the Africans who were skilled and semi-skilled professionals settled in the urban areas. Apart from the occupational and settlement patterns, however, there were also major cultural differences between the two groups.

While under British rule, there was a measure of distrust among these groups, yet this was contained since the "enemy" to be feared and respected was the largely white British elite. However, as the colonies prepared for independence in the 1960s, the animosity between the two groups increased. As Despres (1967)[20] and Ryan (1972)[21] suggested, political mobilisation for electoral purposes appealed to the primordial instincts of both groups. Partly, too, it can be argued, the spoils of the country such as housing, resources and other opportunities could be distributed to the membership of the group that attained political power. Thus, understandably, political rivalry between the two groups was intense and as Brown (1999, p. 6) appropriately described it, became decisively rooted in ethnic cleavages. Prior to the General Elections of 1962, then, there were a number of outbreaks of ethnic violence as the two majority groups fought for the control of the state. La Guerre's (1993, p. 18)[22] interpretation of this situation was that along with race relations, there was also a challenge with respect to the dominance of one group and unequal incorporation of the other.

What emerged as a run-up to the 1961 elections in Trinidad and Tobago was that while a number of splintered groups and individuals contested the General Elections yet the two major protagonists were the

[19] Derek Brown. 1999. *Ethnic politics and public sector management in Trinidad and Guyana*. Paper delivered at Sheffield University Seminar on the Caribbean. Sheffield, 9 March 1999.

[20] Leo Despres. 1967. *Cultural pluralism and nationalist policies in British Guiana*. Chicago, IL: Rand McNally.

[21] Selwyn Ryan. 1972. *Race and nationalism in Trinidad and Tobago*. Toronto, ON: Toronto University Press.

[22] John Gaffar La Guerre. 1993. "A review of race and class in the Caribbean." In *Race, class and gender in the future of the Caribbean*, edited by J. E. Greene. Kingston, Jamaica: ISER.

Democratic Labour Party (DLP) (which drew its rank and file from the East Indian group) and the People's National Party (PNM) which was African-based. In the General Elections of 1961, the PNM won twenty seats with a total vote of fifty-seven per cent of the votes compared with its primary opposition, the DLP which won ten seats with a total of forty-one per cent of the votes cast. What was clearly indicative of this and the pattern of the other elections which were to follow was the geographical spread of the two major ethnic groups which determined the number of seats won by each ethnic party. While this spread was a major influential factor, by itself, however, this does not fully explain why the African-based PNM took control of government for more than two decades (1962–1986). One factor according to Lewis (1962) was the electioneering techniques employed by the PNM as opposed to the ad hoc and aggressive manner in which the DLP conducted their campaigns. Lewis (1962) wrote:

> ...The DLP, by contrast, although technically a party, was, in behavior, nothing much more than an assorted group of old-style political individualists. One of the most telling of PNM campaign bulletins consisted of a damning collection of quotations, both within the Legislative Council and outside, in which DLP members laid bare their uncomplimentary opinions of each other in a vein of gross scurrility; Mr. Simboonath Capildeo's charge that his colleagues a vein of gross scurrility; Mr. Simboonath Capildeo's charge that his colleagues Mr. Maharaj and Mr. Seukeran were seeking to "divide people against people, race against race, and with the evil, malignant, wicked, sinful, vile, despicable and nefarious news mongering they are trying to divide brother against brother" was typical. As a party, again, the group had little of the respect for the public that a genuine party should surely possess, and not the least fantastic aspect of a generally fantastic election was the fact that, using violence as a pretext, its candidates refused to hold a single public meeting for the last three weeks of the campaign.[23]

---

[23] The Trinidad and Tobago General Election of 1961 Author(s): Gordon K. Lewis Source: *Caribbean Studies*, Vol. 2, No. 2 (July 1962): 2–30, Published by: Institute of Caribbean Studies, UPR, Rio Piedras Campus Stable URL: https://www.jstor.org/stable/25611702. Accessed: 27 March 2019, 20:25 UTC: 16.

He noted:

> ...*the public utterances of Dr. Capildeo, unlike those of the Premier, constituted an open and reckless incitement to civil disorder. There could be no other construction put on his widely publicized invitation to his followers to "come forward on election day and smash up a thousand voting machines" or to 'get ready now to march to Government House"; and of his threat that the 'the day we are ready we will take over this country and not a thing will stop us. "The only remedy", he told a private house meeting is "to adopt the South American method of bloodshed and riot and revolution or civil disobedience until you grind government operations to a full stop and you then get possession." It is small wonder that many of his colleagues became thoroughly alarmed at their leader's temperamental outbursts and that according to report, many of the Indian pundits turned against him.*

The end result though was that the PNM party continued in power during the period 1962–1986. This trend was to have an impact on the management of the state and of course the distribution of state resources. Scholarships, awards and employment opportunities were also found, afterwards, to be vehicles of patronage.

ETHNIC IMBALANCES IN THE PUBLIC SECTOR 1962–1986

In Trinidad and Tobago, statistics revealed that the majority of senior positions were held by Afro-Trinidadians. Criticisms emerged suggesting that membership in the PNM provided a direct entry to key positions in the public services and state-owned enterprises and also provided houses, resources, as well as scholarships for supporters and their families. In the case of neighbouring Guyana where a similar situation had emerged, many of the policies of the state with respect to the appointment of persons in the public sector and state enterprises were vehemently opposed by the East Indian population leading to the establishment of a Commission of Enquiry in 1965. In the case of Trinidad and Tobago, the claims while not vociferous were nonetheless aired. For example, the *Trinidad Express Newspaper* reported on 22 October 1970 that of the one hundred employees of the Central Bank of Trinidad, eighty-four were Afro-Trinidadians, ten were Indo-Trinidadians, three were of Chinese descent, two were of Portuguese descent and one was of Caucasian descent.

This inequity was further highlighted in 1989 when the *Trinidad Express Newspaper* published statistics on June 25th revealing that of the total number of persons employed in all government organisations, twenty-nine per cent were Indo-Trinidadians. In the Police Force, the Regiment of the Defense Force, the Coast Guard and the Port Authority, respectively, the percentage of Indo-Trinidadians was twenty-five per cent, five per cent, sixteen per cent and six per cent, respectively. It is also important to note that according to the census data, Indo-Trinidadians at that time comprised 40.3% of the country's population while Afro-Trinidadians made up 39.6%.

The first attempt to initiate a commission to enquire into the ethnic composition of the public sector of Trinidad and Tobago went unheeded. Indeed, in 1987, one of the seven commissioners appointed to review the Constitution of the Republic of Trinidad and Tobago was rebuffed when he proposed that an Equal Opportunity Commission be established. His justification for the establishment of such an institution was that certain Associations such as the African Association of Trinidad and Tobago, the United National Congress, the President of the Bar Association as well as organisations and individuals had been vociferous in their call for such an institution. He argued, then, that to ignore the demand is to fail to come to grips with the forces which stimulate such a demand. He advised that grievances unless they were channeled, investigated and dealt with were likely to explode in diffuse directions as happened in 1970.

He further explained:

> ...*One might contend that the existing Constitution already provides protection against discrimination on the grounds of sex or race, or that an Ombudsman exists to investigate all cases of maladministration. The truth is, however, that constitutional motions are beyond the reach of those ordinary means; whilst the Ombudsman is empowered to investigate only the public sector and is usually subject to a number of limitations.*[24]

By 1992, though, it was felt that given the claims of ethnic imbalances some form of action should be taken. Accordingly, in 1992, a Centre

[24] Report of the Constitution Commission of Trinidad and Tobago. 1987. Presented to his Excellency, the President on 1st June 1990. Reservation by John Gaffar La Guerre, 286.

for Ethnic Studies was established at the University of the West Indies, St Augustine Campus by the Government of the Republic of Trinidad and Tobago. The mandate of the Centre was to provide statistical data with respect to the ethnic composition of both the private as well as the public sector as well as to interrogate those persons who were awarded scholarships by the Government of Trinidad and Tobago.

To a large extent, claims of ethnic imbalances in senior positions in the public sector were confirmed by the reports from the Centre of Ethnic Studies (see Tables 2.1 and 2.2).

By contrast as, as Table 2.3 in the professional fields such as medicine and finance Indo-Trinidadians reached and surpassed the equity ratio. In the latter category, it should be noted that the criteria for employment and advancement was clearly based on qualifications and technical skills.

Table 2.1 Distribution of posts by race (%; 1970–1992)

Year	Range 60+		Range 46–59		Range 35–45		Under 35	
	East Indian	Other	East Indian	Other	East Indian	Other	East Indian	Other
1970	20.7	79.3	25.6	74.4	33.5	66.5	25.1	74.9
1980	27.1	72.9	28.9	71.1	5.8	74.2	35.6	64.4
1992	35.6	64.4	41.3	58.7	37.0	63.0	41.0	59.0

Source Ethnicity and Employment Practices in Trinidad and Tobago: 1994. Centre for Ethnic Studies, St Augustine, Trinidad and Tobago: 93

Table 2.2 Racial representation in senior administrative positions (%; 1992)

Classification	Non-Indo Trinidadians	Indo-Trinidadians
Administrative Officer V	87.5	12.5
Administrative Officer 1 V	90.5	9.5
Administrative Officer 11	70.6	29.4

Note Ethnicity and Employment Practices: 98
Source Ethnicity and Employment Practices in Trinidad and Tobago: 1994. Centre for Ethnic Studies, St Augustine, Trinidad and Tobago: 98

Table 2.3 Racial representation in selected professional positions (%; 1992)

Post	Non-Indo Trinidadians	Indo-Trinidadians
Doctors	45.2	54.8
Engineers	56.3	43.7
Research and planning officers (Public sector)	74.8	25.2

Note Ethnicity and Employment Practices: 98
Source Ethnicity and Employment Practices in Trinidad and Tobago: 1994. Centre for Ethnic Studies, St Augustine, Trinidad and Tobago: 98

OFFERING EXPLANATIONS FOR ETHNIC IMBALANCES IN THE PUBLIC SECTOR 1962–1992

No doubt a number of arguments may be offered to explain the disproportion in numbers between the two major groups in the public sector during the period 1962–1992. One major explanation was the way the two groups were assimilated in the core sectors of the society. For instance, it was found that the African—descended population applied and were accepted for positions into the public sector while the Indo-descended population remained in the agricultural sector or sent their children into educational streams such as medicine, engineering or accounting. While this explanation addressed the issue of imbalances in certain sectors including the public sector, it did not, however, explain other types of imbalances that emerged. The Centre for Ethnic Studies noted, for instance, that from their research, East Indian applicants were often bypassed for scholarship opportunities. There were other claims of state resources, for example, the paving of roadways, the erection of community centres, being more pronounced in constituencies that demonstrated strong support for a ruling party. Following up on continuing allegations of inequity, on the 20th October 2011, the incoming Attorney General of the country (representing an Indo-majority government) had this to say on the issue and referred to the Report of the Centre for Ethnic Studies:

> ...*The findings of the Commission raise a prima facie case of political and racial discrimination. The mysterious, secretive process used to grant assistance facilitated this unjustifiable discrimination. The lack of transparency and integrity in the distribution of public funds is a cause for grave concern.*

Such an inequitable and biased distribution of State resources contravenes the spirit and letter of the constitutional right to equality of treatment......there can be no greater injury to the public interest than the conceptualization and execution of a scheme designed to use state funds so as to bestow political patronage and then to seek to cover up this elaborate scheme of misleading both the commission and the Parliament of Trinidad and Tobago.[25]

The conclusion was, therefore, that even as late as 2010 certain sectors of the population had not been accorded equal opportunity. The perception of the East Indian group was, understandably, because the African government, the People's National Movement remain in power from 1956 to 1986; 1991–1995 and then from 2001 to 2010 the resources of the state as it related to employment opportunities, scholarships, housing and allocation of funds had been dispersed to the supporters of that party.

EVALUATING THE MECHANISMS TO ALL FOR EQUAL OPPORTUNITY OF ETHNIC GROUPS IN TRINIDAD AND TOBAGO

A number of mechanisms were and more recently has been established in the twin-island state to allow for equal representation in the public sector as well as the wider society. These included:

- The Public Service Commissions;
- The Public Service Appeal Board/Appellate Tribunal;
- The Office of the Ombudsman;
- Public Service Unions;
- Judicial Review;
- The Establishment of an Equal Opportunity Commission (2000);
- The Freedom of Information (2000).

It has been suggested, however, that even the introduction of these mechanisms has done little to minimise unequal treatment particularly when a new government assumes power. An examination and some assessment of these mechanisms/instruments will accordingly follow.

[25] The Trinidad Express Newspaper: The AG Comments on the Findings of the EOC. 20 October 2011, p. 2.

The Public Service Commissions

The Public Service Commission was established in 1950 by Order of Council and was closely modelled along the institution that had been established in Britain in 1855. According to one academic, Collin (1967) the initial justification for establishing the Commissions in ex-colonial territories included:

- It was felt by the departing colonials that political independence for the colonies would prove dangerous for the integrity of the public services. Hence the need to introduce measures that protected the public servants from political interference.
- Service Commissions were necessary in order to maintain public service neutrality.[26]

When Trinidad and Tobago attained independent status in 1962, the Public Service Commission became an executive agency and was vested with a number of powers. The powers included the capacity to make appointments, promotions, acting appointments, discipline and transfer staff throughout the public service. They were also vested with the authority to regulate their own procedures and they promulgated regulations with setting out the principles and guidelines to be followed in making appointments, promotions, transfers and the exercise of disciplinary procedures. The various Chairmen of the Commissions claimed that inherent in these regulations were considerations of equality, fairness and justice.

However, the Commissions were subject to a number of criticisms. It was contended, for instance, that the selection method of using competitive interviews employed by the Service Commissions was biased against Indo-Trinidadians as well as women. According to the report by the Centre for Ethnic Studies (1992) the bias appeared to have existed in the composition of the interviewing panel which primarily comprised Afro-Trinidadian males. The report suggested that even if the greatest objectivity was maintained, the impression may have been given, and unsuccessful Indo-Trinidadian would claim that they were victims of racial discrimination.[27]

[26]B. A. N. Collins. 1967. "Some notes on the public service commissions in the Commonwealth Caribbean." *Social and Economic Studies*, Vol. 16, No. 1: 1–16.

[27]Centre for Ethnic Studies. 1992. *Ethnicity and employment practices in Trinidad and Tobago.* The University of the West Indies, St Augustine, Trinidad, p. 8.

Other criticisms levelled against the Commissions were that of inefficiency and of placing "square pegs in round holes". The system of appointment and promotion based on the criterion of seniority also ensured that the status quo was maintained. Indeed, it has been suggested by many that what the policy of maintaining the status quo might have done was to reinforce what is referred to as "institutional racism". The phenomenon of institutional racism occurs where the institutions themselves become imbued with prejudices, conventions, biases and world views which inform their visions of groups and what group relations should be. In other words, the practice of discrimination may be reinforced by the processes and procedures of the institutions. By maintaining the principle of seniority of service, therefore, the Various Commissions ensured that the groups who first entered the public services would attain the top-level positions irrespective of their ability to lead or their capacity to function at the higher level.

More recently, however, the Commissions have introduced other mechanisms to allow for a wider pool of candidates to different positions including interviews, examinations and interviews and advertisement of the positions. As early as 1990, also, there was a move by the Commission to introduce contract positions.

The Public Service Appeal Board

This Board, it has been suggested, also became a "creature" which promoted "institutional racism". Matters coming to this Board were constrained to appeals relating specifically to disciplinary matters forwarded to it by the Public Service Commission. In essence it was an ineffective mechanism to ensure that equality reselection of groups was in place.

The Effectiveness of Unions

The unions representing workers have also been criticised on a number of fronts. It is alleged, for instance, that the unions representing workers are vociferous only during wage bargaining and matters of discrimination or unequal treatments are not given priority. In their defense, these unions claim that while sometimes they do investigate the matters, the final decisions are taken by the various service commissions. They argue, though, that many matters are forwarded to the Ministry of Labour or the Industrial Court and the costs of expenses are defrayed by them. While this is true, some may argue that in a plural society such as Trinidad and Tobago, it is surprising that during the period 1962–2010, these unions had not submitted one case of ethnic discrimination. One may therefore question if incidents of ethnic discrimination exist or whether the unions are merely reluctant to address such claims.

Brown (1999) asserted that the Public Services Association the Union was representing, public servants avoided issues pertaining to race and ethnicity preferring inaction to taking sides. Yet, in the case of Trinidad and Tobago, that was not quite true. In 1999, the Public Services Association was quite vociferous in their allegations of racial discrimination. Their claim was that Indo-Trinidadians were getting top positions at the airport authority (this was because an Indo-based party was in power during this period and there were claims that top-level positions were allocated to supporters of this party). While it may be argued that this may have been an effort by the Union to maintain equity, counter to this may very well be the question, why, *when the shoe is on the other foot,* similar claims were not made by the union which comprised mainly of Afro-Trinidadians.

The Office of the Ombudsman

A major institution that has been described by a number of writers as a *toothless bulldog*[28] has been the office of the Ombudsman. This institution, as elsewhere, has as its major aim the undertaking to address claims of maladministration and discrimination. Yet, investigations by these institutions have been stymied by a number of challenges including:

- Limited resources;
- Inadequacy of record-keeping by ministries and departments;
- The lack of authority to impose sanctions against ministries/ departments.

---

[28] Haller W. (2010). The place of the Ombudsman in the world community, Fourth International Ombudsman Conference Papers, Canberra, Canadian Federal Corrections 15(5), 15–24; L. Ademolekun and E. L. Ogunkule. 1985. *Nigeria's Ombudsman system: Five years of the public complaints.* Ibadan: Heineman.

However, a far more critical consideration has been the limitations imposed upon this office by the existing Constitution. Section 93 of the Constitution of Trinidad and Tobago circumscribes the jurisdiction of the ombudsman limiting his investigations to decisions and recommendations made or acts done or omitted by government departments and authorities in the exercise of administrative functions. Also in the Third Schedule to the Constitution, some matters are not subject to investigation, namely the conduct of civil or criminal proceedings in any court, action taken relating to contractual or other commercial transactions and actions taken in respect of appointments or removals, pay, discipline, superannuation or personal matters. Yet, as the Ombudsman in 1998 report pointed out, the bulk of the complaints were from public officers and employees of statutory and local authorities alleging discrimination in employment practices such as preferment of acting appointments and promotions, which, it was alleged, contravened the Public Service Regulations and departmental policies and procedures. These were the procedures from which the Ombudsman and his office were constitutionally debarred from investigating. Table 2.4 consists of excerpts taken from the Fortieth Annual Report of the Ombudsman for the period January 2017–December 2017.

Table 2.4 Complaints received by the office of the Ombudsman (2017)

	Number	Percentage
Total number of complaints brought forward from previous years	1516	
Total number of complaints received in 2017	957	
TOTAL	2473	100
Less total number of complaints without jurisdiction	(82)	33
Less enquiries and feedback	(362)	14.6
Less total of freedom of information Act matters	(13)	0.5
Total number of complaints pursued	2016	81.5
Total number of complaints concluded	(804)	39.9
Complaints sustained	400	19.8
Complaints not sustained	29	1.5
Complaints withdrawn	295	14.6
Complaints advised	76	3.8
Complaints with no jurisdiction	4	0.2
Total number of complaints under investigation as at 31 December 2017	1212	60.1

Source Report of the Ombudsman, 2017, Office of the Ombudsman, Trinidad and Tobago (A compilation)

Table 2.4 illustrated the total number of cases brought forward to 2017 together with new complaints received in the same year. It can be seen that a total of one thousand, two hundred and twelve cases (1212) or 60.1% were under investigation as of 31 December 2017.

It should be noted, though, that these cases did not involve any complaints of injustice as a result of discrimination. Even with its limited mandate, however, lack of resources continue to stymie the effectiveness of this Office and the challenges facing the Ombudsman continues as outlined in the 2017 report. The challenges cited include:

i. The lack of action by Parliament in dealing with both Annual Reports and Special Reports. According to the Office of the Ombudsman this leads to the non-implementation of recommendations made by the Ombudsman in those Reports;

ii. The tendency of Government Departments and State Agencies to respond to Ombudsman matters and recommendations in a lackadaisical and untimely manner. The report from the Ombudsman suggested that departments and agencies had taken the cue from the perceived inaction and behaviour of Parliament in dealing with Annual Reports and Special Reports; and

iii. The denied opportunity for financial autonomy. The Report of the Ombudsman noted that this Office required approval from Parliament (the line Organisation), where financial matters were concerned. Consequently, this stifled various activities which the Office desired to undertake. The Report concluded:

> However, in light of the present economic climate, it is unlikely that the Office will be given full control of its budget[29]

No doubt the latter remarks from this report speak volumes about the limitations of the Office of the Ombudsman.

Judicial Review

Prior to the year 2000, public officers were unable to seek judicial review on matters deliberated by the Service Commissions. However, with

---

[29] Ombudsman 40th Annual Report (2017), Office of the Ombudsman, Trinidad and Tobago.

the introduction of a new government, by Act 60 of 2000, the Judicial Review Act Chapter 7:08 was introduced. The Act accordingly established the following Judicial Review Procedure as follows:

(1) An application for judicial review of a decision of an inferior Court, tribunal, public body, public authority or a person acting in the exercise of a public duty or function in accordance with any law shall be made to the Court in accordance with this Act and in such manner as may be prescribed by Rules of Court.

(2) The Court may, on an application for judicial Review, grant relief in accordance with this Act—
  (a) To a person whose interests are adversely affected by a decision; or
  (b) To a person or a group of persons if the Court is satisfied that the application is justifiable in the public interest in the circumstances of the case.

(3) The grounds upon which the Court may grant relief to a person who filed an application for judicial review includes the following:
  (a) That the decision was in any way unauthorised or contrary to law;
  (b) Excess of jurisdiction;
  (c) Failure to satisfy or observe conditions or procedures required by law;
  (d) Breach of the principles of natural justice;
  (e) Unreasonable, irregular or improper exercise of discretion;
  (f) Abuse of power;
  (g) Fraud, bad faith, improper purpose or irrelevant consideration;
  (h) Acting on instructions from an unauthorised person;
  (i) Conflict with the policy of an Act;
  (j) Error of law, whether or not apparent on the face of the record;
  (k) Absence of evidence on which a finding or assumption of fact could reasonably be based;
  (l) Breach of or omission to perform a duty;
  (m) Deprivation of a legitimate expectation;
  (n) A defect in form or a technical irregularity resulting in a substantial wrong or miscarriage of justice; or
  (o) An exercise of a power in a manner that is so unreasonable that no reasonable person could have so exercised the power.

(4) An applicant is not limited to the grounds set out in the application for judicial review but if the applicant wishes to rely on any other ground not so set out, the Court may, on such terms as it thinks fit, direct that the application be amended to specify such other ground.

With the introduction of the Judicial Review Act 60 of 2000, there was clearly an increase in the number of cases filed, 38 in 2000 and 32 in 2001. In 2002, there was an increase to 58 and in 2003 a very sharp increase to 109. This was followed by a further increase to 142 in 2004 and a slight decline to 125 in 2005.[30]

The awards by the Courts to employees have been well accepted by employees both in the public as well as the private sectors. In addition to increasing public confidence in the judiciary the intense scrutiny of the Commissions has led to improvements in the actual functioning of the ministries and departments.

The Freedom of Information Act

The Freedom of Information Act Chapter 22:02, Act 26 of 1999 (amended by 92 of 2000 and 14 of 2003) extends the right of members of the public to access to information in the possession of public authorities by—

a. making available to the public information about the operations of public authorities and, in particular, ensuring that the authorisations, policies, rules and practices affecting members of the public in their dealings with public authorities are readily available to persons affected by those authorisations, policies, rules and practices; and

b. creating a general right of access to information in documentary form in the possession of public authorities limited only by exceptions and exemptions necessary for the protection of essential public interests and the private and business affairs of persons in respect of whom information is collected and held by public authorities.

However, it has been evident in many cases that the request of information under the Act was not straightforward but rather applicants had to forward their cases to the Court by way of Judicial Review in order to allow for an interpretation of the Act. Two cases stand out. One of the early cases was in 2005, the case of **Ashford Sankar v Public Service**

---

[30] "Judicial Supervision of Executive Action in the Commonwealth Caribbean." *Michael de la Bastide*, Commonwealth Law Bulletin, Vol. 33, No. 2 (2007): 177–189.

Commission (High Court of Justice of Trinidad and Tobago—Claim No CV 2006-00037). The two cases are accordingly recorded in depth in order to present a scenario about the machinations that emerge when persons apply for information under this Act.

The Applicant, Sankar, was an Acting Deputy Permanent Secretary with the Public Services on 15th November 2005 the Applicant, pursuant to the provisions of the Freedom of Information Act ("FOI Act"), applied for certain documents from the Public Services Commission ("PSC") which were used to assess his suitability for promotion to the post of Deputy Permanent Secretary, namely:

1. The results of the screening interview/assessment conducted by Symcom Systems Management Consultants Limited on behalf of the PSC in 1997 for the filling of the office of Deputy Permanent Secretary.
2. The names of all public officers whose names were retained for future reference arising from the exercise by Symcom Systems Management in 1997 as above at (1).
3. His position in the overall ranking of the Assessment Exercise conducted by the Personnel Psychology Centre ("PPC") of Canada for the office of Deputy Permanent Secretary.
4. Recommendations/staff reports made on his behalf since 1997 for the offices of Deputy Permanent Secretary by the Permanent Secretary.
5. Public advertisements for the filling of the offices of Deputy Permanent Secretary and Permanent Secretary with effect from January 1997 by the PSC.
6. Minutes of the meetings of the PSC at which the issue(s) of appointment/promotion to the office of Deputy Permanent Secretary and/or Permanent Secretary were discussed/determined relative to the appointments made in October 2005.
7. The score sheets or other documents of all public officers who were assessed or evaluated by the PPC of Canada for appointments/promotion relative to the appointments made in October 2005.
8. Agreement between the PPC of Canada and the PSC (or whichever party) with respect to the Assessment Centre Exercise for, the filling of the post of Deputy Permanent Secretary and/or Permanent Secretary which appointments were made in October 2005.

On 19 November 2005, the Human Resource Adviser Π in the Service Commissions Department, in a telephone conversation with the Applicant, orally confirmed receipt of the application (para. 7 of her affidavit.) By letter dated 29 November 2005, the PSC acknowledged receipt of the application and informed the Applicant that the matter was receiving attention and that the Applicant would be informed as soon as possible. By letter dated 16 December 2005 and hand-delivered on the said date, the Applicant informed the Defendant that the statutory time frame for providing the information requested had elapsed, and agreed without prejudice to an extension until 5 January 2006. By letter dated 22 December 2005 the Applicant's Attorney wrote to the Designated Officer in the Freedom of Information Unit, Service Commissions Department, enquiring about the application and giving notice of judicial review proceedings if the information was not provided within seven (7) days of the date of the letter.

On 6 January 2006, the Applicant commenced proceedings for judicial review seeking inter alia:

1. An order of mandamus to compel the Respondent to provide the Applicant with the information requested on 15 November 2005 in his application under the FOI Act.
2. A declaration that the Applicant is entitled to the information.
3. An order directing the Respondents to provide the Applicant with the requested information free of charge within seven (7) days hereof.
4. Alternatively, an order directing the Respondent to forthwith prepare and supply notice in accordance with Section 23 of FOI Act.
5. A declaration that there has been an unreasonable delay on the part of the Respondent in making a decision on the Applicant's request under FOI Act. Some of the documents and/or information were supplied before trial.

The Applicant did not pursue Request 7, namely the score sheets or other documents of all public officers who were assessed or evaluated by the PPC of Canada for appointments/promotion to the offices of Permanent Secretary or, Deputy Permanent Secretary. The PSC had contended that the disclosure of this information would infringe on Section 30 of the FOI Act since it would involve the disclosure of information relating to other public officers. The Respondent also contended that those documents relating to Requests Nos. 1 and 2 could not be found, but that searches were continuing for same. With respect to Request No. 6, namely minutes of the meetings of the PSC at which the issue(s) of appointment/promotion to the office of Deputy Permanent Secretary and/or Permanent Secretary were discussed/determined relative to the appointments made in October 2005, the PSC was contending that the minutes are exempt under Section 27 of FOI Act.

The case concluded in April of 2007 with the Judge agreeing that the PSC should provide the relevant information and that they should pay the applicant costs.

In another case, Claim **NO CV 2007-03288 between Darren Baptiste and the Police Service Commission**, Mr Baptiste had applied for but by letter dated 14th November 2005 ("D.B.1"), was informed that he was omitted from the list of persons selected for promotion to the rank of Corporal and was invited to make representations to the Police Service Commission (the First Defendant) within 14 days.

By letter dated 5th December 2005 ("D.B.1") the PSC acknowledged receipt of his representations. By further letter dated 17th May 2006 ("D.B.1") the PSC further informed the Claimant that they had considered his representations and had requested the comments of the Commissioner of Police (the Second Defendant). They also notified him that since they were in the process of receiving the comments of the Second Defendant, they would consider his claim for promotion when next consideration was being given to recommendations for promotion to the rank of Corporal and that offices will not be filled until the First Defendant makes a final decision on his representations. By letter dated 7th June 2006 ("D.B.1") the Claimant was informed that he had not achieved the score needed for promotion.

By another letter dated 6th November 2006 ("D.B.1"), further representations were submitted, this time on the Claimant's behalf from the Trinidad and Tobago Police Service Social and Welfare Association. These representations make a case for the Claimant to receive one (1) point under Academic Qualifications for either his training course at Roytec or his certificate in Bible and Theology studies thereby bring his total score to seventy-four (74) points which, in the opinion of the Welfare Association, would qualify the Claimant for promotion to the rank of Corporal. The First Defendant responded to this letter on 16th May 2007 saying that the Claimant still had not achieved the score needed for promotion.

The Claimant requested information under the Freedom of Information Act ("FOIA"), Chapter 22:02, as a precursor to determining whether he had been unfairly bypassed for promotion to the position of Police Corporal. The Claimant's request was made on 4 June 2007 via two FOIA request forms accompanied by covering letters dated 5 June 2007, all of which was sent to the First and Second-named Defendants by registered mail. The Claimant requested access to:

i. Copies of any correspondence in connection with his claim for promotion to the rank of Police Corporal;
ii. Copies of academic qualifications, certificates and diplomas for Police Officers #14807 and #13468 who, though junior to the Claimant, were successful in their respective applications for promotion;
iii. Copies of any letters of recommendation for promotion in respect of the two officers named in the foregoing paragraph.

The contention was that even under the FOIA, academic qualifications, certificates and diplomas were considered "personal" and therefore could not be shared under the Act. Accordingly, Mr Baptiste sought the opinion of the court. After a period of four years (6th November 2009) the case was concluded as follows by the sitting Judge:

> By reason of the foregoing, the Claimant is entitled to access to copies of the academic qualifications, certificates and diplomas of the successful candidates but shall be denied access to the letters of recommendations requested. Costs of the Claim are to be paid by the Defendants to the Claimant as assessed in accordance with the budgeted costs application, namely the sum of seventy-five thousand dollars ($75,000).

As an overview of both cases presented above illustrate, the Freedom of Information Act certainly does not provide information in an open and transparent manner. Rather it is clear, that if these cases, at great expense to both Applicants, were not subject to Judicial Review, the information requested would not have been provided.

The Equal Opportunity Act 2000

This Act sets out as its mandate the prohibition of certain kinds of discrimination, the promotion of equality of opportunity between persons of different status, and the establishment of an Equal Opportunity Commission and an Equal Opportunity Tribunal was assented to on the 20th October 2000. Part 111 of the Act accordingly sets out the grounds for discrimination, in relation to employment, education, the provision of goods and services and the provision of accommodation.

According to the 2008–2013 statistics from Reports of the Equal Opportunity Commission, what emerges is that while discrimination on the basis of race still stands out as a significant factor, increasingly discrimination based on other factors such as gender, disability and religion are also emerging (Table 2.5).

While these claims have been forwarded for the consideration to the EOC, it is evident that in arriving at a solution, the EOC has involved the Ministries and Departments in a number of discussions which may have raised awareness on these issues. Most of the cases filed, too, have indicated that the majority are based on maladministration and very few cases were based on actual race discrimination.

Table 2.5 Statistical data drawn from the EOC reports (2008–2013)

Type of Complaint	2008	2010	2011	2012	2013
Racial	11	38	40	15	24
Gender	0	6	10	11	6
Religious	2	6	10	8	8
Employment	11	0	0	0	0
State services	18	0	0	0	0
Education	2	0	0	0	0
Other	9	0	0	0	0
Disability		3	3	13	5
Origin		3	9	3	2
Marital Status		0	0	1	1

Source Author created with statistics drawn from Equal Opportunity Reports 2008–2013

CONCLUSION

Apart from these remedies, a number of other reports were accordingly commissioned including *The International Convention on the Elimination of Discrimination Against Women* (Office of the Attorney General, Trinidad and Tobago 2000a), *The International Convention on the Elimination of all Forms of Racial Discrimination* (Office of the Attorney General, Trinidad and Tobago 2000b) and the *International Covenant on Civil and Political* Rights (Office of the Attorney General, Trinidad and Tobago 2000c). The legislation was also enacted including legislation which established Joint Select Committees to investigate the workings of the Administrative Apparatus of State (Act 29 of 1999).

While all these remedies have been introduced the larger question that remains is whether, in the future, the question of representation will continue to be relevant. While during the 1960–2000, governments around the world continued to maintain an active role in the distribution of resources as well as providing employment opportunities, increasingly that role has diminished due to a number of factors including migration, international treaties, limited resources by the state, privatisation and contracting out of major sectors. As states continue to contract and thus opportunities in state departments and agencies are reduced, increasingly charges of racial discrimination may decline and other claims based on sexual preference, psychographic characteristics, cultural or team tenure may emerge. Indeed, as Tschirthart (2000)[31] had noted in 2000 and it has become more relevant in 2019, interpretations of the concept of managing diversity may vary widely and should be treated as a self-conscious programmic approach affecting the politics, culture and structure of an organisation. As states move away from welfare considerations to entrepreneurial considerations, increasingly emphasis will not be placed on seniority of service but would focus on specialisations and efficiency in a particular field. The challenge for governments, therefore, is how given the mainstreaming of the educational sectors, to prepare potential employees for limited employment opportunities and for the competition that will eventually emerge for the few positions that will exist. No doubt, within this limited space, new mechanisms will have to be designed to allow for representation and access by various groups.

---

[31] Louis Rescascino Wise and Mary Tschirthart. 2000 September/October. "Examining empirical evidence on diversity effects: How useful is diversity research for public sector managers?" *Public Administration Review*, Vol. 60, No. 5: 386–396.

REFERENCES

Agyapong, E. (2018, February 28). Critical assessment of representative bureaucracy: Toward a more expanded theory. *PA Times*. https://patimes.org/a-critical-assessment-of-representative-bureaucracy-toward-a-more-expanded-theory/.

Brown, D. (1999, March 9). *Ethnic politics and public sector management in Trinidad and Guyana*. Paper delivered at Sheffield University Seminar on the Caribbean, Sheffield.

Collins, B. A. N. (1967). Some notes on the public service commissions in the Commonwealth Caribbean. *Social and Economic Studies, 16*(1), 1–16.

Dauda, B. (1990). Fallacies and dilemmas: The theory of representative bureaucracy with a particular reference to the Nigerian Public Service 1950–1986. *International Review of Administrative Sciences, 56*, 467–495.

Despres, L. (1964). The implications of nationalist politics in British Guiana for the development of cultural theory. *American Anthropologist, 66*(5), 1051–1077.

Despres, L. (1967). *Cultural pluralism and nationalist policies in British Guiana*. Chicago, IL: Rand McNally.

Evans, J. (1974). Defining representative bureaucracy. *Public Administration Review, 34*(6), 628–631.

Furnival, J. S. (1948). *Netherland Indies*. London: Cambridge University Press.

Hitzen, P. (1994). The Colonial Foundations of race relations and Ethno-politics in Guyana. *Guyana History Gazzette*, No. 65.

Kelsall, R. K. (1955). *Higher civil servants in Britain*. London: Routledge and Keagan Paul.

Kim, P. S. (1994). A theoretical overview of representative bureaucracy: Synthesis. *International Review of Administrative Sciences, 60*(385–397), 386.

Kingsley, J. D. (1944). *Representative bureaucracy*. Yellow Springs, OH: Antioch Press.

La Guerre, J. G. (1974). *Calcutta to Caroni: The East Indians of Trinidad*. New York: Longman Inc.

La Guerre, J. G. (1993). A review of race and class in the Caribbean. In J. E. Greene (Ed.), *Race, class and gender in the future of the Caribbean*, 18. Kingston, Jamaica: ISER.

Long, N. (1952). Bureaucracy and constitutionalism. *American Political Science Review, 46*, 808–818.

Long, N. (1958). Implementing equal opportunities in the 1980s: An overview. *Public Administration, 67*, 7–18.

Mosher, F. C. (1968). *Democracy and the public service*. New York: Oxford University Press.

Office of the Attorney General, Trinidad and Tobago. (2000a). The International Convention on the Elimination of Discrimination Against Women.

Office of the Attorney General, Trinidad and Tobago. (2000b). The International Convention on the Elimination of all Forms of Racial Discrimination.

Office of the Attorney General, Trinidad and Tobago. (2000c). The International Covenant on Civil and Political Rights.

Ryan, S. (1972). *Race and nationalism in Trinidad and Tobago*. Toronto, ON: Toronto University Press.

Smith, M. G. (1965). *The plural society in the British West Indies*. Berkeley: University of California Press.

Smith, R. T. (1971). Race and political conflict in Guyana. *Race and Class, 12*(4), 415–427.

Subramaniam, V. (1967). Representative bureaucracy: A reassessment. *The American Political Science Review, LXI*(4), 1010–1019.

Van Riper, P. P. (1958). *History of the United States Civil Service*. Evanston, IL: Row Peterson.

CHAPTER 3

Equality and Discrimination
on the Basis of Sex

The prevailing culture in the Anglophone Caribbean is inherently patriarchal, such that relative to women, men generally hold more influential organisational, political and societal roles. Conversely, women overpopulate supportive, administrative and service-based occupations, which are comparatively the lowest paid and least skilled (Bissessar 2014; CDB 2016; ILO 2018a, b). This may be attributed in part, to the region's history of colonisation and enslavement, where enslaved and indentured males were regarded as more valuable than females. Over time, these perceptions have been embedded into accepted societal practice and as such have become social norms which are ubiquitous across the Caribbean region. As a consequence, in the home, women continue to be expected to (and do) perform the role of the primary caregiver (Mahabir and Ramrattan 2015; Seguino 2008), which may adversely affect their availability to actively engage in the formal labour market and earn competitive remuneration in relation to their male counterparts. Consequently, these gender expectations also exist within organisations, which lead to a divergence in the type of employment which is available to men and women, particularly as it relates to leadership, management and access to developmental and promotional opportunities (Acker 1990, 2006). This chapter will examine sex discrimination and employment in the Caribbean region. In an attempt to redress the balance of inequities, some Caribbean islands have: included sex as one of the prohibited

© The Author(s) 2020
J. H. Stephenson et al., *Diversity, Equality,
and Inclusion in Caribbean Organisations and Society,*
https://doi.org/10.1007/978-3-030-47614-4_3

grounds in enacted anti-discrimination laws, implemented equal pay legislation and have become signatories to international conventions which promote gender equality and non-discrimination on the basis of sex.

CURRENT STATUS OF WOMEN IN EMPLOYMENT IN THE CARIBBEAN REGION

The United Nations Convention on the Elimination of All Forms of Discrimination Against Women (1979), which has been signed and ratified by most Caribbean member states, compels signatories to take appropriate measures to eliminate discrimination against women (see Table 3.1). Further to this, enacted equality legislation in the Caribbean, namely: Trinidad and Tobago's Equal Opportunity Act, 2000[1]; St. Lucia's Equality of Opportunity and Treatment in Employment and Occupation Act, 2000[2]; and Guyana's Prevention of Discrimination Act, 1997,[3] prohibit discrimination on the basis of sex, *inter alia*.

Moreover, with a view of redressing the balance in terms of remuneration and employment rights, some Caribbean islands have also implemented equal pay and labour standards legislation, these include: Antigua and Barbuda (*Antigua and Barbuda Labour Code,* 1975); Anguilla (*Anguilla, Labour Code,* 2003); Dominica (*Labour Standards Act,* 1977); Guyana (*Equal Rights Act,* 1990); St Vincent and the Grenadines (*Equal Pay Act,* 1994); and Jamaica (*Employment-Equal Pay for Men and Women Act,* 1975). The effect of these laws is to provide a mandate that all men and women are entitled to equal rights and equal remuneration for the same work, or work of the same nature and generally makes unlawful, disparate treatment in employment on the grounds of sex.

[1] Trinidad and Tobago's Equal Opportunity Act, 2000—The protected grounds are sex, race, ethnicity, origin, religion, marital status, disability.

[2] St. Lucia's Equality of Opportunity and Treatment in Employment and Occupation Act, 2000—The protected grounds are race, sex, religion, colour, ethnic origin, family responsibilities, pregnancy, marital status, or age.

[3] Guyana's Prevention of Discrimination Act, 1997—The protected grounds are race, sex, religion, colour, ethnic origin, indigenous population, national extraction, social origin, economic status political opinion, disability, family responsibilities, pregnancy, marital status or age except for purposes of retirement and restrictions on work and employment of minors.

Table 3.1 Signatories to the Convention to End All Forms of Discrimination against Women (CEDAW 1979)

Country	Accession/ratification
Anguilla	
Antigua and Barbuda	1st August 1989
Bahamas	6th October 1993
Barbados	16th October 1980
Belize	7th March 1990
Bermuda	–
British Virgin Islands	UK Overseas Territory CEDAW extended
Dominica	15th September 1980
Grenada	30th August 1990
Guyana	17th July 1980
Jamaica	19th October 1984
St. Kitts and Nevis	25th April 1985
St. Lucia	5th October 1985
St. Vincent	4th August 1981
Trinidad and Tobago	12th January 1981
Turks and Caicos	UK Overseas Territory-CEDAW extended

Notes The Convention on the Elimination of All Forms of Discrimination against Women (CEDAW) (1979) and General Recommendation No. 19 (1992) which is directed towards eliminating discrimination against women and which recognises gender-based as a form of discrimination against women
Source CEDAW website

According to the International Labour Organisation (ILO), the rate of female labour force participation has increased over the past decade in the Bahamas, Guyana, Jamaica, St. Lucia, and St. Vincent and the Grenadines. The findings from the ILO's 2017 Caribbean survey on gender and employment, found that the "leaking pipeline", i.e. where women exit their career paths during their ascent from junior levels to executive roles (Alper and Gibbons 1993; Xie and Shauman 2004), results in the occupation of less than 10% of senior executive roles in the Caribbean region, by women. However, the levels of engagement are higher at lower levels of management as follows: junior management (30%); middle management (30%) and senior management (30%) (ILO Caribbean company survey, 2018b—see Table 3.2).

These outcomes for women may be attributed to women becoming organisationally plateaued due to the surplus of qualified staff at their current organisations, in their field or by virtue of the pyramid structure of their organisations, where promotional opportunities become less

Table 3.2 Share of women managers (%) at different management levels and median of selected Caribbean countries (2017)

Country	Junior management	Middle management	Senior management	Top executive
Antigua and Barbuda	37	38	45	25
Bahamas	45	25	25	10
Barbados	25	23	20	2
Belize	21	20	27	6
Dominica	2	23	50	13
Grenada	32	50	40	20
Guyana	28	25	26	20
Jamaica	50	50	40	33
Saint Kitts and Nevis	14	4	0	0
St. Lucia	28	25	32	18
St. Vincent and the Grenadines	24	17	11	4
Suriname	30	30	25	10
Trinidad and Tobago	37	50	33	20
Sub regional median	**30**	**30**	**30**	**10**

Source ILO Caribbean Company survey; Women in business and management: Gaining momentum in the Caribbean, October 2018; Bureau for Employers' Activities (ACT/EMP), International Labour Organisation 2018b

abundant at higher levels of the organisational ladder. Furthermore, lack of access to flexible and alternative working arrangements, and child/senior care facilities may also limit participation by women at the influential levels of organisational leadership and decision making. In addition to the stereotypical lens through which organisations perceive women in employment, further barriers are encountered in relation to promotional and developmental opportunities. This is because of concerns by organisations that they will not realise a positive return on their training and development investments, as in the long term, it is believed that women are likely to leave the organisation for family-related reasons (ILO 2018a, b). In short, barriers may be deliberate or unconscious with organisations either blatantly contravening the non-discrimination legislation, policies or international conventions or making more discrete efforts to do so.

Largely the stereotypes facing women in employment and within society are gender based, and arise from culturally accepted norms, in relation to the roles and characteristics appropriate for women. Hence, women are perceived not to be as competitive as men in the workplace, and not as capable of performing roles traditionally filled by men. Consequently, where women are engaged in organisational roles in which they are required to be assertive, dominant and focused on achievement, they are denigrated and marginalised, unlike the response to women who are perceived to be more *appropriately* employed in sectors and roles in which they are able (and expected) to demonstrate empathy, kindness, thoughtfulness and consideration for others (Glick et al. 1988; Heilman 2012; Heilman and Okimoto 2007). In short, factors which determine which individuals will experience discrimination include the gender of the employee, the personality of the employee and the accepted sex type of the job (Eagly and Karau 2002; Fagenson and Marcus 1991; Heilman and Okimoto 2007).

The male/female composition of the islands of the Anglophone Caribbean is shown in Table 3.3, along with their labour force participation segmented by sex. A review of these statistics illustrates gender disparities across the populous and by extension the labour force. Further, the World Economic Forum's (WEF) 2016 Global Gender Gap Index has identified gender gaps in the Caribbean region in "education, economy, health and politics". This is supported by analysis conducted by the United Nations Development Programme (UNDP) (see Table 3.4), which indicates that although gender disparities still exist, the gap continues to narrow (albeit marginally) over the assessed period i.e. 1995–2018.

In the WEF's global gender gap index, the region has been represented in the Index according to their ranking of 144 countries globally, the Caribbean is represented by Barbados (ranked 28th), the Bahamas (ranked 37th), Jamaica (ranked 42nd) and Trinidad and Tobago (ranked 44th). The global gender gap index analyses each country's economic participation and opportunity, educational attainment, health and survival and political empowerment to determine their overall global ranking. In each of these categories are also useful sub-indexes (see Table 3.5), the labour force participation ratio of these islands as 0.92, 0.91, 0.83 and 0.74, respectively, which suggests that for every man in Barbados who is an active participant in the labour force, there are 0.92 active women in the labour force, as it relates to the Bahamas, 0.91 active women, in Jamaica 0.83 active women and in Trinidad and Tobago 0.74 active women. The findings in relation to wage equality for similar work (female/male) ratio was 0.71 in Barbados, 0.63 in Jamaica and 0.64 in Trinidad and Tobago (i.e. for every dollar earned by a man,

Table 3.3   Population statistics for Caribbean islands

Island states	Male	Female	Total	Labour force participation
Anguilla	6469 (49.6%)	6568 (50.4%)	13,037 (100%)	M-81.2%; F-65.8%
Antigua and Barbuda	40,007 (48%)	43,271 (52%)	83,278 (100%)	M-47%; F-53%
Barbados	133, 018 (47.9%)	144,803 (52.1%)	277, 821 (100%)	M-73.1%; F-62.1%
Dominica	34,973 (51%)	33,940 (49%)	68,913 (100%)	M-58.4%; F-41.6%
Grenada	53,008 (50.23%)	52,531 (49.77%)	105,539 (100%)	M-2011: 67.4%; F-2011: 53.5%;
Montserrat	2498 (51.58%)	2345(48.43%)	4843(100%)	M-1485; F-1233
St. Kitts and Nevis	22,846 (49.2%)	23,552 (50.8%)	46,398 (100%)	M-St. Kitts-78% Nevis-76.2% F-St. Kitts-70.3% Nevis-66.3%
St. Lucia	82,227 (49.7%)	83,368 (50.3%)	165,595 (100%)	M-76%; F-65%
St. Vincent and the Grenadines	56,419 (51.2%	53,572 (48.8%)	109,991 (100%)	M-29,383 (56%) F-22,631 (44%)

Source Country Gender Assessments—Synthesis Report—Caribbean Development Bank (January 2016)—Based on Census for each island in 2010/2011

a woman in the same post would earn 0.71 cents in Barbados, 0.63 cents in Jamaica and 0.64 cents in Trinidad and Tobago). The female to male ratio of employment for senior officials and managers is 1.00 in Barbados; 0.80 in the Bahamas; 1.00 in Jamaica and 0.78 in Trinidad and Tobago. These findings indicate that in for every male in a senior official and management position, in Barbados, there is one woman, in the Bahamas, there are 0.8 women, in Trinidad and Tobago, there are 0.78 women and in Jamaica, the trend is reversed in favour of women, such that for every one man in management and senior roles, there are 1.45 women. These disparities are explained in part by the Caribbean Development Bank's (CDB) Country gender assessment report findings

Table 3.4   Gender inequality index (GII)

Island state	1995	2000	2005	2010	2011	2012	2013	2014	2015	2016	2017	2018
Bahamas	–	0.387	0.36	0.386	0.385	0.383	0.379	0.379	0.374	0.372	0.353	0.353
Barbados	0.372	0.356	0.347	0.32	0.314	0.307	0.296	0.293	0.295	0.289	0.283	0.256
Guyana	–	0.544	0.534	0.523	0.517	0.514	0.509	0.506	0.503	0.5	0.495	0.492
Jamaica	0.479	0.47	0.469	0.455	0.444	0.44	0.435	0.427	0.423	0.412	0.408	0.405
St. Lucia	–	–	–	–	–	–	0.356	0.355	0.341	0.339	0.336	0.333
Trinidad and Tobago	0.426	–	0.353	0.354	0.352	0.349	0.348	0.348	0.334	0.328	0.327	0.324

Source United Nations Development Programme Gender Inequality Index webpage (http://hdr.undp.org/en/indicators/68606#)

Table 3.5 World economic forum rankings by indicators (2016)

Labour force participation

Country	Female	Male	Female to male ratio	F/M percentage	Rank
Barbados	75	81	0.92	092	21
Bahamas	77	84	0.91	0.91	24
Jamaica	63	76	0.83	0.83	60
Trinidad and Tobago	60	81	0.74	0.74	88

Employment—Legislators, senior officials and managers

Country	Female	Male	Female to male ratio	F/M percentage	Rank
Barbados	50	50	1.00	1.00	1
Bahamas	44	56	0.80	0.80	7
Jamaica	59	41	1.45	1.00	1
Trinidad and Tobago	44	56	0.78	0.78	9

Professional and technical workers

Country	Female	Male	Female to male ratio	F/M percentage	Rank
Barbados	57	43	1.31	1.00	1
Bahamas	63	37	1.74	1.00	1
Jamaica	–	–	–	–	–
Trinidad and Tobago	56	44	1.25	1.00	1

Enrolment in tertiary education

Country	Female	Male	Female to male ratio	F/M percentage	Rank
Barbados	91	40	2.25	1.00	1
Bahamas	–	–	–	–	–
Jamaica	39	17	2.80	1.00	1
Trinidad and Tobago	–	–	–	–	–

Women in Parliament

Country	Female	Male	Female to male ratio	F/M percentage	Rank
Barbados	17	83	0.20	0.20	93
Bahamas	13	87	0.15	0.15	108
Jamaica	17	83	0.21	0.21	87
Trinidad and Tobago	31	69	0.45	0.45	39

Women in ministerial positions

Country	Female	Male	Female to male ratio	F/M percentage	Rank
Barbados	12	88	0.13	0.13	99
Bahamas	20	80	0.25	0.25	61
Jamaica	20	80	0.25	0.25	61
Trinidad and Tobago	10	90	0.11	0.11	115

Years with female head of state (last 50 years)

Country	Female	Male	Female to male ratio	F/M percentage	Rank
Barbados	6	44	0.12	0.12	24
Bahamas	0	50	0.00	0.00	61
Jamaica	6	44	0.13	0.13	23
Trinidad and Tobago	5	45	0.12	0.12	26

Source The Global Gender Gap Report 2016 (World Economic Forum)

that sex stereotyping and occupational segregation continues to facilitate a labour market with uneven employment for men and women, where the period of unemployment is more sustained for women relative to men (Seguino 2013) and where men typically receive higher wages for doing the same jobs as their female peers (Mahabir and Ramrattan 2015). Further, because of their proliferation in the informal sector, cumulative wages and salaries of women are inferior to that of their male colleagues which contributes to limitations in their economic success (Sookram and Watson 2008). This has a multiplier effect on the economy, this is because many households in the Caribbean are headed by females, and therefore failure to obtain and retain full employment at comparable levels of remuneration, results in their dependence on state welfare payments (Mahabir and Ramrattan 2015), which could ultimately have an adverse effect on their standard of living (as well as that of their dependants).

Where workplaces pursue the goal of diversity management, they may pursue employment practices which are inclusive, irrespective of immutable differences (for example sex, race, age, etc.) as a means of achieving competitive advantage. The intended impact of the applicable Caribbean legislation and Conventions to which the islands are signatories, is to not treat one person less favourably than another as a consequence of their sex/gender (*inter alia*), which should mean that the individuals with the most relevant skills, experience and qualifications are appointed to vacancies and employed. This approach should facilitate diverse organisations.

Business Case Arguments Related to Sex Discrimination

The business case is one of the primary arguments which may be advanced in support of sex diversity (Barmes and Ashtiany 2003). The traditional approach to a business case justification is to encourage workplaces to support non-discrimination/equality initiatives because of the multiple ways in which workplaces benefit from so doing, for example, through an enhanced customer base; increased profitability; offset labour and skill shortages; preserving and extending the positive image of an employer; enhanced organisational performance; enhanced creativity; better decision making and problem-solving; flexibility; better work environment and employee satisfaction; a workforce which represents the composition in society and consequently the goods and/or services produced by the workplace are likely to have greater appeal to a wider cross-section of society; and a workplace where there is a combination of sexes could mean a greater level of innovation and ideas (Allard 2002; Cornelius et al. 2001; Kochan et al. 2003; Liff 1999; Robinson and Dechant 1997; Singh et al. 2002; Subeliani and Tsogas 2005). Consequently, where non-discriminatory practices are perceived as being in the employers' interest, such employers are more likely not to discriminate on the basis of sex, when making human resource decisions. However, the success of the business case is not inevitable and perhaps may be more accurately regarded as a contingent approach (Dickens 2005), which may depend on the size and type of the workplace as well as the economic sector in which it is categorised. Further, there is inconclusive evidence about whether and the extent to which the pursuit of non-discrimination will benefit workplaces (Noon 2007; Wise and Tschirhart 2000). Without tangible evidence, it continues to be a challenge to convince workplaces of the definitive benefits which will result from non-discrimination (Duncan 2003; Noon 2007; Stoney and Roberts 2003). Moreover, it has been contended that discrimination (on the basis of sex) is largely irrational thus, when workplaces realise this they will cease to discriminate and abandon their exclusionary practices, in favour of non-discrimination and potential business benefits (Rubenstein 1987). However, this simplistic and somewhat idealistic view has been challenged (Bendick et al. 1991; Hayles and Mendez 1997). Indeed, there exists mediating factors which determine whether workplaces are likely to realise purported benefits including: the environment in which the workplace functions (Kochan et al. 2003); the culture of the workplace; the commitment of management to non-discrimination; the way in which non-discriminatory practices are implemented; the gender composition of the workforce; the way in which human resources are perceived and managed; and the competitive nature of the sector in which the business functions (Dickens 1999; Kirton and Greene 2005). Thus, where a workplace emphasises the value of its workers (both men and women), equality is more likely to be positively associated with business benefits and as such, more likely to be pursued (Dickens 2005).

According to Kirton and Greene (2005) the business case rationale is more closely associated with managing diversity and inclusion, than the attainment of equality. Competitive pressures to stay ahead may also be considered a determinant in whether non-discriminatory practices towards inclusion and diversity of both sexes are pursued by workplaces. Indeed, it has been noted that "discrimination may arise" (Weller 2007, p. 437), as a direct result of decisions made by employers to be aligned with accepted industry practices. This is supported by Dickens (2005) who notes that competition may extend from the product/service provided, to the availability of labour market resources. Further, a shift in the discrimination discourse from equality to diversity has, to some extent, been influenced by increasing product competition locally and abroad, and the desire of employers to remain competitive and as such utilise the workplace as a "primary source of competitive advantage, valuing workforce diversity as the route to organisational success" (Kirton and Greene 2005, p. 202).

Some critics of the business case suggest that if the benefits to be gained are seen as specific and identifiable, once the particular inequality and/or discrimination issue has been addressed by the organisation and the benefits of that change realised, the business case reasons to pursue non-discrimination will no longer exist (Kirton and Greene 2005). Otherwise stated, once the desired business benefits have been realised then there is no longer a need for an anti-discrimination approach to employment practice relating to sex, because the intended goal has been attained (Dickens 1994; Kirton and Greene 2005). Further, given the complexity of the environment in which workplaces function, some business case arguments will be more relevant and applicable than others at any given point in time, depending on the nature of the business, the strategy of the business, the state of the economy and the influence of other stakeholders *inter alia* (Dickens 2005).

Notwithstanding this, business case rationales may not solely be responsible for non-discrimination within the workplace and indeed, business case arguments, the social justice rationale and legislative compliance are not mutually exclusive (Dickens 2005). Thus, consideration could be given to their collective and simultaneous influence. Additionally, though business and social justice reasons are thought to theoretically operate simultaneously, the reality is that there is typically a systematic order in which such issues are considered, with the result that objectives associated with social justice and responsibility are considered only subsequent to those of efficiency (Dickens 2007). The legislative factors for workplaces to consider vis-à-vis inclusion and non-discrimination as it relates to sex are now considered.

LEGISLATIVE CONSIDERATIONS

The enactment of anti-discrimination legislation makes explicit society's disapproval of discriminatory behaviour as morally unacceptable, and raises the profile of sex discrimination where it occurs (Bennington and Wein 2000). Although the legislation will not obliterate every occurrence of discrimination, its enactment is likely to result in a decline of its incidence, particularly the most obtrusive and reprehensible forms (Neumark 2003; Rowe 1990). For workplaces hiring, retaining and developing workers, these decisions should be based on merit, irrespective of whether the owners of the required skills and competencies, are in the form of men or women (Weller 2007). Equality laws therefore act as an important catalyst for change, where they mandate employers to remove sexist policies and practices and in turn, employers realise the benefits of engaging employees of diverse sexes and other diverse characteristics (Kirton and Greene 2005).

In the Caribbean, the equality legislation enacted in Guyana, Trinidad and Tobago and St. Lucia all prohibit discrimination on the basis of sex, *inter alia*. The primary exception in these Acts is the genuine and determining occupational requirement (GDOR, also referred to as the *bona fide occupational qualifications exception*), which allows employers to discriminate in situations where they can prove that there was a genuine occupational requirement. Otherwise stated, employers are permitted to discriminate in employment if they can show that having a particular protected characteristic (i.e. sex in this case), is an occupational requirement and further that this requirement is a proportionate means of achieving a legitimate aim. The equality/anti-discrimination legislation in the indicated Caribbean islands, allow for discrimination on the basis of sex, in situations where the job can only be performed by persons with specific physical attributes; where a particular sex is required for authenticity in a dramatic performance or the production of a work of art; and to provide privacy and decency where personal services are performed and/or required.

It has been argued that exceptions may offer legitimacy to discrimination and as such stymie compliance objectives (Hornstein 2001; Sargeant 2006), hence, legal exceptions may weaken efforts towards non-discrimination (Dickens 2007). This means that within workplaces, instead of pursuing the objective of non-discrimination within employment practice, where determined to do so, employers may persist in treating persons differently as a consequence of their sex, while utilising and relying on the exception of "genuine and determining occupational requirements" permitted by the law. Where workplaces can show that they have not treated one person less favourably than another as a consequence of their sex, or where they have been discriminatory in their practices but their actions can be objectively justified, these workplaces are unlikely to be found in breach of the anti-discrimination legislation. The importance of the recourse available to those workers/applicants who have experienced sex discrimination in employment cannot be overstated. Indeed, the existence and use of remedies which are punitive such that they discourage discrimination within workplaces is considered a factor which could potentially contribute to the efficacy of anti-discrimination legislation (Dickens 1992). Thus, such measures would arguably be more effective than the vindication of employees through the declaration of rights for example or acknowledgement by the workplace of wrongdoing (Kirton and Greene 2005).

Anti-discrimination legislation in the Caribbean region, in an effort to deter prohibited behaviour, has allowed for remedies to be imposed in favour of the aggrieved parties. Once it is determined by the courts or tribunals, that the discrimination case is well founded, the remedies which could be imposed in relation to the complaint include the imposition of a penalty on the offending workplace in the amount of $20,000 Guyana$ (~USD $98) in Guyana, and $5000 Eastern Caribbean$ (~USD $1852) in St. Lucia, however in the Trinidad and Tobago legislation, specific penalties are not outlined but where workplaces fail to comply with the directives of the legislation, they could be subject to the imposition of compensation, fines or damages. In addition, further remedies which may be imposed include a judgement of damages imposed on the employer; an order directing the employer to reinstate the aggrieved complainant; or an order voiding any decision made in relation to the aggrieved party. As it relates to legislative guidance regarding equality in remuneration, Section 6 of the St. Lucia Act and Section 9 of the Guyana Act mandates equal remuneration for men and women performing work of equal value. Further, Jamaica (*The Employment, Equal Pay for Men and Women Act, 1975*) and St. Vincent and the Grenadines (*The Equal Pay Act, 1994*) have enacted specific legislation to prohibit discrimination in the rates of remuneration of men and women in paid employment to further address related disparities in pay. Failure to comply with the dictates of these laws means that financial penalties can be imposed, in Jamaica this includes a maximum fine of $ 300JCA (~$2.07 USD) or six months' imprisonment and in St. Vincent the fine is a maximum of $2000ECD (~$740 USD) or six months' imprisonment.

These fines, it may be argued, are not sufficiently punitive, therefore where so minded!, and relying on the exceptions provided, employers may continue to discriminate or engage in inequitable practices, until it costs them more not to discriminate than to engage in such heinous practices. Therefore, one way which has been suggested for improving the existing remedies in relation to breaches of anti-discrimination legislation, is "the adoption of a deterrent rather than compensatory approach to damages" (Dickens 1986, p. 29). The law requires aggrieved parties to take the initiative to file a claim against an offending workplace and to present evidence in support of their claim of discrimination on the basis of sex. Such evidence is not easily accumulated as offending workplaces are unlikely to blatantly practice discrimination, with a view of making the relevant documents available to evidence such unlawful practices (Riach and Rich 2006). The failure of the legislative stick to encourage employment equality could explain the emergence of the carrot approach of the business case but both have their limitations, most employers will continue to discriminate, until it costs them more to discriminate than not to discriminate (Rubenstein 1987). Costs, however, are a single consideration and it has been argued (Vickerstaff et al. 2007), that dependence on cost considerations for decision making, may have the impact of creating short-term solutions, hence not adequately resulting in decisions which result in long-term change.

Where the effects of legal regulation are considered collectively, it has been suggested that large workplaces appear to comply with legislation in a more systematic and comprehensive manner than do smaller workplaces (Brown et al. 2000), where workplaces have limited knowledge of available anti-discrimination legislation, its impact may be limited because of this lack of knowledge but also because of the supposition that the legislation is not relevant to their workplace (Edwards et al. 2004; Marlow 2003). Furthermore, the extent of the impact of the legislation appears to be influenced by the competitive nature of the market, thus "where conditions are benign, regulations can be absorbed, but in other circumstances, employment regulations can exacerbate competitive pressures" (Edwards et al. 2004, p. 245). These examples suggest the likelihood of slow, incremental adjustments made to workplace practice over time subsequent to the enactment of anti-discrimination laws, and perhaps more fundamental changes made in relation to workplace practice over time, compared to a greater level of policy changes after the initial enactment of the legislation.

OTHER CONSIDERATIONS

The International Labour Organisation's (ILO) Caribbean company survey, 2017 (see Table 3.6) suggests that greater organisational support should be given in relation to organisational policies and practices relative to the following human resource concerns, with a view of promoting greater participation of women in management, namely: maternity leave; recruitment, retention and promotion; training and development opportunities; and mentoring *inter alia*. Efficient and effective human resources are vital in organisations at every level of responsibility but these are not homogeneous, hence, it is critical that consideration is given to the fundamental differences between the career patterns of both men and women (ILO 2018b). It is further argued that (Mahabir and Ramrattan 2015) consideration could be given to the implementation of affirmative action policies, in order to improve the success of women in the labour market. The challenge with policies such as quotas, positive

Table 3.6 Prevalence of initiatives on gender diversity among respondent companies in the Caribbean (2017)

Ranking	Company initiative	Percentage of companies
1	Maternity leave	76
2	Recruitment, retention and promotion	66
3	Skills training and executive training	64
4	Remuneration	52
5	Mentoring	45
6	Flexible working hours	44
7	Sexual harassment	42
8	Paternity leave	29
9	Part-time working hours	23
10	Remote work or telework	20
11	Career breaks	18
12	Re-entry programmes	14
13	Child care or elder care	6

Source ILO Caribbean company survey, 2017; Women in business and management: Gaining momentum in the Caribbean; International Labour Organisation 2018b

discrimination and affirmative action is that these are not required by the enacted anti-discrimination and equality legislation in the Caribbean region and evidence from larger jurisdictions have shown that this approach can result in undesired outcomes for the protected groups. The anti-discrimination laws currently mandate organisations not to treat women less favourably than men, but it does not require organisations to take proactive steps to ensure that there is an equal distribution of sexes within the organisation, or to increase the participation of underrepresented groups (Sloane, Grazier and Jones 2005; McNamara and Basit 2004). In fact, in the USA where affirmative action has been extensively researched in relation to race, it has been found that policies which advance the careers of racial minorities can exacerbate racial conflict, antagonism and resentment against them by members of other races including dominant racial groups, such policies therefore, do not benefit from large scale support, as they are seen as giving opportunities to those who are *"undeserving and unqualified"* (Archibong and Sharps 2013; McNamara and Basit 2004). The lesson here is that it may be beneficial to have ongoing monitoring of staffing and gender composition as it relates to the staff and management complement across organisations, with a view of determining whether the criteria for accessing training and development opportunities are equally available to both men and women. Notwithstanding this, an equal distribution of men and women is not necessarily the best outcome for organisations, but instead engaging and retaining the most efficacious employees to achieve the goals of the organisation, irrespective of their sex. Where relevant legislation is not enforced, workplaces are free to include equality policies in their espoused practices which are not translated to enacted practices and as such do not result in a reduction of disparate treatment and inequitable outcomes and/or opportunities on the basis of sex.

CONCLUSION

Sex is an immutable characteristic and as such where an employee possesses the requisite skills, talents and attributes to effectively perform a role within an organisation, their sex should not determine whether they gain and retain employment (Weller 2007). Moreover, extant anti-discrimination laws provide that unless specific physical attributes are required by an employer, or a particular sex is required for a dramatic or artistic production, or for reasons of privacy, employment decisions which are made on the basis of sex are discriminatory. Notwithstanding this, the clear demarcation of the types of jobs and industries which are considered suitable for men and women, and the widespread acceptance of stereotypes, continues to result in disparate treatment on the basis of sex in the Caribbean.

Arguments have been advanced in favour of legislative approaches to mandate non-discrimination, while the concept of the business case is associated with the benefits which can accrue to organisations who pursue non-discrimination on the basis of sex. However, there are challenges with both suggestions, indeed within the organisational context, non-discriminatory policies and practices have not universally produced the advantages anticipated, in part because of ineffective implementation and lack of commitment by management (Pitts 2005). Similarly, the implementation of anti-discrimination laws and the mandates of the United Nations Convention on the Elimination of All Forms of Discrimination Against Women, have not effectively deterred discriminatory organisational policies and practices, this may be attributed to the lack of compliance enforcement and toothless fines allowed by the legislation, which are not sufficiently punitive as to deter discriminatory policies and practices.

Typically sex discrimination results in pay disparities and the inequitable experience of women at work, however, stereotypical attitudes can also have an adverse impact on male employment, for example in instances where men pursue careers which require the demonstration of empathy, compassion and thoughtfulness, in the fulfilment of their duties, which are attributes generally associated with women (Weichselbaumer 2004). Nevertheless, an examination of contemporary society reveals that the extant binary culture is slowly changing and incrementally more women are entering previously male-dominated industries, while similarly more men than before, are entering previously female-dominated occupations (Heckman 2002). Continued cultural change will require commitment from societal stakeholders, including but not limited to organisations, government policymakers and legislators, to the pursuit of equality and non-discrimination on the basis of sex.

REFERENCES

Acker, J. (1990). Hierarchies, jobs, bodies: A theory of gendered organisations. *Gender and Society, 4*(2), 139–158.

Acker, J. (2006). Inequality regimes: Gender, class, and race in organizations. *Gender and Society, 20*(4), 441–464.

Allard, M. (2002). Theoretical underpinnings of diversity. In C. Harvey & M. Allard (Eds.), *Understanding and managing diversity*. Upper Saddle River, NJ: Prentice-Hall.

Alper, J., & Gibbons, A. (1993). The pipeline is leaking women all the way along. *Science, 260*(5106), 409–415.

Anguilla, Labour Code (2003).

Antigua and Barbuda Labour Code. (1975).

Archibong, U., & Sharps, P. W. (2013). A comparative analysis of affirmative action in the United Kingdom and United States. *Journal of Psychological Issues in Organizational Culture, 3*(S1), 28–49.

Barmes, L., & Ashtiany, S. (2003). The diversity approach to achieving equality: Potential and pitfalls. *Industrial Law Journal, 32*(4), 274–296.

Bendick, M., Jackson, C. W., Reinoso, V. A., & Hodges, L. A. (1991). Discrimination against Latino job applicants: A controlled experiment. *Human Resource Management, 30*(4), 469–484.

Bennington, L., & Wein, R. (2000). Anti-discrimination legislation in Australia: Fair, effective, efficient or irrelevant? *International Journal of Manpower, 21*(1), 21–33.

Bissessar, A. M. (2014). Challenges to women's leadership in ex-colonial societies. *International Journal of Gender and Women's Studies, 2*(3), 13–35.

Brown, W., Deakin, S., Nash, D., & Oxenbridge, S. (2000). The employment contract: From collective procedures to individual rights. *British Journal of Industrial Relations, 38*(4), 611–629.

Caribbean Development Bank (CDB). (2016, January). *Country gender assessment—Barbados*. Prepared by Caroline Allen and Juliette Maughan (CDB)s.

Cornelius, N., Gooch, L., & Todd, S. (2001). Managing difference fairly: An integrated 'partnership' approach. In M. Noon & E. Ogbonna (Eds.), *Equality, diversity and disadvantage in employment*. Palgrave: Basingstoke.

Dickens, L. (1986). Equal opportunity: A *more* encouraging approach. *Employee Relations, 8*(4), 27–32.

Dickens, L. (1992). Anti-discrimination legislation: Exploring and explaining the impact on women's employment. In W. McCarthy (Ed.), *Legal intervention in industrial relations: Gains and losses*. Oxford: Blackwell.

Dickens, L. (1994). The business case for women's equality—Is the carrot better than the stick? *Employee Relations, 16*(8), 5–18.

Dickens, L. (1999). Beyond the business case: A three-pronged approach to equality action. *Human Resource Management Journal, 9*(1), 9–19.

Dickens, L. (2005). Walking the talk? Equality and diversity in employment. In S. Bach (Ed.), *Managing human resources: Personnel management in transition* (4th ed., pp. 179–208). London: Blackwell.

Dickens, L. (2007). The road is long: Thirty years of equality legislation in Britain. *British Journal of Industrial Relations, 45*(3), 463–494.

Dominica Labour Standards Act. (1977).

Duncan, C. (2003). Assessing anti-ageism routes to older worker re-engagement. *Work, Employment & Society, 17*(1), 101–120.

Eagly, A. H., & Karau, S. J. (2002). Role congruity theory of prejudice toward female leaders. *Psychological Review, 109*(3), 573.

Edwards, P., Ram, M., & Black, J. (2004). Why does employment legislation not damage small firms? *Journal of Law and Society, 31*(2), 245–265.

Equal Opportunity Act. (2000). Trinidad and Tobago.

Equality of Opportunity and Treatment in Employment and Occupation Act. (2001). St. Lucia.

Fagenson, E. A., & Marcus, E. C. (1991). Perceptions of the sex-role stereotypic characteristics of entrepreneurs: Women's evaluations. *Entrepreneurship Theory and Practice, 15*(4), 33–48.

Glick, P., Zion, C., & Nelson, C. (1988). What mediates sex discrimination in hiring decisions? *Journal of Personality and Social Psychology, 55*(2), 178.

Guyana Equal Rights Act. (1990).

Hayles, R., & Mendez, R. A. (1997). *The diversity directive.* New York: McGraw Hill.

Heckman, D. (2002). Glass sneaker: Thirty years of victories and defeats involving title IX and sex discrimination in athletics. *Fordham Intellectual Property Media and Entertainment Law Journal, 13,* 551.

Heilman, M. E. (2012). Gender stereotypes and workplace bias. *Research in Organizational Behavior, 32,* 113–135.

Heilman, M. E., & Okimoto, T. G. (2007). Why are women penalized for success at male tasks? The implied communality deficit. *Journal of Applied Psychology, 92*(1), 81.

Hornstein, Z. (Ed.). (2001). *Outlawing age discrimination: Foreign lessons, UK choices.* Bristol: Policy Press.

International Labour Organisation. (2018a). *Gender at work in the Caribbean— Synthesis report for five countries.* International Labour Organization.

International Labour Organisation. (2018b, October). *Women in business and management: Gaining momentum in the Caribbean.* Bureau for Employers' Activities (ACT/EMP). International Labour Organization.

Jamaica Equal Pay for Men and Women Act. (1975).

Kirton, G., & Greene, A. (2005). *The dynamics of managing diversity* (2nd ed.). Oxford: Elsevier Butterworth Heinemann.

Kochan, T., Bezrukova, K., Ely, R., Jackson, S., Joshi, A., Jehn, K., et al. (2003). The effects of diversity on business performance: Report of the diversity research network. *Human Resource Management, 42,* 3–21.

Liff, S. (1999). Diversity and equal opportunities: Room for a constructive compromise? *Human Resource Management Journal, 9*(1), 65–75.

Mahabir, R., & Ramrattan, D. (2015). Influences on the gender wage gap of Trinidad and Tobago: An economic concept or a social construct? *World Journal of Entrepreneurship, Management and Sustainable Development, 11*(2), 140–151.

Marlow, S. (2003). Formality and informality in employment relations: The implications for regulatory compliance by smaller firms. *Environment and Planning C: Government and Policy, 21*(4), 531–547.

McNamara, O., & Basit, T. N. (2004). Equal opportunities or affirmative action? The induction of minority ethnic teachers. *Journal of Education for Teaching, 30*(2), 97–115.

Neumark, D. (2003). Age discrimination legislation in the United States. *Contemporary Economic Policy, 21*(3), 297–317.

Noon, M. (2007). The fatal flaws of diversity and the business case for ethnic minorities. *Work, Employment & Society, 21*(4), 773–784.

Pitts, D. W. (2005). Diversity, representation, and performance: Evidence about race and ethnicity in public organizations. *Journal of Public Administration Research and Theory, 15*(4), 615–631.

Prevention of Discrimination Act. (1999). Guyana.

Riach, P. A., & Rich, J. (2006). An experimental investigation of sexual discrimination in hiring in the English labor market. *The BE Journal of Economic Analysis & Policy, 6*(2).

Robinson, G., & Dechant, K. (1997). Building a business case for diversity. *The Academy of Management Executive, 11*(3), 21–31.

Rowe, M. P. (1990). Barriers to equality: The power of subtle discrimination to maintain unequal opportunity. *Employee Responsibilities and Rights Journal, 3*(2), 153–163.

Rubenstein, M. (1987). Modern myths and misconceptions. *Equal Opportunities Review,* 16(November/December).

Sargeant, M. (2006). The Employment Equality (Age) Regulations 2006: A legitimisation of age discrimination in employment. *Industrial Law Journal, 35*(3), 209–227.

Seguino, S. (2008). Micro-macro linkages between gender, development, and growth: Implications for the Caribbean region. *Journal of Eastern Caribbean Studies, 33*(4), 8.

Seguino, S. (2013). *Financing for gender equality: Reframing and prioritizing public expenditures.* UN Women. Retrieved from http://www.gender-budgets.org/index.php.

Singh, V., Kumra, S., & Vinnicombe, S. (2002). Gender and impression management: Playing the promotion game. *Journal of Business Ethics, 37*(1), 77–89.

Sloane, P. J., Grazier, S., & Jones, R. J. (2005). *Preferences, gender segregation and affirmative action* (No. 1881). IZA Discussion Papers.

Sookram, S., & Watson, P. (2008). The informal sector and gender in the Caribbean: The case of Trinidad and Tobago. *Journal of Eastern Caribbean Studies, 33*(4), 43–68.

St Vincent and the Grenadines Equal Pay Act. (1994).

Stoney, C. and Roberts, M. (2003). *The case of older workers at Tesco: An examination of attitudes, assumptions and attributes* (Working Paper No. 53). Carleton University School of Public Policy and Administration.

Subeliani, D., & Tsogas, G. (2005). Managing diversity in the Netherlands: A case study of Rabobank. *International Journal of Human Resource Management, 16*(5), 831–851.

Vickerstaff, S., Loretto, W., & White, P. (2007). *The future for older workers: Opportunities and constraints.* The future for older workers. New Perspectives, 203–226.

Weichselbaumer, D. (2004). Is it sex or personality? The impact of sex stereotypes on discrimination in applicant selection. *Eastern Economic Journal, 30*(2), 159–186.

Weller, S. A. (2007). Discrimination, labour markets and the labour market prospects of older workers: What can a legal case teach us? *Work, Employment & Society, 21*(3), 417–437.

Wise, L. R., & Tschirhart, M. (2000). Examining empirical evidence on diversity effects: How useful is diversity research for public-sector managers? *Public Administration Review, 60*(5), 386–394.

Xie, Y., & Shauman, K. A. (2004). Women in science: Career processes and outcomes. *Social Forces, 82*(4), 1669–1671.

CHAPTER 4

Sexual Orientation and Inclusivity in the Caribbean Region

Introduction

As a patriarchal, heteronormative region, the islands of the Caribbean regard any divergence by its populous, away from the dominant heterosexual orientation as deviant and unacceptable. Hence, acknowledgement of the existence of sexual diversity does not equate to its celebration in practice (Maiorana et al. 2013). Indeed, the Caribbean remains one of the jurisdictions, with active legislation which criminalises same-sex relations, and for which offenders (*where found guilty*) can be imprisoned or subjected to capital punishment. The Caribbean region has been found to be homophobic (Holness 2013; Martin-Mack 2012; Skeete 2010), consequent on the established expected patterns of behaviour in relation to gender groups, religious beliefs, heteronormative cultural norms and extant legislation which prohibits same-sex conduct. This results in disparate treatment routinely meted out to members of the LGBTQ (Lesbian, Gay, Bisexual, Transgender, Queer) community, which affects their ability to live tranquil and productive lives. Thus, this group faces challenges in relation to education, gaining and retaining full employment, accessing goods and services and experiencing full integration in society. There is currently a paucity of research and literature on diverse sexualities in the Caribbean (Murray 2009), this chapter examines the current situation in the Caribbean region as it relates to discrimination on the basis of one's sexual orientation, the criminalization of members of the LGBTQ community and offers a timely catalyst through which issues related to sexual minorities may be discussed and understood, particularly as it relates to work. This chapter also facilitates opportunities to consider societal change, and amendments to employment policies and legislative mandates, in relation to this group.

ENGAGEMENT WITH SEXUAL MINORITIES IN THE REGION

There is currently an absence of comprehensive, national and/or regional statistics in relation to the LGBTQ community in the Caribbean region. Inquiries in relation to sexual orientation are not made during decennial census exercises, however, if such queries were made, knowledge of prevailing cultural norms would preclude respondents from giving accurate data, deferring instead to responses regarded as socially desirable (Jackman 2017).

Homophobia or hatred, prejudice and discrimination towards sexual minorities (Maiorana et al. 2013), has been exhibited in varying ways and pervasiveness in the island states which comprise the Caribbean (Atluri 2001; CADRES 2013a, b, c; Gaskins 2013; Holness 2013; Martin-Mack 2012; Sharpe and Pinto 2006; Skeete 2010). As such, homosexuality is considered an alternative form of sexual orientation, which is contrary to accepted norms and values, and persons who are identified as part of the LGBTQ community are often stigmatised and discriminated against (Jackman 2016; Maiorana et al. 2013). The International Lesbian, Gay, Bisexual, Trans and Intersex Association's Homophobia report (2015), identified over 70 countries globally where same-sex relationships are prohibited by law. Included in this Report are many of the islands of the English-speaking Commonwealth Caribbean, with the exception of the Bahamas, where buggery has been decriminalised since 1991, and Belize in 2016.

In the Caribbean, heterosexuality is regarded as natural, moral and superior and hence any behaviour which is incongruous with this orientation is perceived as unacceptable and inferior (Atluri 2001). Within patriarchal societies such as the Caribbean a family unit which consists of a man as the head of the household with the woman having the subordinate, supporting role (Atluri 2001), is regarded as the accepted norm, hence households which deviate away from this tradition are considered abnormal. Consequently, the idea of members of the LGBTQ community, living with the expectation that they can get married, raise children, be engaged in gainful employment and contribute to their communities by being engaged in community activities is rejected by the status quo, even though the fundamental difference between the heterosexual and LGBTQ communities, is what they do in the privacy of their bedrooms (Murray 2009), which does not adversely affect their ability to be a contributing member of society. The taboo associated with sexual minorities means that, in the main, members of this community deliberately remain hidden, in fear of the challenges which they may encounter because their lifestyles are not embraced or tolerated.

Indeed, sexual diversity in the Caribbean is both closeted and observable, and many people adopt a *don't ask, don't tell* mentality (Kempadoo 2009). Indeed, where it is likely that revealing one's membership of the LGBTQ community would result in being ostracised, marginalised, precluded from accessing goods and services, education and employment, remaining silent about one's authentic sexual orientation is the option most often chosen. Moreover, overt association with members of the LGBTQ community is avoided by heterosexuals, in an effort not to have their *allyship* misinterpreted as support for, or endorsement of the sexual practices of this marginalised group (CADRES 2013a, b, c; Kempadoo 2009; Murray 2009).

Sexual praxis is the term used to refer to visible indicators of sexuality, to include behaviour, activities and interactions between people (Kempadoo 2009). Thus, there are lifestyle characteristics which typify that which is expected from a Caribbean male, based on the current binary heterosexist system (Atluri 2001; Maiorana et al. 2013). A man in the Caribbean is therefore expected to have early engagement in sexual activity (adolescent engagement is not uncommon), objectify women, be sexually involved simultaneously with multiple women, have several children, establish an independent household and rely primarily on female partners to fulfil parental and domestic responsibilities (Atluri 2001; Kempadoo 2009; Lewis and Kertzner 2003; Maiorana et al. 2013). Consequently, if men adopt roles traditionally associated with women in households, this is seen as an attempt to undermine hypermasculinity and as such subordinate the hegemony of masculine dominance (White and Carr 2005). It is argued therefore that the disparate treatment of persons within the LGBTQ community, intended to exclude those whose lifestyle is incongruent with the cultural norm of heterogeneity, are justified and manifested through violence, ridicule, harassment and disparagement, indeed, such males are regarded as soft, weak and deplorable (Maiorana et al. 2013;

Murray 2009). Therefore, to keep up appearances and avoid marginalisation, in the Caribbean it is not unusual for men who have sex with men, to also have sexual and domestic relationships with women, similarly, women who are in relationships with other women, also typically have relationships—sexual and domestic—with men, for the furtherance of reproduction and to avoid suspicion or discrimination, and to appear to have a lifestyle which is consistent with extant norms and mores of the heteronormative society in which they live and work (Kempadoo 2009; White and Carr 2005). However, it must be noted that same-sex relationships between women do not attract the same consternation, aversion and objection, as same-sex male relations (White and Carr 2005), nonetheless such relationships are kept hidden and *"their suppression is often integral to the maintenance of the patriarchy"* (Atluri 2001).

FACTORS WHICH INFLUENCE ATTITUDES TOWARDS SEXUAL MINORITIES

It has been argued that one's demographic and religious background, existing legislation, the extent of interpersonal contact with persons of alternative sexual orientations, and beliefs about the origin of homosexuality are some of the factors which may influence a person's beliefs about, engagement with and attitudes in relation to members of the LGBTQ community, including whether individuals have negative perceptions of homosexuals, discriminate against homosexuals and believe it is important to maintain laws which prohibit buggery (CADRES 2013a, b, c; Jackman 2017). Thus, persons with negative views of gay men and lesbians are more likely to be religious, older, less well educated and have had little to no known interpersonal contact with gay men or lesbians (CADRES 2013a, b, c; Chadee et al. 2013; Griffith and Wickham 2016; Gromer et al. 2013; Jackman 2017; White and Carr 2005). Men are also more aggressively discriminatory, specifically towards other men who are known or thought to be homosexual (CADRES 2013a, b, c). This is because of the traditional gender roles that men are believed to have a responsibility to fulfil, and further to remove any interpretation of their objection to unfair and disparate treatment, as support for, identification with or membership of the LGBTQ community (Hope 2010; Jackman 2017; Maiorana et al. 2013).

The current Sexual Offences laws which prohibit buggery in the Commonwealth Caribbean, are also influential in how sexual minorities are perceived. The failure by the LGBTQ community to adhere to the status quo of heterosexism is perceived as immoral, and contrary to the governing laws which criminalise engagement in specific sexual behaviour to the exclusion of others. Moreover, in the Caribbean region, in the absence of evidence to support it, homosexuality seems to be increasingly equated with paedophilia, immorality and HIV (Rutledge and Abell 2005; White and Carr 2005; Wiley and Bottoms 2013). Consequently, when advocacy groups for the LGBTQ community, agitate for changing or removal of anti buggery laws, this is often perceived to mean the inevitable corruption of public morals, and the increased manifestation of sexual orientations other than the status quo (Jackman 2017). However, deviant and morally reprehensible behaviour is not the exclusive domain of persons with an alternative sexual identity, indeed, individuals with a heterosexual orientation, have also been arrested, charged and imprisoned for engaging in paedophilia, are immoral and have contracted and died from HIV/AIDS (Drakes 2016).

Turning to business-related justification for embracing non-discriminatory and inclusive organisational policies and practices in the Caribbean region, many of the economies of the island states depend on tourism for their success, hence, where tourists feel that less favourable treatment has been meted out to them primarily due to their membership of the LGBTQ community, this could result in the curtailment of holiday or business visitors to the region, and as such decreased foreign exchange earnings and business investments (White and Carr 2005). Such exclusions could also limit ongoing business relations, customer patronage and business sustainability, insofar as organisations cultivate a reputation where only persons of a heterosexual orientation are welcome.

It is also appropriate to consider the pursuit of social justice objectives by employers in relation to sexual minorities. The social justice approach considers employment inequalities as unjust and deems workplaces to have a duty to address any disparate treatment which may exist (Kirton and Greene 2006). Thus, the pursuit of non-discrimination within the workplace may be viewed as a valid consideration (Dickens 1999; Humphries and Rubery 1995). Social justice motives are not seen as mutually exclusive from other motives and are certainly not divorced from business imperatives and legislative objectives. Indeed, because discrimination is a moral issue, arguments against it are inherently aligned with the pursuit of social justice (Dickens 2007; Liff and Dickens 2000).

DISCRIMINATION IN PRACTICE

Across many of the Caribbean islands referred to above, once sexual preferences and behaviour are kept private, criminal prosecution is unlikely. However, where individuals openly identify themselves as having an alternative sexual orientation, they are more likely to be ridiculed and ostracised, and the likelihood of legal action against them is enhanced.

Within the Caribbean region, Jamaica, has been repeatedly referred to as one of the most homophobic islands (Maiorana et al. 2013; White and Carr 2005), this was further sensationalised by an article written in *Time* magazine in 2006. Though based on anecdotal rather than empirical evidence, the article tarnished the country's image, which is further damaged by reports of physical beatings, verbal abuse and homelessness faced by sexual minorities on the island (White and Carr 2005). One such incident is the case of Gareth Henry (an LGBTQ advocate), who in 2008 was routinely beaten and abused by fellow citizens and members of the Jamaican constabulary (Bowcott and Wolfe-Robinson 2012). Subsequent to this, Mr. Henry fled Jamaica, sought and was granted asylum in Canada as a result of the persecution he faced. Similarly, reports in the Trinidadian press recount incidents of serious violent assaults of gay individuals, who were living otherwise normal lives (Broome 2011). Although offenders could have been prosecuted for common assault and battery, victims have no recourse in relation to being discriminated against on the grounds of sexual orientation (Wahab 2012). Turning to St. Lucia, where there is widespread discrimination against homosexuals, the religious and conservative nature of the island has resulted in closeted homosexuals there. Gay men are discriminated against in all aspects of society including employment, are routinely refused medical care and may be subjected to abuse, threats, violence and murder. According to the United Nations Refugee Agency, vulnerable homosexuals in St. Lucia may face a life of fear, discrimination and persecution, simply by reason of their sexual orientation. In Guyana, there has been an ongoing national debate on whether to overhaul laws that discriminate against gays, lesbians and transgender people. In the Hindu and Islamic faith which represents Guyana's most prominent religious groups, the legal-isation of homosexuality is strongly opposed. Based on their sexual ori-entation, persons from the LGBTQ community in Guyana have limited access to health care and social services including accommodation and face discrimination at work, fear of being fired, harassed or victimised by colleagues. Failure to obtain and retain gainful employment may result in dependence, by this group, on non-traditional economic activities or the welfare system and state payments in order to meet their financial needs.

Legislative Mandates

In seeking justice whether for oneself or others, the law is a stand-ard tool upon which civilised societies rely. As indicated, the Caribbean has enacted, only in a limited number of islands, anti-discrimination legislation which prohibits discrimination on wide-ranging grounds to the exclusion of sexual orientation. As noted, protections for this group are not addressed in the legislation and could not logically be, as laws prohibiting buggery are still current and active legislation in the Commonwealth Caribbean (with the exception of Belize and the Bahamas). As such until these buggery laws are repealed or otherwise amended, it would be futile to seek to enact anti-discriminatory laws which include protection for sexual minorities. Notably, the act of bug-gery is not unique to same-sex relationships, but may also be engaged in by heterosexual couples, however, societal rejection of proposed leg-islative amendments to the decriminalisation of buggery is based largely on the belief that to do so will encourage homosexuality and therefore erode public morals. Otherwise stated, maintaining the current bug-gery laws is a thinly veiled attempt at prohibiting homosexuality (Griffith and Wickham 2016; Jackman 2016). Moreover, "*the outmodedness* (of these laws) *is evident in the lack of prosecutions made for infractions of the said laws and the disregard of such laws is also evident in the actions and attitudes of those supposedly guided by* them" (Griffith and Wickham 2016). Indeed, penalising such acts would mean self-reporting would be required or a willingness of witnesses, to illegal sexual acts, to report the offending parties (to law enforcement officials) and give evidence when required at trial, which is unlikely. As developing states, human rights infractions if they persist, are likely to have an adverse impact on the way in which the Caribbean region is perceived internationally, which in turn could negatively impact the islands' economies.

LGBTQ Employment

The obvious absence of prohibition of the discrimination on the grounds of sexual orientation in the region's current anti-discrimination legislation (Trinidad and Tobago,[1], Guyana,[2] St. Lucia[3]) is due to the existing legislation within these jurisdictions (see Table 4.1), which prohibits same-sex relationships, and does not consider gender identity, gender re-assignment or any related grounds. The primary problem with the existing laws, is that they contribute to, and significantly exacerbate the difficulties faced by members of the LGBTQ community, leaving them vulnerable to violence, harassment and discrimination. Consequently, where discrimination has been institutionalised in a society or an organisation, prejudicial patterns of employment practice may be followed without question, as a result of expectations within the workplace (Renskin 2000). Indeed, the existence of widespread discrimination within society (Banaji 1999) may make it more challenging for changes to be made to attitudes and practices within organisations or other social institutions.

Across the region (specifically in Jamaica, Trinidad and Belize), LGBTQ (Lesbian, Gay, Bisexual, Transgender and Queer) advocacy groups have filed court cases to have sections of these buggery laws struck down, or ruled unconstitutional, however to date, relevant sections of these laws have only been repealed in Belize and the Bahamas. In the main, these laws are remnants of the colonial era, when British law governed the islands and buggery was prohibited, even after the UK amended their buggery laws and extended protections on the grounds of sexual orientation within their Equality Act, 2010. In Jones *v* Attorney General of Trinidad and Tobago (2017), Jones challenged the constitutionality of sections 13 and 16 of the Sexual Offences Act, 1986, which

---

[1] Trinidad and Tobago, *Equal Opportunity Act, 2000,* prohibits discrimination on the grounds of sex, race, ethnicity, origin, religion, marital status, disability.

[2] Guyana, *The Prevention of Discrimination Act, 1997, prohibits* discrimination on the grounds of race, sex, religion, colour, ethnic origin, indigenous population, national extraction, social origin, economic status political opinion, disability, family responsibilities, pregnancy, marital status or age.

[3] St. Lucia, *Equality of Opportunity and Treatment in Employment and Occupation Act,* 2000, prohibits discrimination on the grounds of race, sex, religion, colour, ethnic origin, social origin, political opinion, disability, family responsibilities, pregnancy, marital status or age.

Table 4.1 Laws prohibiting buggery in the Commonwealth Caribbean

#	Island	Laws prohibiting buggery	Maximum penalties for buggery
1	Antigua & Barbuda	Sexual Offences Act, 1995	*Imprisonment for:* • for life, if committed by an adult on a minor • for 15 years, if committed by an adult on another adult • (c) for 5 years, if committed by a minor
2	Barbados	Sexual Offences Act, 1992	Imprisonment for life
3	Dominica	Sexual Offenses Act, 1998	*Imprisonment for:* • 25 years, if committed by an adult on a minor • 10 years, if committed by an adult on another adult • 5 years, if committed by a minor; and if the Court thinks it fit, the Court may order that the convicted person be admitted to a psychiatric hospital for treatment
4	Grenada	Grenada Criminal Code, 1987	Imprisonment for 10 years
5	Guyana	Criminal Law (Offences) Act of Guyana, 1998	Imprisonment for life
6	Jamaica	Offences Against the Person Act OAPA), 1864	Imprisonment and kept to hard labour for a term not exceeding 10 years
7	St Kitts & Nevis	St. Kitts and Nevis, Offences Against the Person Act, 1998	Imprisonment and kept to hard labour for a term not exceeding 10 years
8	St Lucia	St Lucia Criminal Code, 2004	*Imprisonment for:* • life, where committed with force and without the consent or • 10 years where the circumstances of commission are different
9	St Vincent & the Grenadines	Criminal Code, 1990	Imprisonment for 10 years
10	Trinidad & Tobago	Sexual Offenses Act, 1986	*Imprisonment for:* • 5 years (if the act is committed by a minor) • 25 years (if the act is committed by an adult on another adult) • life (if the act is committed by an adult on a minor)

Source Excerpts from legislation identified in this table

prohibits buggery and imposes penalties including imprisonment for those found guilty of such offences. The High Court of Trinidad and Tobago ruled in favour of Jones and supported the unconstitutionality of those sections of the Act, thus supporting Jones' assertions that the legislation violated his privacy, liberty and freedom of expression. This decision has since been appealed by the Attorney General of Trinidad and Tobago. As a consequence of this appeal, sections 13 and 16 of Trinidad and Tobago's Sexual Offences Act (1986) are in abeyance and cannot be enforced until the decision of the Appeal Court has been handed down (*at the time of writing, this decision had not yet been determined*).

CHANGES WHICH COULD PROMOTE THE INCLUSION OF SEXUAL MINORITIES AT WORK

In the face of opposition, by LGBTQ advocacy groups, the anti-gay notion which prevails within the Caribbean region, pervades every aspect of society including the workplace. The absence of anti-discrimination legislation on the grounds of sexual orientation, means that employers can discriminate against applicants and employees on the grounds of their sexual orientation, without fear of prosecution. However, not all employers are inclined to discriminate in this way. For some employers, hiring the most qualified and efficient employees outweighs any consideration of the person's sexual preference, notwithstanding this, the prevailing heteronormative culture, could make the organisational environment quite uncomfortable for persons in the LGBTQ community, particularly where there is harassment, victimisation and bullying, property vandalism, verbal and physical abuse primarily because of their sexual orientation. Thus, where organisations are desirous of hiring, training and developing the best employees, without regard to their sexual orientation, institutionalised prejudicial practices which are accepted as part of societal and workplace culture would need to be changed, as failure to do so could result in an unsuccessful transition towards employment policies and practices which are non-discriminatory and inclusive (Kirton and Greene 2006). There have been reported cases, where employees who are outwardly flamboyant LGBTQ community members have courted increased attention from the public (Murray 2009). This disrupts the normal course of business, may discourage legitimate patrons from frequenting the establishment, and may dissuade employers from hiring overt or flamboyant members of the LGBTQ community. It is equally important for legislators, businesses and other relevant stakeholders to have a realistic expectation of the type and extent of change likely to be realised, in the absence of relevant, enforced anti-discrimination legislation. Such expectations could in turn, serve as an indicator of the type and intensity of further action required by workplaces (for example training or education) or legal amendments which would be necessary in order to enhance the sustainability of the change (see Dickens 2005; Dickens and Hall 2006).

POSSIBLE TYPES OF WORKPLACE CHANGE

Wide-ranging workplace change in relation to discrimination against sexual minorities is largely dependent on broader societal changes. One significant change which could have an immediate impact, is a change in the current legislation across the Caribbean region which criminalises buggery and where prohibition of discrimination against sexual minorities is included as one of the acknowledged grounds of discrimination in the extant anti-discrimination laws. Laughlin's (1991) change model predicts the likely response by workplaces to environmental disturbances. For the purposes of this discussion, the environmental disturbance would be a change within the legislation to decriminalise buggery (i.e. a proxy for homosexuality), which would allow members of the LGBTQ community to live without fear of being imprisoned, harassed or discriminated against as a consequence of their sexual orientation (Abramschmitt 2008). According to Laughlin's (1991) model, prior to incidences of environmental disturbance, workplaces are in a state of inertia or equilibrium and consequently, the likely change responses may be categorised as follows: (i) *rebuttal*, where despite the environmental change there is an attempt by the workplace to maintain the status quo; (ii) *reorientation*, where environmental change is accepted and incorporated into the way in which the workplace functions but is managed such that existing beliefs, values and norms remain unchanged; (iii) *colonisation*, which occurs where change is imposed on the workplace and consequently beliefs and norms change along with the workplace ethos; and finally (iv) the *evolution* response to environmental change, is where change occurs as a consequence of the relevant stakeholders within the workplace agreeing to adopt and pursue a new direction. Hence, should a change in legislation occur in the future, organisations could decide to maintain their human resource practices and continue to mete out disparate treatment to sexual minorities (*rebuttal*); make efforts to make surface-level changes to ensure that their human resource policies and practices are consistent with the new legislative guidance, but the foundational norms and values remain unchanged (*reorientation*); make both surface and deep-level changes to ensure that their erroneous discriminatory beliefs are discredited, and policies and practices are consistent with a desire to make the workplace more inclusive and diverse (*colonisation*); organisational stakeholders including organisational decision makers, leaders and managers decisively agree to adopt and pursue a new direction away from discrimination, in so doing the organisation will create a new ethos and strategy, which they will follow and with which all employees will be expected to comply (*evolution*). Consistent with the Laughlin (1991) model is the assertion by Goss and Adam-Smith (2001), that workplaces could respond to environmental changes by maintaining the status quo, implementing workplace changes (i.e. changes in policy but not in practice) and as such do not significantly alter the existing equilibrium, or finally noncompliance. It is clear from these studies that there is more likely to be a range of organisational responses, from the nonresponsive workplace to those workplaces which embrace non-discriminatory practices.

Workplace changes which result from significant environmental disturbances, are likely to be wide and varied and this is due in part to the complex environment in which workplaces function. The workplace environment is one where there are several factors which, along with the legislation, are likely to influence employment practice. These may be broadly categorised as factors which are internal and external to the workplace. In this regard, the internal factors include knowledge of equal opportunity issues in the organisation, attitudes of managers, organisational members and trade unions, and previous workplace practice (see Claes and Heymans 2008; Smedley and Whitten 2006). Additionally, those potential influences which may be regarded as external to the workplace include competitive pressures, economic growth/recession, demographic changes and legislative rulings (see Dickens 2007; Kirton and Greene 2006). Finally, there are issues of organisational context and mediating factors which are likely to influence compliance with legislative requirements. These may include, but are not limited to the competitive nature of the market, the workplace culture and structure, trade union influence, management style, management strategies and current practice (Dickens 1999; Wood et al. 2004). Thus for example, where societally and culturally accepted workplace practices are in contravention with the updated anti-discrimination legislation in the future, ensuring compliance will be challenging, as adapting to legislative requirements may necessitate comprehensive societal and organisational adjustments, which occur incrementally over time (see Heery and Simms 2005).

CONCLUSION

This chapter examined diverse sexualities and discrimination in the Caribbean. As indicated in the foregoing discussion, members of the LGBTQ community in the Caribbean continue to experience challenges in varying aspects of their lives, including employment, as a consequence of their sexual orientation. This is largely due to the prevailing heterosexist culture in the islands of the Caribbean region. Therefore, efforts towards a more inclusive and diverse society, will include taking decisive action to make changes in the extant societal culture and buggery legislation, which reinforce the belief that disparate treatment is appropriate *vis-à-vis* sexual minorities. It is acknowledged that making changes in culturally embedded attitudes, values and mores is challenging and such a transition is unlikely to occur in the short term, notwithstanding this, initial efforts which are being made regionally, are significant. In the Bahamas and Belize, such efforts have already resulted in the decriminalization of consensual sexual activities of sexual minority groups, and as it relates to Trinidad and Tobago, the decision is still outstanding (in a similar matter) in the Court of Appeal decision *re*: Jones *vs* Attorney General of Trinidad and Tobago.

There are a few island states in the Commonwealth Caribbean which have enacted anti-discrimination legislation, but due to the extant buggery laws, these anti-discrimination laws exclude the prohibition of discrimination on the basis of sexual orientation. This means that currently, it is legal for members of the LGBTQ community to be discriminated against, and there is no available recourse, when such disparate treatment is meted out to them. Where change is desired, it is important for legislators to acknowledge the existence of a dominant patriarchal, heteronormative and heterosexist culture, and the incremental changes which will need to be taken in order to effect changes in attitudes in society and employment practice in relation to sexual minorities. Arguably, efforts to expedite changes will include the decriminalisation of buggery, the enactment of anti-discrimination legislation with sufficiently punitive measures for any breaches; the application of social justice; and a cultural change towards fostering, respecting and valuing difference (irrespective of its origin or nature). In the workplace, this will require the commitment by management to non-discrimination and the implementation of non-discriminatory practices, however, within the wider societal context, change necessitates a collective effort by all social institutions to the re-education and reorientation of the populous, as it relates to their preconceived notions of members of the LGBTQ community. This includes dispelling some of the erroneous stereotypical beliefs which hitherto have been accepted without opposition, replacing them with accurate facts about members of the LGBTQ community and their capabilities, and recognising that this is not a homogeneous group, but it reflects heterogeneity in the same manner as other societal groupings.

References

Abramschmitt, C. (2008). Is Barbados ready for same-sex marriage? Analysis of legal and social constructs. *Social and Economic Studies, 57*(2), 61–88.

Atluri, T. L. (2001). *When the closet is a region: Homophobia, heterosexism and nationalism in the Commonwealth Caribbean.* Cave Hill: Centre for Gender and Development Studies, University of the West Indies.

Banaji, M. R. (1999). *The roots of prejudice.* Kendon Smith Lectures. Greensboro, NC: University of North Carolina.

Bennington, L., & Wein, R. (2002). Aiding and abetting employer discrimination: The job applicant's role. *Employee Responsibilities and Rights Journal, 14*(1), 3–16.

Bowcott, O., & Wolfe-Robinson, M. (2012). Gareth Henry: 'I saw my friends killed … There's no safe place in this country'. Accessible: https://www.theguardian.com/world/2012/oct/26/jamaican-gay-petitioner-gareth-henry. Published on October 12, 2012.

Broome, J. (2011). *Despite ratifying core international and regional labour standards, Trinidad and Tobago's labour legislation is deficient in dealing with employment discrimination.* What reform is necessary? (Unpublished Master's dissertation). Middlesex University.

Budd, J. W., & Mumford, K. (2004). Trade unions and family-friendly policies in Britain. *Industrial and Labor Relations Review, 57*(2), 204–222.

Caribbean Development Research Services Inc. (CADRES). (2013a). *Attitudes toward homosexuals in Guyana.* Bridgetown, Barbados: CADRES.

Caribbean Development Research Services Inc. (CADRES). (2013b). *Attitudes toward homosexuals in Trinidad.* Bridgetown, Barbados: CADRES.

Caribbean Development Research Services Inc. (CADRES). (2013c). *Attitudes toward homosexuals in Barbados.* Bridgetown, Barbados: CADRES.

Carrico, C. (2012). *The University of the West Indies Faculty of Law under the UWI Rights Advocacy Project* (URAP). Report on the Social Impact of Laws Affecting Lesbians, Gays, Bisexuals and Transgender (LGBT) Persons in Guyana.

Chadee, D., Brewster, D., Subhan, S. L., Palmer, D., De Gannes, A., Knott, D., et al. (2012). Persuasion and attitudes towards male homosexuality in a University Caribbean sample. *Journal of Eastern Caribbean Studies, 37*(1), 1–21.

Chadee, D., Joseph, C., Peters, C., Sankar, V. S., Nair, N., & Philip, J. (2013). Religiosity, and attitudes towards homosexuals in a Caribbean environment. *Social and Economic Studies, 62*(1), 1–28.

Claes, R., & Heymans, M. (2008). HR professionals' view on work motivation and retention of older workers: A focus group study. *Career Development International, 13*(2), 95–111.

Colling, T., & Dickens, L. (1998). Selling the case for gender equality: Deregulation and equality bargaining. *British Journal of Industrial Relations, 36*(3), 389–411.

Dawson, P. (1996). Beyond conventional change models: A processual perspective. *Asia Pacific Journal of Human Resources, 34*(2), 57–70.

Dickens, L. (1999). Beyond the business case: A three-pronged approach to equality action. *Human Resource Management Journal, 9*(1), 9–19.

Dickens, L. (2005). Walking the talk? Equality and diversity in employment. In S. Bach (Ed.), *Managing human resources: Personnel management in transition* (4th ed., pp. 179–208). London: Blackwell.

Dickens, L. (2007). The road is long: Thirty years of equality legislation in Britain. *British Journal of Industrial Relations, 45*(3), 463–494.

Dickens, L., & Hall, M. (2006). Fairness—Up to a point. Assessing the impact of New Labour's employment legislation. *Human Resource Management Journal, 16*(4), 338–356.

Dickens, L., Hall, M., & Wood, S. (2005). *Review of research into the impact of employment relations legislation* (Employment Relations Research Series No. 45). Department of Trade and Industry (DTI).

Drakes, N. (2016). *Examining stigma and discrimination experienced by key populations.* Barbados: HIV/AIDS Commission.

Equal Opportunity Act, 2000—Trinidad and Tobago.

Equality of Opportunity and Treatment in Employment and Occupation Act, 2001—St. Lucia.

Fennell, S., & Arnot, M. (Eds.). (2008). *Gender education and equality in a global context: Conceptual frameworks and policy perspectives.* London: Routledge.

Gagnon, S., & Cornelius, N. (2000). Re-examining workplace equality: Applying Sen and Nussbaum's capability approach. *Human Resource Management Journal, 10*(4), 68–87.

Gaskins, J. (2013). Buggery and the Commonwealth Caribbean: A comparative examination of the Bahamas, Jamaica and Trinidad and Tobago. In C. Lennox & M. Waites (Eds.), *Human rights, sexual orientation and gender identity in the Commonwealth: Struggles for decriminalisation and change* (pp. 429–454). London School of Advanced Study, University of London.

Genrich, G. L., & Brathwaite, B. A. (2005). Response of religious groups to HIV/AIDS as a sexually transmitted infection in Trinidad. *BMC Public Health, 5*(1), 121.

Goss, D., & Adam-Smith, D. (2001). Pragmatism and compliance: Employer responses to the working time regulations. *Industrial Relations Journal, 32*(3), 195–209.

Gray, R., Walters, D., Bebbington, J., & Thompson, I. (1995). The greening of enterprise: An exploration of the (non) role of environmental accounting and environmental accountants in organizational change. *Critical Perspectives on Accounting, 6*(3), 211–239.

Greenwood, R., & Hinings, C. R. (1988). Organizational design types, tracks and the dynamics of strategic change. *Organization Studies, 9*(3), 293–316.

Griffith, A., & Wickham, P. (2016). Attitudes towards homosexuals in Trinidad & Tobago and the southern Caribbean. *Sargasso Journal Issue on Love: Hope: Community: Sexualities and Social Justice, 2014–2015,* 107–128.

Gromer, J. M., Campbell, M. H., Gomory, T., & Maynard, D. M. (2013). Sexual prejudice among Barbadian University students. *Journal of Gay & Lesbian Social Services, 25*(4), 399–419.

Gutzmore, C. (2004). Casting the first stone!: Policing of homo/sexuality in Jamaican popular culture. *Interventions, 6*(1), 118–134.

Heery, E., & Simms, M. (2005). Union organising under certification law in the United Kingdom. In G. Gall (Ed.), *Union recognition: Organising and bargaining outcomes.* London: Routledge.

Herek, G. M. (2007). Confronting sexual stigma and prejudice: Theory and practice. *Journal of Social Issues, 63*(4), 905–925.

Herek, G. M. (2012). *Facts about homosexuality and child molestation.* Sexual Orientation: Science, Education, and Policy.

Holness, T. (2013). Lesbian, gay, bisexual, trans and intersex rights in the Caribbean: Using regional bodies to advance culturally charged human rights. *Brooklyn Journal of International Law, 38*(3), 926–957.

Hope, D. (2010). *Man Vibes: Masculinities in the Jamaican Dancehall.* Kingston: Ian Randle Publishers.

Humphries, J., & Rubery, J. (Eds.). (1995). *The economics of equal opportunities.* London: HMSO.

Immigration Act, 1995—Trinidad and Tobago.

Jackman, M. (2016). They called it the 'abominable crime': An analysis of heterosexual support for anti-gay laws in Barbados, Guyana and Trinidad and Tobago. *Sexuality Research and Social Policy, 13*(2), 130–141.

Jackman, M. (2017). Protecting the fabric of society? Heterosexual views on the usefulness of the anti-gay laws in Barbados, Guyana and Trinidad and Tobago. *Culture, Health & Sexuality, 19*(1), 91–106.

Jewson, N., & Mason, D. (1986). The theory and practice of equal opportunities policies: Liberal and radical approaches. *The Sociological Review, 34*(2), 307–334.

Kempadoo, K. (2009). Caribbean sexuality: Mapping the field. *Caribbean Review of Gender Studies, 3*, 1–24.

Kirton, G., & Greene, A. M. (2006). The discourse of diversity in unionised contexts: views from trade union equality officers. *Personnel Review, 35*(4), 431–448.

Laughlin, R. (1991). Environmental disturbances and organisational transitions and transformations—Some alternative models. *Organisational Studies, 12*(2), 209–232.

Lewis, L. J., & Kertzner, R. M. (2003). Toward improved interpretation and theory building of African American male sexualities. *Journal of Sex Research, 40*(4), 383–395.

Liff, S. (1999). Diversity and equal opportunities: Room for a constructive compromise? *Human Resource Management Journal, 9*(1), 65–75.

Liff, S., & Dickens, L. (2000). Ethics and equality: Reconciling false dilemmas. In D. Winstanley & J. Woodall (Eds.), *Ethical issues in contemporary human resource management*. London: Macmillan.

Liff, S., & Wajcman, J. (1996). Sameness and difference revisited—Which way forward for equal opportunity initiatives. *Journal of Management Studies, 33*(1), 79–94.

Maiorana, A., Rebchook, G., Kassie, N., & Myers, J. J. (2013). On being gay in Barbados: 'Bullers' and 'Battyboys' and their HIV risk in a societal context of stigma. *Journal of Homosexuality, 60*(7), 984–1010.

Martin-Mack, C. J. (2012). *Homophobic attitudes and stigma toward gay men and lesbians in the Caribbean: A systematic review of the literature* (Doctoral dissertation). University of Pittsburgh.

Meager, N., Tyers, C., Perryman, S., Rick, J., & Willison, R. (2002). *Awareness, knowledge and exercise of individual rights*. Employment Relations Research Series, No. 15. London: DTI and IES.

Murray, D. A. (2009). Bajan queens, nebulous scenes: Sexual diversity in Barbados. *Caribbean Review of Gender Studies, 3*, 1–20.

Nelson, L. (2003). A case study in organisational change: Implications for theory. *The Learning Organisation, 10*(1), 18–30.

Noon, M. (2007). The fatal flaws of diversity and the business case for ethnic minorities. *Work, Employment & Society, 21*(4), 773–784.

Prevention of Discrimination Act, 1999—Guyana.

Race Relations Act, 1968—United Kingdom.

Renskin, B. F. (2000). The proximate causes of employment discrimination. *Contemporary Sociology, 29*, 319–328.

Rutledge, S. E., & Abell, N. (2005). Awareness, acceptance, and action: An emerging framework for understanding AIDS stigmatizing attitudes among community leaders in Barbados. *AIDS Patient Care & STDs, 19*(3), 186–199.

Sharpe, J., & Pinto, S. (2006). The sweetest taboo: Studies of Caribbean sexualities; A review essay. *Signs: Journal of Women in Culture and Society, 32*(1), 247–274.

Skeete, G. (2010). Representations of homophobic violence in anglophone Caribbean literature. *Caribbean Review of Gender Studies, 4,* 1–20.

Smedley, K., & Whitten, H. (2006). *Age matters—Employing, motivating and managing older employees.* Hampshire: Gower Publishing.

Smith, C., & Kosobucki, R. (2011). Homophobia in the Caribbean: Jamaica. *Journal of Law and Social Deviance, 1,* 1–55.

Standing, H., & Baune, E. (2000, December 9–12). *Equity, equal opportunities, gender and organization performance.* Paper presented for the Workshop on Global Health Workforce Strategy: Annecy, France, World Health Organization, Geneva, 2001.

Stoney, C., & Roberts, M. (2003). *The case of older workers at Tesco: An examination of attitudes, assumptions and attributes* (Working Paper No. 53). Carleton University School of Public Policy and Administration.

Taylor, P., & Walker, A. (1998). Policies and practices towards older workers: A framework for comparative research. *Human Resource Management Journal, 8*(3), 61–76.

The Sexual Offenses Act, 1986—Trinidad and Tobago.

Wahab, A. (2012). Homophobia as the state of reason: The case of postcolonial Trinidad and Tobago. *GLQ: A Journal of Lesbian and Gay Studies, 18*(4), 481–505.

West, K., & Cowell, N. M. (2015). Predictors of prejudice against lesbians and gay men in Jamaica. *The Journal of Sex Research, 52*(3), 296–305.

West, K., & Hewstone, M. (2012). Culture and contact in the promotion and reduction of anti-gay prejudice: Evidence from Jamaica and Britain. *Journal of Homosexuality, 59*(1), 44–66.

Wheatle, S. (2013). *Adjudication in homicide cases involving lesbian, gay, bisexual and transgendered (LGBT) persons in the Commonwealth Caribbean.* Report to the Faculty of Law UWI Rights Advocacy Project. University of the West Indies, Cave Hill Campus, Barbados.

White, R. C., & Carr, R. (2005). Homosexuality and HIV/AIDS stigma in Jamaica. *Culture, Health & Sexuality, 7*(4), 347–359.

Wiley, T. R., & Bottoms, B. L. (2013). Attitudinal and individual differences influence perceptions of mock child sexual assault cases involving gay defendants. *Journal of Homosexuality, 60*(5), 734–749.

Wood, G., Harcourt, M., & Harcourt, S. (2004). The effects of age discrimination legislation on workplace practice: A New Zealand case study. *Industrial Relations Journal, 35*(4), 359–371.

CHAPTER 5

Disability: Disparate Treatment or Inclusion in Caribbean Organisations

Introduction

The United Nations Universal Declaration of Human Rights (Article 7) provides that all persons are equal before the law and entitled to equal protection against discrimination. This entitlement to protection from discrimination is also reflected in each Constitution of the island states of the Commonwealth Caribbean. Specifically, as it relates to persons with disabilities, the islands of the Commonwealth Caribbean have further signalled their commitment to inclusion and the reduction of disparate treatment in relation to persons with disabilities, by becoming signatories to the United Nations (UN) Convention on the Rights of Persons with Disabilities (CRPD), which aims to "*promote, protect and ensure the human rights, dignity and fundamental freedoms of all persons with disabilities*". To date, the following islands are signatories to and have ratified this UN Convention: Antigua and Barbuda, The Bahamas, Barbados, Dominica, Grenada, Guyana, Jamaica, St. Vincent and the Grenadines and Trinidad and Tobago (see Table 5.1), and consequently, they are legally bound by the directives outlined therein.

In the Caribbean region, there are three islands which have enacted anti-discrimination legislation which includes the prohibition of

© The Author(s) 2020
J. H. Stephenson et al., *Diversity, Equality, and Inclusion in Caribbean Organisations and Society,*
https://doi.org/10.1007/978-3-030-47614-4_5

Table 5.1 Rates of disability in Caribbean islands

	Independent English-speaking Commonwealth Caribbean islands	Population at last census (year in brackets)	Rate of disability as at last census date[c] (%)	Signatory to the UN Convention on the rights of the disabled[a,b]	Ratification of the UN Convention on the rights of the disabled[a,b]
1	Antigua and Barbuda	86,295 (2011)	2.5	30 March 2007	7 January 2016
2	The Bahamas	351,461 (2010)	2.9	24 September 2013	28 September 2015
3	Barbados	277,821 (2010)	5.3	19 July 2007	27 February 2013
4	Dominica	71,293 (2011)	6.1	30 March 2007	1 October 2012
5	Grenada	105,075 (2011)	4.2	12 July 2010	27 August 2014
6	Guyana	746,955 (2012)	3.0	11 April 2007	10 September 2014
7	Jamaica	2,697,983 (2011)	3.0	30 March 2007	30 March 2007
8	St. Kitts and Nevis	53,000 (2011)	5.0	NO	NO
9	St. Lucia	165,595 (2010)	4.9	22 September 2011	NO
10	St. Vincent and the Grenadines	109,341 (2011)	4.4	29 October 2010	29 October 2010
11	Trinidad and Tobago	1,328,019 (2011)	4.3	27 September 2007	25 June 2015

Source [a]Schmid et al. (2008); [b]https://www.disabled-world.com/disability/discrimination/crpd-milestone.php; [c]World Report on Disability 2011

discrimination on the basis of disabilities, these are Guyana[1] (Prevention of Discrimination Act, 1999); St. Lucia[2] (Equality of Opportunity and Treatment in Employment and Occupation Act, 2001) and Trinidad and Tobago[3] (Equal Opportunity Act, 2000). The prohibition relates to employment, education and the provision of goods and services. Additionally, Jamaica, Antigua and Barbuda and the Bahamas have enacted legislation solely to prohibit discrimination on the grounds of disabilities, *to wit*: The Disabilities Act, 2014 (Jamaica); the Persons with Disabilities (Equal Opportunities) Act, 2014 (The Bahamas) and Antigua and Barbuda (Disabilities and Equal Opportunities Act, 2017); (see Table 5.2). However, though the enactment of legislation outlawing the discrimination of persons with disabilities is not widespread in the Caribbean, these initial efforts to establish legislation to prohibit it, are positive steps towards recognition of the need to achieve inclusion and accept the diversity of the Caribbean populous (Karpur et al. 2014). Moreover, there are additional island states which have proposed disability bills and policy papers for consideration in Parliament, with a view of establishing guidance on the practice of discriminating against persons with disabilities, however to date, relevant legislation has not yet been enacted in these jurisdictions, namely: Barbados (Persons with Disabilities Bill); and *Grenada* (Rights and Freedoms Bill).

The CRPD is legally binding on all signatories, hence in the Caribbean, where there is an absence of an anti-discrimination Act which specifically prohibits discrimination on the basis of disabilities, signatory states have an obligation to ensure that their policies and practices align with the mandates of the Convention. Notably, even though the medical model is still the prevailing lens through which persons with disabilities are viewed in the Caribbean, the spirit of the Convention is to encourage

[1] Guyana, *The Prevention of Discrimination Act, 1997, prohibits* discrimination on the grounds of race, sex, religion, colour, ethnic origin, indigenous population, national extraction, social origin, economic status political opinion, disability, family responsibilities, pregnancy, marital status or age.

[2] St. Lucia, *Equality of Opportunity and Treatment in Employment and Occupation Act*, 2000, prohibits discrimination on the grounds of race, sex, religion, colour, ethnic origin, social origin, political opinion, disability, family responsibilities, pregnancy, marital status or age.

[3] Trinidad and Tobago, *Equal Opportunity Act, 2000*, prohibits discrimination on the grounds of sex, race, ethnicity, origin, religion, marital status, disability.

Table 5.2 Caribbean countries and relevant laws prohibiting discrimination on the basis of disability

Countries Relevant laws	Objective of the law	Grounds of discrimination prohibited	Definition of disability
Guyana Prevention of Discrimination Act, 1999	An Act to provide for the elimination or discrimination in employment, training, recruitment and membership or professional bodies and the promotion of equal remuneration to men and women in employment who perform work of equal value, and for matters connected therewith	Race, sex, religion, colour, ethnic origin, indigenous population, national extraction, social origin, economic status, political opinion, disability, family responsibilities, pregnancy, marital status or age except for purposes of retirement and restrictions on work and employment or minors	A "disabled person" means an individual whose prospects or securing, retaining and advancing in suitable employment are substantially reduced as a result of a duly recognised physical or mental impairment
St. Lucia Equality of Opportunity and Treatment in Employment and Occupation Act, 2001	An Act to provide for equality of opportunity and treatment in employment and occupation	Any characteristic which appertains generally or is generally imputed to persons of a particular race, sex, religion, colour, ethnic origin, social origin, political opinion, disability, family responsibility, pregnant state, marital status or age except for purposes of retirement and restrictions on work and employment of minors or for the protection of minors	A "disabled person" means a person who is disadvantaged by virtue of intellectual, communicative, behavioural, physical or multiple exceptionalities

(continued)

Table 5.2 (continued)

Countries Relevant laws	Objective of the law	Grounds of discrimination prohibited	Definition of disability
Trinidad and Tobago Equal Opportunity Act, 2000	An Act to prohibit certain kinds of discrimination, to promote equality of opportunity between persons of different status, to establish an Equal Opportunity Commission and an Equal Opportunity Tribunal and for matters connected therewith	"Protected status", in relation to a person, means— (a) the sex; (b) the race; (c) the ethnicity; (d) the origin, including geographical origin; (e) the religion; (f) the marital status or (g) any disability of that person	"Disability" means: (a) total or partial loss of a bodily function; (b) total or partial loss of a part of the body; (c) malfunction of a part of the body including a mental or psychological disease or disorder or (d) malformation or disfigurement of part of the body
Jamaica Disabilities Act, 2014	An Act to Promote, protect and ensure the full and equal enjoyment by persons with disabilities, of privileges, interests, benefits and treatment, on equal basis with others. A person with a disability shall not, by reason of such disability, be subject to any form of discrimination	Protection from discrimination on the basis of disability in the following areas: (a) Education and training; (b) Employment; (c) Political Office and Public Life; (d) Health Care and Facilities; (e) Premises and Housing; (f) Public Passenger Vehicles; (g) Provision of services	A "person with a disability" includes a person who has a long-term physical, mental, intellectual or sensory impairment which may hinder his full and effective participation in society, on an equal basis with other persons

(continued)

Table 5.2 (continued)

Countries Relevant laws	Objective of the law	Grounds of discrimination prohibited	Definition of disability
The Bahamas Persons with Disabilities (Equal Opportunities) Act, 2014	An Act to achieve equalisation of opportunities for persons with disabilities, to eliminate discrimination on the basis of disabilities, to provide rights and disabilities, to provide rights and rehabilitation and habilitation of persons with disabilities, to establish the national commission for persons with disabilities and for connected purposes	Protection from discrimination on the basis of disability in the following areas: (a) Employment; (b) Education, training and development; (c) Health care services; (d) Housing; (e) Transportation; (f) Social services; (g) Sports and recreation	"Persons with disability" means persons with a long-term disability including physical, mental, intellectual, developmental or sensory impairments and other health-related illnesses, which in interaction with various barriers may hinder full and effective participation in society on an equal basis with others
Antigua and Barbuda Disabilities and Equal Opportunities Act 2017	An Act to make provision for the protection of the rights of persons with disabilities and for connected matters; to improve the standard of living for persons with disabilities; to provide facilitate the elimination of discrimination against persons with disabilities; to promote the entitlement of equal rights for persons with disabilities and to ensure full societal participation for persons with disabilities	Protection from discrimination on the basis of disability in the following areas: (a) Employment, (b) Housing, (c) Education, (d) Transportation, (e) Communication, (f) Recreation, (g) Healthcare services, (h) Voting and (i) access to various public services	A "person with a disability" includes a person who has a physical, mental, intellectual or sensory impairment which has a long-term adverse effect on the ability of that person to participate fully and effectively in society on an equal basis with other persons

Source Extracts from the Acts indicated above

change towards viewing persons with disabilities not as their limitations but through the social model paradigm, where adjustments are made to remove the barriers faced and appropriate accommodations are implemented to make work, education and society engagement accessible. The core principles of the CRPD include respect, dignity and inclusion of persons with disabilities, the pursuit of non-discrimination and equality of opportunity for persons with disabilities (PWD) and to ensure accessibility for this marginalised group. These principles if pursued and reinforced in practice will work towards full engagement of persons with disabilities in each segment of society (Morris 2018).

The objective of this chapter is to offer a systematic review of research in relation to persons with disabilities in the Caribbean, primarily within contemporary organisations, it will examine the challenges encountered, the potential benefits which may be realised by organisations and the scope of protections available to PWD who are subjected to discrimination within the organisational context. As a consequence, it will also offer insight to relevant stakeholders (including but not limited to human resource managers, government policymakers and legislators) as to how to create and foster a more inclusive and reflective of diversity, as it relates to this heterogeneous, often marginalised group.

Understanding Disabilities

There are three (3) primary models of disability, namely the medical, social and the economic models. The medical model of disability focuses on the physical and/or mental impairment with which an individual has been diagnosed. It defines disability as "the attribute(s) of a person who is functionally and biologically limited" (Jongbloed 2003), these may be categorised as physical, visual, auditory, psychosocial and intellectual. This perspective of disability aligns the disability with the individual and as a result, the individual is seen as defective, dependent and stigmatised (Foster and Scott 2015; Sullivan 2011). The medical model was the initial approach to understanding disabilities, however, its limited and exclusive focus on an individual's physical and mental impairments, facilitated the development of a more evolved understanding of disabilities. Hence, the social model of disability emerged which identifies society as having a role to play in relation to the barriers which are faced by persons with disabilities. The social model argues that extant "social systems and societal structures are responsible for creating barriers which exclude consideration for people with impairments"

(Newton et al. 2007). Thus with this model, the physical limitations of an individual are less important than the social environment in which they live, particularly where societies do not accommodate and include persons with disabilities and in fact result in their oppression (Barnes 2000; Foster and Scott 2015; Sullivan 2011). The *human rights model* of disability is an iteration of the social model and identifies the primary challenge for persons with disabilities "within society and outside of persons with disabilities", otherwise stated, the model suggests that disability is socially constructed (Gordon and Tavera-Salyutov 2018). Finally, the *economic* model of disability considers it the individual's primary responsibility, to ensure they are in compliance with the employer's requirements, hence the employer is not expected to accommodate the employee's differences by making changes, instead it is assumed that an employee's "ability to work is determined by their functional capacities", the further aim of the model is to "distribute and reduce the costs associated with limited productivity" (Jongbloed 2003; Mack 2014).

Within the island states of the Caribbean, the medical model is prominently relied on and as such, physical or mental impairments are perceived to differentiate persons with disabilities from persons with no known disabilities. This is reflected in the legislation enacted to prohibit discrimination on the basis of disabilities, for example Trinidad and Tobago's Equal Opportunity Act, 2000 (Part 1), defines disability as, *"total or partial loss of a bodily function; total or partial loss of a part of the body; malfunction of a part of the body including a mental or psychological disease or disorder; or malformation or disfigurement of part of the bo*dy". Similarly, St. Lucia's Equality of Opportunity and Treatment in Employment and Occupation Act, 2000 (Part 1), defines a disabled person *"as a person who is disadvantaged by virtue of intellectual, communicative, behavioural, physical or multiple exceptionalities"*. Turning to Guyana, Guyana's Prevention of Discrimination Act, 1999 (Part 1), refers to a disabled person as an *"individual whose prospects of securing, retaining and advancing in suitable employment are substantially reduced as a result of a duly recognized physical or mental impairment"*. The disability legislation in Antigua and Barbuda,[4]

---

[4]Antigua and Barbuda—Disabilities and Equal Opportunities Bill, 2017, Part 1(2): "person with a disability includes a person who has a physical, mental, intellectual or sensory impairment which has a long term adverse effect on the ability of that person to participate fully and effectively in society on an equal basis with other persons".

Table 5.3 Prevalence of disability by type (all persons), 2010/11 (Number of persons with disabilities per thousand)

	Seeing	Hearing	Communicate	Remembering or concentrating	Self-care	Walking	Upper body
Antigua and Barbuda	10	3	3	4	5	12	3
Bahamas	3	2	1	2	0	4	1
Barbados	9	5	2	8	3	23	16
Grenada	18	5	6	8	8	21	6
Guyana	12	4	4	5	0	10	5
Jamaica	14	5	4	6	7	12	11
St. Lucia	13	4	6	4	8	17	5
Trinidad and Tobago	16	5	8	6	8	18	4
Caribbean	13	5	5	6	7	14	8

Source Economic Commission for Latin America and the Caribbean (ECLAC) on the basis of national population and housing censuses and United Nations, Department of Economic and Social Affairs

Jamaica[5] and the Bahamas[6] rely on a similarly categorised definition of disability. The rates of disability across the Commonwealth Caribbean are outlined in Table 5.1 as reported in the national census data for the most recent decennial exercise (i.e. 2010–2012). The highest rate of prevalence of persons with disabilities is reported in Dominica (6.1%), the lowest rate is on the twin islands of Antigua and Barbuda (2.5%), the other island states reported rates as follows: Barbados (5.3%); St. Kitts and Nevis (5.0%); St. Lucia (4.9%); St. Vincent and the Grenadines (4.4%); Trinidad and Tobago (4.3%); Grenada (4.2%); the Bahamas (2.9%). As it relates to the types of disabilities, data collected during the census exercises 2010–2012, suggest that across the Caribbean,

[5] Bahamas—Persons with disabilities (Equal Opportunities Act), 2014, Part 1: "persons with disabilities means persons with a long term disability including physical, mental, intellectual, developmental or sensory impairments and other heath related illnesses, which in interaction with various barriers may hinder full and effective participation in society on an equal basis with others".

[6] Jamaica—The Disabilities Act, 2014, Part 1: "persons with disabilities includes persons with long term physical, mental, intellectual or sensory impairment, which may hinder his full and effective participation in society on an equal basis with other persons".

prevalence rates are higher for disabilities related to sight and mobility (specifically walking and upper body challenges), remembering and concentrating and ability to take care of one's self (as outlined in Table 5.3). In the Caribbean region, the causes of disabilities include accidents (work related and vehicular), chronic illnesses (e.g. diabetes) and other health conditions, gun violence and gender-based violence (ECLAC 2019; Gayle and Palmer 2005; World Health Organization 2019). Future projections for 2020–2050 based on current population census statistics suggest a continued upward trend in the current prevalence rates of disabilities in the Caribbean (Jones and Luanne 2018).

Many of the challenges faced by persons with disabilities, within the context of employment, may be attributed to discrimination based largely on stigmatisation, resentment, negative bias, accepted societal stereotypes as to their abilities, limitations, accommodation costs, absenteeism and turnover rates (Stone and Colella 1996). Further reasons for the disparate treatment of persons with disabilities within organisations, include anxiety over the possibility that one might also become disabled, which in turn results in avoidance, adoption of prevailing cultural (societal and/or organisational) norms of exclusion of members of this group, and belief in the *just world hypothesis,* i.e. where PWD are blamed for their disabilities or thought to be deserving of their disabilities (Colella and Bruyère 2011). Either one or a combination of any of these challenges may result in unfavourable outcomes for persons with disabilities in the workplace and, in the Caribbean these are compounded by lack of access to or inadequate transportation, disincentives to seek employment as a result of receiving income support payments from the state, limitations in education or training, reluctance by employers to make accommodation adjustments and hostile corporate cultures (Ali et al. 2011; Blanck et al. 2007; Ren et al. 2008; Morris 2004). As it relates to stereotypes, these cannot be applied to all persons with disabilities as this is not a homogeneous group. Research has found that persons with disabilities perform as well as non-disabled employees, do not have higher rates of absenteeism, have comparable or better safety records and accommodations—where required—are not typically prohibitively costly (Stone and Colella 1996). Conversely, favourable organisational outcomes for persons with disabilities can be realised where other organisational members interact with them in a paternalistic manner and where previous engagements with persons with disabilities have been positive (Ren et al. 2008).

In addition to the discrimination faced by this group due to their perceived limitations, within the context of employment, PWD experience social categorisation as out-group (subordinate) members rather than in group (superordinate) members (Carvalho-Freitas and Stathi 2017; Halevy et al. 2012; Waldzus and Mummendey 2004). They are not often regarded as part of the in-group (i.e. preferred groups in the workplace with high levels of homogeneity and acceptance), where members are offered opportunities for development, with greater levels of responsibility, direct contact with and influence on supervisory and management staff and enhanced rewards. In fact, due to their differences (real or perceived), PWD are often subjected to exclusion from the in-group and the attendant benefits, and instead are given less responsibility, receive less attention from supervisory and management staff, limited opportunities for career development and rewards and are collectively regarded as members of the polarised out-group (Carvalho-Freitas and Stathi 2017; IADB 2019). Largely as a consequence of these challenges, persons with disabilities are likely to experience social exclusion, be more inactive economically, underemployed, self-employed, employed in the informal sector, engaged in low wage-earning jobs with limited opportunities for advancement and to experience higher levels of poverty (ECLAC 2019; World Health Organization 2004, 2019).

When thinking about employment opportunities, some reasons which have been advanced for embracing the diverse skills of this marginalised group and pursuing non-discrimination include the moral argument, where the provision of equal access to opportunities and non-discrimination is pursued. The legal case has also been tabled where employers are committed to complying with the extant legislation and where none exists the CRPD provides guidance which the employers should consider, namely respect, dignity and inclusion of persons with disabilities, the pursuit of non-discrimination and equality of opportunity for PWD and ensure accessibility for this marginalised group. Such legal arguments will be bolstered by reinforcing the punitive measures which have been put in place in order to deter discriminatory policies and practices. Finally, the economic case argues in favour of treating persons with disabilities as a heterogeneous group, such that not all persons with disabilities are considered to have the same limitations, abilities, attitudes and behaviour. Indeed, in the same way that other marginalised groups would be examined on merit, this group, arguably, should be afforded the same opportunities. Moreover, an assumption should not be made as to the type and costs of accommodations that PWD are likely to need and each individual should be assessed as such and not as part of a collective. Hence the same access to training and developmental opportunities should be accessible as well as mentorship guidance (IADB 2019). It is

important to note that even though legislation may be an important catalyst in the process of changing prejudicial attitudes and behaviour, the
law in itself is not a panacea and is insufficient to eliminate the problem
of discrimination within employment or wider society, simply by virtue
of its enactment, it is more likely to reduce discrimination, in its most
offensive and obtrusive forms (Neumark 2003), which implies that sub-
tler forms of discrimination may continue to persist.

Seminal Model and Influential Factors

One of the most influential disability models was developed by Stone
and Colella (1996), in which they highlighted several factors which may
affect the treatment of disabled individuals in organisations as well as
those seeking employment. These factors include the antecedents of relevant legislation and organisational characteristics (including size, structure, design and prevailing values); intervening influential factors such
as: attributes of persons with disabilities (including the nature and origin of their disability); personal attributes of colleagues and supervisors
(including their demographic composition); nature of the job and the
skills required; psychological consequences for colleagues and supervisors;
job-related expectations of colleagues and supervisors and as it relates to
the workplace, the treatment of persons with disabilities by colleagues
and supervisors and the responses of persons with disabilities, to the
treatment meted out to them. The goal of the model is to "provide a
framework for understanding and studying the way persons with disabilities are perceived and treated at work" (Stone and Colella 1996). This
model is supported by Wang et al. (2006), who, in addition to considering environmental antecedents which may impact whether a person with
disabilities successfully gains employment, assert that their employment
trajectory may be influenced by similar moderating and mediating factors.

As it relates to mediating or intermediate factors, limitations due to
the nature of a person's physical or mental disability, may adversely affect
their ability to take advantage of developmental opportunities (e.g. training programmes), which in turn could restrict their career advancement
and the ability to avail themselves of development of other job-related
opportunities and skills (Ren et al. 2008; Wang et al. 2006). This could
result in career stagnation, demotivation and withdrawal from the labour
force (Boardman 2003). In short, in addition to the physical and/or
mental limitations faced by persons with disabilities, positive engagement

and experiences within work, are dependent on contextual organisational and environmental factors (Gjaltema and Moonie 2011; Heron and Murray 2003; Ren et al. 2008; Vornholt et al. 2017), espoused diversity and inclusion policies which are consistent with enacted practice (Blanck et al. 2007) and a well-established and dependable support system are essential to ensure organisational success.

DISABILITIES AND EMPLOYMENT

Globally, employment rates for persons with disabilities are significantly lower when compared with those for persons without known disability (*all things being equal*, i.e. the same economy, with comparable skills, knowledge and experience) (Barnes 2012; Blanck et al. 2007; Wang et al. 2006). This suggests that for persons of working age, having a disability may prove challenging when trying to secure full-time stable employment, this is because they are perceived negatively (Beatty et al. 2019), in part due to the acceptance of stereotypes (as representative of reality) by employers as it relates to PWD and their capabilities and the other limitations outlined above. Indeed, within the context of work, persons with disabilities experience greater levels of discrimination, including less confirmation and support from supervisors and peers, less opportunities for learning and development, less reinforcement of their self-concept, lower levels of remuneration, less inclusion and participation in decision making (William et al. 2019; Zhu et al. 2019).

The rates of employment and unemployment are outlined in Table 5.4. Across the Caribbean region, the employment rates of persons aged 15–59 with disabilities are reported as: in relation to seeing (49%); hearing (39%), walking (28%) and the upper body (27%). For the specific islands for which data is available, employment rates are as follows for persons aged 15–59: Antigua and Barbuda (52%); Barbados (36%); Grenada (34%); Jamaica (34%); Guyana (31%); Trinidad and Tobago (30%). Unemployment rates are likely to be higher for persons with disabilities relative to persons without known disabilities for the reasons outlined above (Blanck et al. 2007; ECLAC 2019; Karpur et al. 2014; Newton et al. 2007; Ren et al. 2008). However, this is not exclusive to the Caribbean region, as in developed countries where legislation prohibiting discrimination against persons with disabilities is comparatively more widespread, disparate treatment against this marginalised group continues to exists (Ali et al. 2011).

Table 5.4 Economic activity of persons aged 15–59 with disabilities by type of disability, 2010 (Percentage of persons who are economically active)

Country	Seeing (%)	Hearing (%)	Communicate (%)	Remembering or concentrating (%)	Self-care (%)	Walking (%)	Upper body (%)	All persons aged 18–59 with a disability of any kind (%)	All persons aged 18–59 without a disability (%)
Antigua and Barbuda	66	55	24	46	16	40	36	52	73
Bahamas[a]	–	–	–	–	–	–	–	–	–
Barbados	44	49	27	22	5	39	44	36	76
Grenada	44	34	17	20	6	29	21	34	59
Guyana	47	30	16	10	–	21	21	31	57
Jamaica	46	36	12	14	7	21	21	34	55
St. Lucia[a]	–	–	–	–	–	–	–	–	–
Trinidad and Tobago	48	32	10	16	8	20	19	30	67
Caribbean	49	39	18	21	7	28	27	36	65

Note [a]Data not available for St. Lucia and the Bahamas

Source Economic Commission for Latin America and the Caribbean (ECLAC) on the basis of national population and housing censuses and United Nations, Department of Economic and Social Affairs

Persons with disabilities, though a marginalised group, are not a homogeneous group, hence group members should not be perceived through the same lens. The value of members of this group is assessed through various characteristics including but not limited to their aesthetic qualities, the origin of their disability, the extent to which their disability can be concealed, whether or not making accommodations for the disability is likely to be disruptive and the potential danger which persons with the disability are either known or believed to pose. Consequently, where persons with mental health illnesses are regarded as unpredictable and potentially disruptive in a workplace setting, they are regarded as less desirable employees than persons with physical disabilities (Ali et al. 2011; Ren et al. 2008). If a negative organisational culture as it relates to the capability of persons with disabilities is allowed to prevail, and there are no attempts made to change this erroneous perception, organisational members are likely to expect lower levels of performance from them, believe that their engagement by the company will increase the workload of the existing staff and may perceive any accommodations which are made, to facilitate their productive engagement as breaching the principles of justice and give persons with disabilities which may benefit from said accommodation, an unfair advantage (Ren et al. 2008).

With the continued evolution of technology, efforts have been made to obviate oft-cited objections and reservations by employers, to hiring and retaining persons with disabilities. Innovations in technology have facilitated the development of applications and devices which adapt the physical environment such that the limitations which were previously faced by persons with disabilities can be overcome. Otherwise stated, continuous improvements in technology remove the barriers which previously limited the involvement of persons with disabilities in productive economic engagement and expand the employment opportunities which may be accessible (Blanck et al. 2007; Morris 2018). Moreover, such technology also offers support which may be needed for persons with intellectual and/or developmental disabilities (Morris 2018; Wehmeyer et al. 2006). However, their ability to access the relevant technology will be largely dependent on their awareness of the technology, and the extent to which technologies are accessible in terms of costs, given their limited income status (Morris 2018).

REASONABLE ACCOMMODATION FOR PERSONS WITH DISABILITIES

Given the inaccuracy of many of the widely accepted stereotypes as it relates to persons with disabilities, it is possible for members of this marginalised group to work effectively and productively, when appropriate adjustments are made in order to ensure that their work environment is one which is conducive to their success. Whether or not accommodations are made is one of the most pivotal considerations for PWD seeking employment. Consequently, relevant equality/anti-discrimination legislation which has been enacted in the Caribbean specifically to prohibit discrimination solely on the basis of disabilities (namely the Bahamas[7] and Jamaica[8]) allows for reasonable accommodations to be made to facilitate the productivity and efficacy of persons with disabilities (who are either already employed by the company or are in the process of being recruited). These accommodations when requested, are expected to be reasonable and not to impose hardships or undue burdens on the organisation but *"to ensure to a person with a disability, the enjoyment or exercise on an equal basis with others of privileges, interests, benefits and treatment and the facilitation of such, by the provision of auxiliary aids and services"* Disabilities Act (Jamaica), 2014. Needs for each PWD differ, even where the type and nature of the disability is similar, hence accommodation should be made on a case by case basis. Thus, it would not be prudent for employers to assume that since an individual presents with a disability they would know the needs that they have and the accommodation which they might require (and associated costs). Some persons with disabilities for example have their own software and/technology that they may prefer to use and it is not always the case that they are likely to be dependent on the organisation for such support (IADB 2019).

[7]**Persons with Disabilities (Equal Opportunities) Act, 2014 (The Bahamas)**—*Section 20*: Every person with a disability shall be entitled to a barrier free and disabled friendly environment to enable him to have access to buildings information communication technology roads and other social amenities and assistive or adaptive devices and other equipment to promote his mobility.

[8]**Disabilities Act, 2014 (Jamaica)**—*Section 30*: Where as a result of any employment arrangement made by or on behalf of an employer or feature of a premises occupied by the employer for the purposes of the relevant employment, an employee who is a person with a disability is likely to be at a disadvantage as a result of such arrangement or feature that employer shall take steps to make reasonable arrangements in the circumstances to prevent such disadvantage.

Most accommodations are simple and low costs, for example, reasonable accommodations may include allowances (i.e. allowing additional time for an employee to meet a deadline, replacing a doorknob with one which is accessible), while others may be so costly as to require the organisation to engage a cost–benefit analysis for example a refit of an entire department or building to accommodate a single employee (IADB 2019, United Nations 2019). Typically, accommodations include but are not limited to *environmental adaptations* (e.g. elevators, ramps, automatic doors, special parking) or *assistive devices* (e.g. wheel chairs), *assistive technology or equipment* (e.g. screen readers, adapted keyboards, text to speech software, braille readers), *job restructuring* (e.g. flextime, short breaks, modified work schedules) or *personal assistance* (e.g. coaches, service animals, interpreters, readers), which may influence whether and the extent to which persons with disabilities are able to actively participate in the labour market. Additional accommodation considerations include:- less stimulating work environments (as might be required by persons with epilepsy, or severe asthma), or closer supervision with written task assignments (as might be required by persons with closed head injuries) changes to work schedules and work organisation, development of the work environment, acquisition of assistive technology (AT), assistance of other persons, vocational counselling and guidance, education in self-advocacy, help of others, changes of work schedules, work organisation and special transportation) moderately promotes employment among physically disabled persons (rheumatoid arthritis) and changes in commuting to and from work, and it can focus on a single person or the entire organisation (Colella and Bruyère 2011; Nevala et al. 2015; Ren et al. 2008; Vornholt et al. 2018).

Organisations sometimes indicate their reluctance to make accommodations are as a result of prohibitive costs which the company may incur as a result, however many of the accommodations required by persons with disabilities are not costly and indeed, some of the accommodations may be helpful to other members of staff and/or customers as well, thus for example, installing ramps could help those with temporary mobility issues (e.g. sprained or broken leg), those who are more advanced in age, or mothers with buggies and/or managing multiple children. Moreover, it has been asserted that accommodations can contribute to employee productivity and commitment (Ali et al. 2011). Hence where for example fatigue is a symptom of a medical condition, flexible work arrangements may be an accommodation step which would be appreciated by all staff.

Given the heterogeneity of persons with disabilities, it is not possible for organisations to make a single attempt at reasonable accommodations which makes the workplace more accessible for all employees or potential employees with disabilities indefinitely, since the requirements will vary with the individuals concerned and their specific impairment. Notwithstanding this, to the extent that the accommodations required by the letter and the spirit of the CRPD and extant anti-discrimination legislation, are not intended to be unduly financially burdensome, resulting in an adverse impact on the organisation's sustainability, profitability or productivity. In fact, in practice, "the costs of adjusting to accommodate employees with disabilities are quite low" (Stuart and Hinshaw 2018, p. 121). Moreover, assumptions should not be made by company executives as to what persons with declared disabilities are likely to require in order to be productive, but open communication between the employee and the HR managers should be standard practice, in order to ensure accommodations made are reasonable and helpful to the employee. Vornholt et al. (2018) argue that "work accommodations can make the difference between job loss and a successful employment experience", specifically as it relates to persons with disabilities maintaining their jobs, productivity and job satisfaction. In addition to these considerations, the perceptions of non-disabled colleagues may also be influential, insofar as accommodations where necessary, affect their workload, their performance or their perception of whether these accommodations are congruent with organisational justice (Ren et al. 2008), or whether it is believed to afford persons with a declared disability an unfair advantage over other employees.

From a legal standpoint, workplace accommodations are intended to *"create a barrier free and disabled friendly environment"* Persons with Disabilities (Equal Opportunities) Act, 2014 (The Bahamas). In practice, these workplace provisions help persons with disabilities by improving their performance, removing obstacles to productivity and increasing job satisfaction, relatedly, organisations can access the best candidate for the job, provide conditions at work which will enhance their productivity, this translates to societal benefits of improving inclusion and diversity for persons with disability and offering them the opportunity to contribute to society and contain any cost burdens on the public purse (Morris 2018, Nevala et al. 2015). In order for workplace accommodations to be successful at achieving the outcomes indicated, the culture of the organisation must be conducive to enduring these changes and the organisation must have the capacity to be able to facilitate these changes, there should also be involvement of the employees and the users, support by colleagues and positive open communication. Conversely, barriers to the implementation of accommodations requested include lack of knowledge of accommodations, lack of coordination between stakeholders, inadequate or lack of evaluation efforts, lack of timeliness (Nevala et al. 2015), which can be addressed by the re-education of employers who are willing to make the required changes.

THE WAY FORWARD

There is still considerable work to be done in bringing the islands of the Caribbean up to an internationally acceptable standard, where the requirements of the applicable equality legislation are strictly adhered to and enforced. As it relates to those Caribbean islands where such legislation does not yet exist, it is imperative that the guidance of the United Nations Convention on the Rights of Persons with Disabilities is strictly adhered to, in order to ensure the continued active societal participation of persons with disabilities, including active participation in the labour force (Huggins 2009). In addition, the United Nations has established sustainable development goals with a view of eradicating poverty and hardships currently being endured by persons with disabilities, these include the design and implementation of social protection policies and programmes which include PWD, the removal of barriers which may preclude PWD from benefiting from such programmes (including transportation limitations) and access to public facilities, sensitising persons to barriers and educating them as to how such barriers could be overcome, improving service delivery to include PWD, improving access to banking and other financial services and advice (United Nations 2019). In addition, governments may wish to offer incentives to assist in hiring persons with disabilities such as support for the acquisition of assistive technology or accommodations required, improve data collection to ensure that the needs of this group are known and the possible solutions to their challenges offered by them (Morris 2018). In each Caribbean island, there exists a body representing persons with disabilities and advocating for improvements on their behalf. A published governmental 2016 Human Rights and Equality Report on persons with disabilities in the Caribbean, outlined some of the challenges faced by PWD across the region and which need to be addressed if the goal of inclusion and non-discrimination is to be realised. The challenges include: (i) bus stops and public transportation; (ii) employment; (iii) assistive equipment; (iv) adequate remuneration relative to non-disabled colleagues; (v) built environment and *(vi)* equal opportunity (see also Gjaltema et al. 2011; Jones and Luanne 2018). This is further supported by Beckles and Hanson (2014), who identified the following obstacles faced by persons with disabilities in the Caribbean region: unwillingness of employers to hire persons with disabilities, weak equality legislation and governmental policies, attitudinal barriers, lack of government support, infrastructural barriers, including accessibility of buildings and transport. As it relates to cultural change, while it is important, it is recognised that this is likely to be incremental, and as such will not immediately result in the full employment of persons with disabilities, it is essential as it will facilitate the further elimination of barriers which may be encountered by persons with disabilities as it relates to turnover, social exclusion, dependence on the state, skill acquisition and development and successful careers in a desired area and general contribution to society (Blanck et al. 2007).

The limited enactment of legislation to outlaw discrimination in the Caribbean is commendable but could go further across all regional states with a view of improving the employment opportunities and access to goods and services including health and education (Ali et al. 2011; Blanck et al. 2007; Huggins 2009). The prevailing stereotypes as it relates to the abilities of persons with disabilities and their homogenisation, could be corrected and parameters redefined through re-education campaigns and the inclusion of persons with disabilities in high profile decision making in both the private and public sector (Gayle and Palmer 2005). This includes actively seeking the involvement of persons with disabilities before making needed changes to legislation, government policies and mandates and organisational policies and practice (Morris 2004)

REFERENCES

Ali, M., Schur, L., & Blanck, P. (2011). What types of jobs do people with disabilities want? *Journal of Occupational Rehabilitation, 21*(2), 199–210.

Barnes, C. (2000). A working social model? Disability, work and disability politics in the 21st century. *Critical Social Policy, 20*(4), 441–457.

Barnes, C. (2012). Re-thinking disability, work and welfare. *Sociology Compass, 6*(6), 472–484.

Beatty, J. E., Baldridge, D. C., Boehm, S. A., Kulkarni, M., & Colella, A. J. (2019). On the treatment of persons with disabilities in organizations: A review and research agenda. *Human Resource Management, 58*(2), 119–137.

Beckles, B., & Hanson, D. S. (2014, April 24). *Employment inclusion of persons with disabilities in Trinidad and Tobago.* National Centre for Persons with Disabilities, Trinidad and Tobago.

Blanck, P., Adya, M., Myhill, W. N., & Samant, D. (2007). Employment of people with disabilities: Twenty-five years back and ahead. *Law & Inequalities, 25*(2), 323–353.

Boardman, J. (2003). Work, employment and psychiatric disability. *Advances in Psychiatric Treatment, 9*(5), 327–334.

Campbell, J., & Oliver, M. (2013). *Disability politics: Understanding our past, changing our future.* Routledge.

Carvalho-Freitas, M. N. D., & Stathi, S. (2017). Reducing workplace bias toward people with disabilities with the use of imagined contact. *Journal of Applied Social Psychology, 47*(5), 256–266.

Colella, A. J., & Bruyère, S. M. (2011). Disability and employment: New directions for industrial and organizational psychology. In *APA handbook of industrial and organizational psychology, Vol 1: Building and developing the organization* (pp. 473–503). Washington, DC: American Psychological Association.

Conley, H., Newton, R., Ormerod, M., & Thomas, P. (2007). Disabled people's experiences in the workplace environment in England. *Equality, Diversity and Inclusion: An International Journal, 26*(6), 610–623.

Dickens, L. (2005). Walking the talk? Equality and diversity in employment. In S. Bach (Ed.), *Managing human resources: Personnel management intransition,* 178–208. Oxford, UK: Blackwell Publishing.

Disabilities Act. (2014). Jamaica.

Economic Commission for Latin America and the Caribbean (ECLAC). (2019). *Social Panorama of Latin America, 2018* (LC/PUB.2019/3-P). Santiago, Chile.

Equal Opportunity Act. (2000). Trinidad andTobago.

Equality of Opportunity and Treatment in Employment and Occupation Act. (2001). St. Lucia.

Foster, D., & Scott, P. (2015). Nobody's responsibility: The precarious position of disabled employees in the UK workplace. *Industrial Relations Journal, 46*(4), 328–343.

Gayle, A., & Palmer, D. (2005). The activism of persons with disabilities in Jamaica: An evaluation of the impact. *Social and Economic Studies, 54*(4), 122–142.

Gjaltema, T., Ebbeson, L., & Gonzales, C. (2011). *An analysis of the status of implementation of the Convention on the Rights of Persons with Disabilities in the Caribbean* (No. 15). Naciones Unidas Comisión Económica para América Latina y el Caribe (CEPAL).

Gjaltema, T., & Moonie, S. (2011). *Availability, collection and use of data on disability in the Caribbean Subregion*. ECLAC.

Gordon, J. S., & Tavera-Salyutov, F. (2018). Remarks on disability rights legislation. *Equality, Diversity and Inclusion: An International Journal, 37*(5). Bingley: Emerald Publishing Limited.

Halevy, N., Weisel, O., & Bornstein, G. (2012). "In-group love" and "outgroup hate" in repeated interaction between groups. *Journal of Behavioral Decision Making, 25*(2), 188–195.

Heron, R., & Murray, B. (2003). *Assisting disabled persons in finding employment: A practical guide*. Geneva: International Labour Organisation.

Huggins, J. (2009). The disabled in the Caribbean. *Caribbean Dialogue, 14*(1/2), 13–24.

Inter-American Development Bank (IADB). (2019). *We the people—Inclusion of persons with disabilities in Latin America and the Caribbean*. IDB Publication-Inter-American Development Bank Policy Briefs 2019. IADB, Washington, USA.

Jones, F., & Luanne, S. L. (2018). *Disability, human rights and public policy in the Caribbean: A situation analysis* (No. 64). Economic Commission for Latin America and the Caribbean (ECLAC).

Jongbloed, L. (2003). Disability policy in Canada: An overview. *Journal of Disability Policy Studies, 13*(4), 203–209.

Karpur, A., VanLooy, S. A., & Bruyère, S. M. (2014). Employer practices for employment of people with disabilities: A literature scoping review. *Rehabilitation Research, Policy, and Education, 28*(4), 225–241.

Mack, K. J. (2014). Programs and social supports for adults with a learning disability in Trinidad: Policy review and analysis. *Canadian Journal of Disability Studies, 3*(2), 62–94.

Me, A., & Mbogoni, M. (2006). Review of practices in less developed countries on the collection of disability data. International views on disability measures: Moving toward comparative measurement (pp. 63–87). Oxford: Elsevier.

Morris, F. (2004). Human rights and persons with disabilities in the anglophone Caribbean. *The Parliamentarian, Issue, 4*, 300–304.

Morris, F. (2018). An inclusive, equitable and prosperous Caribbean: The case of persons with disabilities. *Social and Economic Studies, 67*(4), 95–119.

Neumark, D. (2001). Age discrimination legislation in the US: Assessment of the evidence. In Z. Hornstein, S. Encel, M. Gunderson, & D. Neumark (Eds.),*Outlawing age discrimination: Foreign lessons, UK choices* (pp. 43–68). Bristol: The Policy Press.

Neumark, D. (2003). Age discrimination legislation in the United States. *Contemporary Economic Policy, 21*(3), 297–317.

Nevala, N., Pehkonen, I., Koskela, I., Ruusuvuori, J., & Anttila, H. (2015). Workplace accommodation among persons with disabilities: A systematic review of its effectiveness and barriers or facilitators. *Journal of Occupational Rehabilitation, 25*(2), 432–448.

Newton, R. A., Ormerod, M., & Thomas, P. (2007). Disabled people's experiences in the work place environment in England. *Equal Opportunities International Journal, 26*(6), 610–623.

Olkin, R. (2002). Could you hold the door for me? Including disability in diversity. *Cultural Diversity and Ethnic Minority Psychology, 8*(2), 130–137.

Persons with Disabilities (Equal Opportunities) Act. (2014). The Bahamas.

Prevention of Discrimination Act. (1999). Guyana.

Ren, L. R., Paetzold, R. L., & Colella, A. (2008). A meta-analysis of experimental studies on the effects of disability on human resource judgments. *Human Resource Management Review, 18*(3), 191–203.

Schmid, K., Vézina, S., & Ebbeson, L. (2008). *Disability in the Caribbean: A study of four countries: A socio-demographic analysis of the disabled* (Vol. 7). United Nations Publications.

Stone, D. L., & Colella, A. (1996). A model of factors affecting the treatment of disabled individuals in organizations. *Academy of Management Review, 21*(2), 352–401.

Stuart, J., & Hinshaw, W. (2018). The debilitating effects of discrimination: A case study on disability in the workplace. *Florida Atlantic University Undergraduate Research Journal, 7,* 118–124.

Sullivan K. (2011). *The prevalence of the medical model of disability in society.* AHS Capstone Disciplinary.

United Nations. (2019). *Disability and development report realizing the sustainable development goals by, for and with persons with disabilities, 2018.* New York, NY: United Nations.

Vornholt, K., Villotti, P., Muschalla, B., Bauer, J., Colella, A., Zijlstra, F., Van Ruitenbeek, G., Uitdewilligen, S., & Corbiere, M. (2017). Disability and employment—Overview and highlights. *European Journal of Work and Organizational Psychology, 27*(1), 40–55.

Vornholt, K., Villotti, P., Muschalla, B., Bauer, J., Colella, A., Zijlstra, F., et al. (2018). Disability and employment—Overview and highlights. *European Journal of Work and Organizational Psychology, 27*(1), 40–55.

Waldzus, S., & Mummendey, A. (2004). Inclusion in a superordinate category, in-group prototypicality, and attitudes towards out-groups. *Journal of Experimental Social Psychology, 40*(4), 466–477.

Wang, P. P., Badley, E. M., & Gignac, M. (2006). Exploring the role of contextual factors in disability models. *Disability and Rehabilitation, 28*(2), 135–140.

Wehmeyer, M. L., Palmer, S. B., Smith, S. J., Parent, W., Davies, D. K., & Stock, S. (2006). Technology use by people with intellectual and developmental disabilities to support employment activities: A single-subject design meta-analysis. *Journal of Vocational Rehabilitation, 24*(2), 81–86.

William, L., Pauksztat, B., & Corby, S. (2019). Justice obtained? How disabled claimants fare at employment tribunals. *Industrial Relations Journal, 50*(4), 314–330.

Woodhams, C., & Danieli, A. (2000). Disability and diversity—A difference too far? *Personnel Review, 29*(3), 402–417.

World Health Organization (WHO). (2004). World Report on Disability. World Health Organization/World Bank.

World Health Organization (WHO). (2019). World Report on Disability. World Health Organization/World Bank.

Zhu, X., Law, K. S., Sun, C., & Yang, D. (2019). Thriving of employees with disabilities: The roles of job self-efficacy, inclusion, and team-learning climate. *Human Resource Management, 58*(1), 21–34.

CHAPTER 6

Politics and Inclusivity in the Caribbean

INTRODUCTION

One cannot discount that in discussions on inclusivity, particularly of ethnic groups in relation to political parties and structures, much has been written—Duverger (1963),[1] Geertz (1963),[2] Lipset and Rokkan (1967),[3] Bart (1969),[4] Lijphart (1977),[5] Horowitz (1985), and[6] Brass (1991).[7] One of the underlying argument of many of these writers is perhaps best captured by Lipset and Rokkan (1967) who suggested

[1] M. Duverger. 1963. *Political parties: Their organisation and activity in the modern state.* New York: Wiley.

[2] Clifford Geertz. 1963. "The integrative revolution, primordial sentiments, and civil politics in the new states." In *Old societies and new states: The quest for modernity in Asia and Africa,* edited by Clifford Geerts. New York.

[3] Seymour Martin Lipset and Stein Rokkan. 1967. "Cleavage structures, party systems, and voter alignments: An introduction," pp. 1–64. In *Party systems and voter alignments: Cross-national perspectives,* edited by Seymour Martin Lipset and Stein Rokkan. New York: Free Press.

[4] Fredrik Bart, ed. 1969. *Ethnic groups and boundaries.* Boston: Little, Brown.

[5] Arend Lijphart. 1977. "Political theories and the explanation of ethnic conflict in western world: Falsified predictions and plausible postdictions," pp. 46–64. In *Ethnic conflict in the western world,* edited by Milton Esman. Ithaca: Cornell University Press.

[6] Donald L. Horowitz 1985. *Ethnic groups in conflict.* Berkeley: University of California Press.

[7] Brass, Paul R. 1991. *Ethnicity and nationalism: Theory and comparison.* New Delhi: Sage.

© The Author(s) 2020
J. H. Stephenson et al., *Diversity, Equality, and Inclusion in Caribbean Organisations and Society,*
https://doi.org/10.1007/978-3-030-47614-4_6

that political parties emerge more or less spontaneously to organise the political conflicts and represent competing interests. They observed, that as with class, ethnic groups autonomously give rise to political parties that organise politics centred on ethnic-based conflicts over power and resources. Thus, according to these writers, democratic elections in this context amount to nothing more than an 'ethnic census' in which vote distribution is an isomorphic reflection of ethnic group distribution.

Lately, other theorists have carried the discourse further. Mozaffar et al. (2003),[8] discussed the way in which electoral institutions and ethnopolitical cleavages shape the structure of the party system, while Torres (2007)[9] instead looked at the effects of electoral systems on ethnic fractionalisation. While both of these writers attempted to base their arguments on statistical data, yet their research falls short in looking at ethnic groups and parties in the case of Guyana and Trinidad and Tobago, two small island states in the Commonwealth Caribbean. This chapter will re-examine the issue of ethnicity and how this translated into the political structures and processes of these countries. It is inevitable that much of the discussion in the case of both Guyana as well as Trinidad and Tobago will centre on an examination of the outcomes of the General Elections from the period the countries attained independence to present. It was believed that the analyses of the election outcomes were one mechanism to highlight the extent to which tribal voting played a major role in the governance of these countries.

BACKGROUND

Guyana, sometimes referred to as the Cooperative Republic of Guyana, comprises the large shield landmass north of the Amazon River and east of the Orinoco River. Prior to 1787, the country consisted of three Dutch colonies: Essequibo, Demerara and Berbice which were later incorporated. The Republic of Guyana is bordered by Suriname to the east, Brazil to the south and southwest, Venezuela to the west and the Atlantic Ocean to the north. At 215,000 square kilometres it is the

---

[8] Shaheen Mozaffar, James R. Scarritt, and Glen Galaich. 2003. "Electoral institutions, ethnopolitical cleavages, and party systems in Africa's emerging democracies." *The American Political Science Review*, Vol. 97, No. 3: 379–390.

[9] Andres Felipe Torres. 2007, Spring. *Electoral systems and ethnic identity: A constructivist approach*. Department of Politics, New York University, Senior Honours Thesis.

third smallest independent state on the mainland of South America after Uruguay and Suriname. Like its neighbour, Trinidad and Tobago, following the abolition of slavery in 1834 and the mass exodus of the newly freed slaves from the estates, East Indian labour was sourced. In May 1838, the first batch of Indian indentured labourers arrived in Guyana, the scheme was interrupted from July 1839 to 1845 after which it continued uninterrupted until 1917 when the indentured system was abolished. By 1917, though, the Indian population had increased exponentially from a total population of 39,560 persons to 150,761 persons in 1929.[10] In 2018, the estimated population of Guyana was 737,718 persons. East Indians constituted 39.8% of the total population, blacks (African) 29.3%, mixed 19.9%, Amerindian 10.5%, other 0.5% (includes Portuguese, Chinese, white) (2012 est.).[11]

Trinidad and Tobago, is a twin-island Republican State, not a Cooperative Republic as its neighbour Guyana.[12] It is situated eleven kilometres off the northeast coast of Venezuela and one hundred and thirty miles south of the Grenadines. Like Guyana the transplanted populations of the islands are the descendants of East Indian indentured servants who make up 35.4% of the total population (1.3 mn persons), the African descended population which comprises 34.2% of the population, mixed-other 15.3%, mixed African/East Indian 7.7%, other 1.3%, unspecified 6.2% (2011 census estimates).

The settlement pattern in both Guyana as well as Trinidad and Tobago, both classified as plural societies, appeared to have followed similar lines. In the case of Trinidad, for example, the newly freed slaves migrated to the urban areas where they were employed as artisans, craftsmen and vendors. The East Indian indentured labourers, on the other hand, were confined primarily to the estates in the rural farming areas and this factor along with

---

[10] J. E. Greene. 1974. *Race vs politics in Guyana: Political cleavages and political mobilisation in the 1968 general election.* Kingston, Jamaica: Institute of Social and Economic Research, University of the West Indies.

[11] https://www.indexmundi.com/guyana/demographics_profile.html.

[12] Guyana achieved independence in 1966, the then Government stated a desire to become a socialist republic. Then in 1973, there was a change in the constitution, creating an executive president, removal of the vestiges of colonial rule such as the British Monarch as the head of state and the formal creation of the socialist state known as the Cooperative Republic of Guyana. The republican status, and the socialist goal both became enshrined in the name. In the case of Trinidad and Tobago, the country assumed republican status in 1976 in which framed laws and structures allow for the governance of the country.

religious and cultural beliefs prevented them from mixing with other eth-nic communities. Similarly, in the case of Guyana, the African descended population settled in and around the capital city of Georgetown while the East Indian population congregated in the rural, farming or fishing areas. Guyana and Trinidad and Tobago, clearly pattern the characteristics of a plural society or fractured or conflict societies. In these societies there are two or more distinct social orders living in parallel within one political entity without much intermingling. To a large extent, it has been argued that the division of groups within these societies was reinforced by the colonial administrators. Stewart (2004)[13] wrote:

> *The role of European planters implementing indentured servitude had a tre-mendous effect on shaping social attitudes in colonial Trinidad. For instance, Indian indentured labourers were kept apart geographically and culturally from the rest of captive labour force. This separation fostered an atmosphere that perpetuated the negative stereotypes initiated by the white planters. The tactic was to further divide the labour force from uniting. The planter elite rationalized the division of labour by claiming that Afrikans were poor work-ers, lazy, irresponsible and frivolous while East Indians were characterized as industrious, docile, obedient and manageable. Later, some East Indians also adopted this view of the enslaved Afrikans. Hence the perpetuation and insti-tutionalization of hackneyed image of the oppressed by a group in a similar situation. East Indians were also stereotyped as stingy, prone to domestic vio-lence and a heathen for not adopting "western ways." Therefore, the division of labour was created by the planter elite as a means of effectively controlling the labour force.*

The impact of the division of the ethnic groups according to bound-aries as well as occupational lines was to have a major impact on the way associations were established but more importantly it also had a signifi-cant if not long-term impact on voting trends when systems of govern-ment were officially established in both countries.

---

[13] Nakeba Stewart. 2004. "Race and colour in Trinidad and Tobago." *Trinidad and Tobago News Forum.* http://www.trinidadandtobagonews.com/forum/webs_config.pl?md=read; id=1467.

ETHNICITY AND POLITICS IN GUYANA

Pre-independence—The Politics of Divide and Rule?

Prior to 1953, Guyana, then called British Guiana, had a number of well-established political parties and numerous Associations representing the various ethnic groupings, including the Chinese as well as the Portuguese.[14] In 1953, however, Guyana held general elections based on a new franchise which extended the voting age to persons of twenty years and older. At that time, the political structure was a bicameral legislature consisting of the following arms:

- A House of Assembly composed of twenty-four elected representatives and three ex officio members;
- A State Council composed of nine members of whom six were appointed by the Governor on his discretion, two on the recommendation of the Ministers elected from the House of Assembly and one appointed after consultation with the independent and minority party members of the House of assembly;
- An Executive Council in which was vested all the essential powers under the Constitution. The Council consisted of the Governor as president, with a casting vote only, the three ex officio members of the House of Assembly, six Ministers chosen by ballot from among the elected members of the House of Assembly and a member of the State Council.

At this stage, though, it was appeared that ethnic considerations were not the basis for party formation. Rather, it should be noted that the People's Progressive Party (the PPP) (this party won the elections taking 18 of the 24 seats) which was established on 1 January 1950 was a merger of the British Guiana Labour Party led by Forbes Burnham (an Afro-Guyanese lawyer) and the Political Affairs Committee led by Cheddi Jagan (an Indo-Guyanese dentist). At its inception, then, the PPP appeared on the surface to be a multi-ethnic party supported by workers as well as intellectuals incorporating members from not only the majority ethnic segments but including the smaller segments such

---

[14] For instance, organisations included the League of Coloured Peoples, the East Indian Association, the Chinese Association and the Portuguese Club.

as Portuguese and Chinese nationals as well. On 27 April 1953, General Elections were held under the first past the post system for 24 seats in the New House of Assembly. The People's Progressive Party (the PPP) polled 77,695 or 51% of the valid votes and obtained 18 of the 24 seats in the House of Assembly, the National Democratic Party won 2 seats and the independent candidates won 4 seats. However, as with all parties, the critical consideration was the question of who was to lead the party, the PPP. The fight over the position of leader emerged early. It has been argued, that the struggle for leadership had to do with diverse ideological positions taken by Jagan and Burnham. It has also been suggested that Burnham had, in a sense, been "double crossed since he thought he would have been selected as leader of the House when he was in fact appointed as Chairman of the Party. He claimed, then, that he had not been treated as an 'equal partner".[15] The legislature opened on 30 May 1953.

Already suspicious of Jagan and the PPP's radicalism, conservative forces in the business community were further distressed by the new administration's programme of expanding the role of the state in the economy and society. The PPP also sought to implement its reform programme at a rapid pace, which brought the party into confrontation with the governor and with high-ranking civil servants who preferred more gradual change. The issue of civil service appointments also threatened the PPP, in this case from within. Following the 1953 victory, these appointments became an issue between the predominantly Indo-Guyanese supporters of Jagan and the largely Afro-Guyanese backers of Burnham. Burnham threatened to split the party if he were not made sole leader of the PPP. A compromise was reached—members of what had become Burnham's faction received ministerial appointments.

It was claimed that it was the introduction of the Labour Relations Act which provoked a confrontation with the British administration. While the law was ostensibly aimed at reducing the intra-union rivalries which existed at that period, at the same time it was felt that it would favour the Guiana and Industrial Workers Union, a Union which was closely aligned with the ruling party. The British government interpreted this intermingling of party politics and labour unionism as a direct

---

[15]For more on this, see Guyana under Siege. A History of Political Alliances in Guyana 1953–1977 by Hazel Woodford. http://www.guyanaundersiege.com/Historical/Political%20Alliances.htm.

challenge to the constitution and the authority of the governor. The day after the act was passed, on 9 October 1953, London suspended the colony's constitution and, under pretext of quelling disturbances, sent in troops.

It appears, though, that the justifications provided for suspending the Constitution in October 1953 was a mere smokescreen. Rather from recently[16] declassified files, it was evident that there was intense distrust of Jagan by the British. Excerpts from one letter are accordingly produced below for the details it provides through its narrative.

12. REPORT ON BRITISH GUIANA BY THE GOVERNOR, SIR ALFRED SAVAGE

(There is no date on document, but it was written in early September 1953.)
URGENT
NOTE BY GOVERNOR
There is no real political opposition to the party in power. There are too many parties and independents and again no apparent leadership.......

*The European Guianese have not yet recovered from the shock of the elections but they are not prepared to enter politics and indeed anti-white feeling is growing, fed by propaganda, and soon no white candidate will stand a chance of being elected. Unfortunately, there is a fairly strong feeling by local Europeans against overseas Europeans. There is no real leadership in the European community. The majority of the leading business men are employees.
......*

In the above circumstances it is not surprising that the P.P.P. not only won the elections but have met with some success in strengthening their position subsequently. The party members are a very mixed lot ranging from labourers to professional men and owners of substantial property. The six opposition members are of poor quality. Every one of these men has a deep bitterness of feeling against Britain, the past administration and/or against society generally. Jagan, brought up on a sugar estate; Burnham, twice abused publicly overseas for being black;

The attack on overseas officers in the Civil Service is fairly general and has not been relieved by the numerous discussions I have had individually and collectively with Ministers. I fear too that there have been many weaknesses in the

---

[16]The Suspension of the British Guiana Constitution—1953 (Declassified British documents) Editor—Dr. Odeen Ishmael GNI Publications—2004 © Odeen Ishmael http://www.guyana.org/govt/declassified_british_documents_1953.html.

past in the Establishment Section of the Secretariat for which we are now suf-
fering and that the previous Promotion Board was not objective or sufficient.
The most serious impact from a security point of view are the attacks on police
morale.

There is a lot of racial feeling here. In spite of the nationalistic slogans, there is
a deep distrust by the African of the Indian and a physical fear of the African
by the Indian. Many Africans hate the while man, while the Portuguese are
probably more responsible than anybody for racial feelings. The African feels
too that rice, which is predominantly an Indian crop, has received unfair
preference in capital expenditure. "White" clubs are a threat to security.

With the suspension of the Constitution, Guyana retracted to racial moorings with a call for Apaan Jaat as well as demands for the partitioning of the country. Fish and Brooks (2004)[17] suggested that political parties, in heterogeneous societies, usually coalesce along party lines and thus it was not strange when as a breakaway party Burnham entered into alliance with the smaller National Democratic Party which changed its name to The People's National Congress. By 1960, however, attempts were once more made to establish a grand alliance or nationalist government with the People's National Congress and those splinter groups including the National Labour Front, the Progressive Labour Party and the United Force. This attempt met with no success. In 1961, by Order in Council 1961, British Guiana (Guyana) attained full internal self-government. On 18 July 1961, a new Constitution—The Constitution of British Guiana—annexed to The British Guiana (Constitution) Order in Council, 1961, and made on 26 June 1961, by Her Majesty by and with the advice of Her Privy Council—came into operation. This new Constitution revoked the 1953 Constitutional Instruments and the amendments thereto. Provision was made in the new Constitution for a Premier and a Council of Ministers (not called the Executive Council or the Cabinet). Provision was also made for a two-chamber Legislature—a Senate and a Legislative Assembly. Under this arrangement, two chambers were introduced namely the Senate and the Legislative Assembly. The Senate or the Upper House consisted of thirteen senators, eight of whom were appointed by the Governor in accordance with the advice of the premier and three persons

---

[17] Steven Fish and Robin S. Brooks. 2004. "Does diversity hurt democracy?" *Journal of Democracy*, Vol. 15, No. 1: 153–167.

represented the public interest. The Legislative Assembly comprised thirty-five elected members. Executive power was vested in the Council of Ministers led by the Premier and consisting of nine other Ministers of Government.

Following the introduction of self-government, General Elections were held on 21 August 1961. Jagan's party, the People's Progressive Party won twenty seats, the People's National Congress attained eleven seats and the United Force led by a Portuguese, Peter D'Aguiar, won four seats. The overall results of the election indicated that the People's Progressive Party led by Jagan won 42.6% of the total votes cast, while the People's National Congress obtained 41% of the vote and the United Front 16% of the total votes cast. During the period 1960–1964, Guyana was faced with a number of unrests. While the unrests did not lead to an overthrow of the Jagan government, it did lead to the putting together of a conference to discuss revisions to the Constitution. Both the Opposition as well as the Government were adamant that they supported the move for independence at this time and while both parties were firm on this point where they departed was the system of voting. The Jagan faction wanted to maintain the first past the post system of voting while the Burnham faction introduced demands for proportional representation. Coming out of the constitutional discussions, the British government stepped in as arbitrators. The British government refused to fix a date for independence, imposed the Israeli model of proportional representation and proposed new elections in 1964, one year earlier than due. The views of the British Government are according summed up in the following despatch:

> *In October, 1961 both Houses of the British Guiana Legislature passed a Resolution asking Her Majesty's Government to fix a date for independence in 1962. The Resolution was approved by a very substantial majority and unanimously by the two main parties which between them obtained 85% of the votes in the recent General Elections. On December 13, Dr. Jagan asked the Colonial Secretary to give effect to the Resolution. In view of Her Majesty's Government's undertaking to consult further with the United States Government (which could not of course be disclosed) the Colonial Secretary told. Dr. Jagan that although the 1960 Constitutional Conference formula represented the agreed position, the Legislature's Resolution was a new development in so far as at the 1960 Conference there had not been near unanimity on the Guianese side on the question of independence.*

While there are still arguments for adhering to the formula agreed in 1960, the balance of advantage now lies with accelerating the move towards independence. However, divided on other subjects, both British Guiana parties are in agreement in their overwhelming desire for early independence and this is probably the one major issue on which Dr. Jagan could enlist mass support for his Government.

In so far as readiness for independence is concerned British Guiana's claim is as good, ... other territories that have recently attained independenc. Delay would worsen Her Majesty's Government's relations with the present Government of British Guiana. If there are no early indications of progress towards independence and of a greater flow of aid, the present Government of British Guiana will be reinforced in its tendency to suspect the West as a whole. The lack of concrete response so far to Dr. Jagan's request for financial aid which he pressed during his visit to the United States has already aggravated the situation. Anti-British agitation would provide a happy hunting ground for those elements whose aim is to exacerbate racial tension in the Colony. Any outbreak of violence would be extremely difficult to control and Her Majesty's Government would find it difficult to justify the despatch of military reinforcements.[18]

It was evident that both the British Government as well as the Government of the USA while pondering the granting of independence to Guyana, at the same time, they were extremely concerned about the "leanings" of Jagan's government during this period. In 1961, when faced with mounting challenges to develop Guyana, Jagan had sought assistance from the USA only to be rejected. He then sought assistance from the Soviet Union to which the USA responded:

The need for a change in US policy is urgent in British Guyana. The colony's five-year development plan, which is regarded as the minimum that must be done if the economy of the territory is not to regress, is running into financial difficulties, and Dr Jagan has to raise some $BW155 million, if it is to be completed. Moreover, he has ideas for vastly expanded expenditure on development and all his efforts are directed towards finding the finance for such a total. Her Majesty's Government cannot assist him further and

---

[18]Telegram from Foreign Office to the British Ambassador in Washington (4 January 1962) Secret Amended Distribution—12 January 1962 Outward Saving Telegram from Foreign Office to Washington by Bag Foreign Office and Whitehall Distribution No. 61 Saving 4 January 1962.

Dr Jagan is willing to look anywhere for money, including the Soviet Bloc. Dr Jagan, however, got no firm promise of money and only a general undertaking of aid during his recent visit to Washington. He is now distrustful of American intensions and the general atmosphere of bumbling associated with the American efforts to do something does nothing to change his convictions. In spite of their tactful reception of Dr Jagan during his visit to Washington, their handling of the situation contrasts with what we have taken to be their policy of proving to British Guiana that its future lies in association with the west rather than following the path taken by Dr Castro who is one of Dr Jagan's heroes.[19]

In 1964, the Constitution was amended. Provision was made for a single chamber legislative body—called the House of Assembly and consisting of 53 Members to be elected for the first time under the system of proportional representation. General Elections were held in Guyana in 1964. According to one observer it could have been described as a "racial census" in which voting was polarised according to ethnicity. The elections were intense with a high voter turnout of nearly 97%.[20] While the Indian party led by Jagan (the PPP) won 24 of the 53 seats, the joining of the African-party led by Burnham (the People's National Congress (PNC)) which won 22 seats with the United Force (this party led by a Portuguese won 7 seats) were able to form a coalition government with a working majority.

In 1965, an amendment to the Constitution provided for the Office of Prime Minister, in the place of Premier. On 26 May 1966, British Guiana attained Independence as Guyana. A new Constitution came into operation. The Office of Governor-General replaced the Office of Governor. The Governor, Sir Richard Edmonds Luyt, KCMG, DCM, became the First Governor-General. The House of Assembly became the National Assembly of the First Parliament of Guyana. The Members of the House of Assembly became the Members of the

---

[19] Draft brief prepared by British colonial office (undated but prepared in December, 1961) Secret Draft Brief for Prime Minister's visit to Bermuda–Anglo-US approach to the Caribbean Area. Declassified Documents on British Guiana (Extracted from Foreign relations of the USA 1961–1963, Volume XII—American republics. This volume was prepared by the US Department of State, Office of Historian, Bureau of Public Affairs and printed by the United States Government Printing Office, Washington, 1966.

[20] Donald L. Horowitz. 2000. *Ethnic groups in conflict*. London, UK: University of California Press.

new National Assembly of the First Parliament of Guyana. The Office of the Legislature was renamed the Parliament Office. Two new Offices of Clerk of the National Assembly and Deputy Clerk of the National Assembly were established by the Constitution, outside of the Public Service, and replaced the Public Service Offices of Clerk of the Legislature.

It was claimed that as soon as Burnham acquired power, he consolidated his rule through party paramountcy. For instance, whereas in 1964, the total number of persons employed in the armed forces was 2135 by 1977 this number had increased to 21,751. While in 1964 there was approximately one military personnel for every 284 citizens by 1976 there was one for every 37 citizens. There appeared, also, to be a distinct bias in the ethnic composition of the persons appointed to key positions. For instance, in 1965 of the total security force of 3671 persons only 733 (20%) were East Indians. In 1970, of a total of 4145 persons in the Defence Force and police forces, 2840 were of African descent, 994 or 24% were of East Indian descent and 310 or 7% were classified as other. In the Civil Service, 33.1% of the total employed, 27.2% were East Indians, 62.5% African, 13.9% were classified as other. In the Government Agencies, 27.2% were of East Indian origin, 62.5% were of African origin while 10.3% were classified as other.

Burnham was to maintain governmental power from 1964 to 1980 as Prime Minister and later when the country became a Cooperative Republic he assumed the position as President (he died in 1985 at the age of 62). Much has been written about Burnham's methods of governance during this period, gerrymandering, the manipulation of the electoral processes and polarisation of the civil service. It was claimed that his policy of nationalisation was so entrenched with ensuring that spoils went to the supporters of the PNC that this was responsible for the country's economic decline. Indeed, by 1988, Guyana's debt had ballooned to over US$1.7 billion and overdue payment of US$1 billion in 1988. An examination of the election results during the periods 1964—1985, clearly seem to indicate that voter padding under the PNC was a well-crafted. Indeed, it appears that Burnham's leadership was one of the classic leadership types proposed by Hagan (1987). It was dominance by a single party, and in this case a dominant leader, with established autonomous bureaucracies and institutions. The various domestic political

Table 6.1 Per cent of vote allocated to the majority parties and seats obtained

	1964		1968		1973		1980		1985	
Party	% votes	Seats	% votes	Seats	% votes	Seats	% votes	Seats	% votes	Seats
PNC	45.8	24	55.8	30	70.1	37	77.7	41	78.5	42
PPP	40.5	22	36.5	19	26.6	14	19.5	10	15.8	8

Source Author created with Statistics drawn from electoral reports of Guyana 1964–1985

Table 6.2 Vote allocated to the majority parties and seats obtained

	1992		1997		2001		2006		2011	
Party	% votes	Seats	% votes	Seats	% votes	Seats	% votes	Seats	% votes	Seats
PNC	42.3	23	40.5	22	41.6	27	34.0	22	40.81	26
PPP	53.5	28	55.3	29	53.0	34	54.6	36	48.6	32

Source Compiled from election results

arenas, among them the cabinet, the legislature and the civil service thus became a continuing arm of the regime leader.[21]

Apart from claims of gerrymandering the election results, it can also be suggested that the system of government seemed to reinforce the dominance of one group in government (see Table 6.1 for period 1964—1985).

As Table 6.1 indicates the PNC consistently demonstrated a high voter turnout and maintained majority control.

However, by 1992 onwards, election results seemed more closely aligned to the racial composition of the society with the People's Progressive Party taking a slim majority (see Table 6.2).

The reform of the Constitution in 1980, promulgated in October of that year, reaffirmed Guyana's status as a Cooperative Republic within the Commonwealth. A Cooperative Republic was defined as having the following attributes: political and economic independence, state

[21] J. Hagan. 1987. "Regimes, political opposition, and the comparative analysis of foreign policy," pp. 345–346. In *New directions in the study of foreign policy*, edited by Charles Hermann et al. Boston: Allen & Unwin.

ownership of the means of production, a citizenry organised into groups such as cooperatives and trade unions and an economy run on the basis of national economic planning. The constitution stated that the country was a democratic and secular state in transition from capitalism to socialism and that the constitution was the highest law in the country, with precedence over all other laws. The constitution guaranteed freedom of religion, speech, association, and movement, and prohibited discrimination. It also granted every Guyanese citizen the right to work, to obtain a free education and free medical care and to own personal property; it also guaranteed equal pay for women. However, freedom of expression and other political rights were limited by national interests and the state's duty to ensure fairness in the dissemination of information to the public.

The twist to the amendments to the Constitution meant that power was distributed among five "Supreme Organs of Democratic Power": the executive president, the cabinet, the National Assembly, the National Congress of Local Democratic Organs and the Supreme Congress of the People, a special deliberative body consisting of the National Assembly in joint session with the National Congress of Local Democratic Organs. Of these five divisions of government, the executive president in practice had almost unlimited powers. The important constitutional changes brought about by the 1980 document were mostly political: the concentration of power in the position of executive president and the creation of local party organisations to ensure Burnham's control over the PNC and, in turn, the party's control over the people. The constitution's economic goals were more posture than substance. The call for nationalisation of major industries with just compensation was a moot point, given that 80% of the economy was already in the government's hands by 1976. The remaining 20% was owned by Guyanese entrepreneurs.[22]

After Burnham's death in 1985, the new President, Desmond Hoyte, took steps to stem the economic decline, including strengthening financial controls over the parastatal corporations and supporting the private sector. In August 1987, at a PNC Congress, Hoyte announced that the PNC rejected orthodox communism and the one-party state. As the elections scheduled for 1990 approached, Hoyte, under increasing pressure from inside and outside Guyana, gradually opened the political

---

[22]http://countrystudies.us/guyana/75.htm.

system. After a visit to Guyana by former US President Jimmy Carter in 1990, Hoyte made changes in the electoral rules, appointed a new chairman of the Elections Commission, and endorsed putting together new voters' lists, thus delaying the election. The elections, which finally took place in 1992, were witnessed by 100 international observers, including a group headed by Mr. Carter and another from the Commonwealth of Nations. Both groups issued reports saying that the elections had been free and fair, despite violent attacks on the Elections Commission building on Election Day and other irregularities.[23] Griffith (1997) noted that some of the political reforms undertaken by the Hoyte government in 1985 included the abolition of overseas voting, access by the opposition parties to state media for campaigning, the sanitising of the voters list, reconstitution of the Elections Commissions, tabulation of the vote at the place of voting, along with the scrutiny of the elections process by foreign observers.

These reforms were significant, particularly when the outcome of the General Election of 1992, saw the return of the PPP under Jagan (see Table 6.3).

The outcome of this Election was interesting since it clearly demonstrated the continuing role of ethnicity in determining political victory. On 1 December 1994, the National Assembly passed a resolution which established the Special Select Committee to Review the Constitution and directed it to present a proposal for its reform before the 1997 general and regional elections. The Select Committee first met in May 1996. Fifty Public meetings across the 10 regions were convened by the Committee to solicit public participation in the reform process. Many written and oral submissions for constitutional reform were received from all sectors of society. The dissolution of Parliament on 29 October 1997 precluded the Special Select Committee from finishing its work. Early in 1999 an Act of Parliament established the Constitutional Reform Commission. It successfully completed its tasks and submitted its report to the National Assembly by the due date of 17 July 1999. The Commission made 171 recommendations for constitutional amendments. All amendments, with the exception of those requiring a referendum, have been passed into Acts of Parliament.

[23] https://www.globalsecurity.org/military/world/caribbean/gy-politics.htm.

Table 6.3   Results of the 1992 Guyana elections

Presidential candidate	Political party	Ethnic base	Votes won	Percentage of total	Seats awarded
Cheddi Jagan	PPP—Civic	Indian	162,058	53.5	28+8=36
Desmond Hoyte	PNC	African	128,286	42.3	23+3=26
Clive Thomas	WPA	Mixed	6068	1.7	1+1=2
Manzoor Nadir	TUF	Mixed	3138	1.2	1+0=1
Paul Tenassee	DLM	Indian	1157	*	0
Joseph Bacchus	NDF	African	68	*	0
Robert Gangadeen	NRP	Indian	114	*	0
Llewelyn John	PDM	African	298	*	0
Lindley GeBorde	UGI	Mixed	134	*	0
Leslie Ramsammy	URP	Indian	1343	*	0
Winston Payne	UWP	African	77	*	0

Source Griffith (1997)

Between the time of independence in 1966 and the 1980 constitutional change, the legislature comprised 53 members. With the adoption of the new constitution in 1980, only 53 of the 65 members of the legislature were elected directly, while the remaining 12 were indirectly elected from the Regional and National Council of Local Demographic Organs. Under the current system, adopted after considerable legislative action in 2000 and 2001, all members of the assembly are directly elected. Twenty-five members are elected from the ten geographic constituencies, and the remaining 40 are elected from a national list to guarantee a high degree of proportionality. Political parties that contest seats in the assembly must contest in at least six of the ten geographic constituencies and nominate candidates for 13 of the 25 constituency seats. Furthermore, at least one-third of the candidates on a party's geographical lists must be women.[24]

[24] https://freedomhouse.org/report/countries-crossroads/2006/guyana.

CONCLUDING REMARKS

It is evident that in the case of Guyana, ethnicity and politics are closely interconnected and while there have been a number of smaller political parties, these have failed to capture significant power. Over the years, it is true, there have been a number of constitutional amendments and some attempts at coalition government. Yet, what emerges during elections is it that there are significant unrests and the voting trend is based on ethnic affiliation. Arguments for further constitutional reforms, checks and balances, a movement away from proportional representation to the first-past-the-post model of government continue to abound amidst charges of corruption and patronage. Clearly, what emerges, is that even with a hybrid-political system, ethnicity continues to play a major role in determining political outcomes.

ETHNICITY AND POLITICS IN TRINIDAD AND TOBAGO

Unlike Guyana, Trinidad and Tobago have had extremely peaceful transitions during elections, particularly from the 1960s onwards. In 1962, on the granting of independent status, the Westminster Whitehall system of government was introduced in the twin-island colonies. While this model mirrored the Westminster model from Britain, according to Quinn (2015) most analysts characterise it as a modified or "adapted" Westminster model whose key features include constitutionalism; the Prime Minister as head of government, not head of state; Cabinet government with Ministers drawn from an elected legislature; parliamentary sovereignty; competitive elections; pluralist representation; official recognition of the role of the opposition and the assumption of civil service neutrality.[25]

One of the characteristic features of the Westminster Whitehall model was the first past the post system of voting. Also commonly referred to as the "winner takes all", this system awards a seat to the individual candidate who receives the most votes in an election. The first past the post system generally depends on single-member constituencies and allows voters to indicate only one vote on their ballot. The constitutional

[25] Kate Quinn. 2015. "Introduction: Revisiting Westminster in the Caribbean." *Commonwealth & Comparative Politics*, Vol. 53, No. 1: 1–7. https://doi.org/10.1080/14 662043.2014.993146.

requirements, in the case of Trinidad and Tobago, are that all the constituencies be as practically of equal size having regard to the influence of such factors such as population density, geographical barriers and administrative boundaries. Approximate equality of constituency size is critical for satisfying the important principle of equal weight of each ballot. While the first past the post method of voting could be applied in countries where a population is fairly homogenous, in the case of a plural society, it is argued that this system promotes the party with the numerical advantage (In terms of number of constituencies or seats obtained).[26]

In the case of the twin islands of Trinidad and Tobago, the lines were drawn early with the African-based party the People's National Movement (PNM), taking the lead in the elections of 1961 with a total of 190,003 votes. The Democratic Labour Party (DLP), which depended on its support from the East Indian segment of the society formed the Opposition. This trend continued with the PNM remaining entrenched as the Government of the county until 1985. While in some instances, such as the 1981 elections, a newly formed middle-class party the Organisation for National Reconstruction (ONR) captured the highest number of votes in the elections that year, the victory eventually reverted to the PNM since it was the party winning the majority of seats rather than the total number of votes who would form the Government. It was also evident, in the case of Trinidad and Tobago, that the demographic settlement of groups within particular constituencies would determine the outcome of the elections, particularly from 1995.

However, it was evident that by 1986, there was a shift from the regular voting pattern due, no doubt, to a number of factors. Indeed, in an overwhelming victory, a party incorporating a number of factions or groups, the National Alliance for Reconstruction (NAR) led by ANR Robinson, won thirty-three of the thirty-six seats with three seats going to the incumbent government the PNM.[27] The voter turnout at this time could not be described as "swing voting", rather the determinants of this elections had to be many and varied in order to convince the traditional voters to virtually "desert" their party. Some may suggest, that like the General Elections in the USA in 2012, the election in the case

[26] For a more in-depth discussion on the politics of Trinidad and Tobago see my book *Ethnic conflict in developing societies: Trinidad and Tobago, Guyana, Fiji and Suriname.* Palgrave Macmillan, 2017.

[27] The NAR attained 380,029 votes or 66.3% of the total votes cast.

of Trinidad and Tobago, was in no small measure influenced by shifts not only in this case by the country's underlying demographic structure, the increase in the number of marginal communities with incorporated elements of Indo and African middle classes, the increase in the number of younger voters, the increase in educational access, but also by the general apathy in the country and the disappointment with the ruling party. Indeed, some argued that the population was ready for a change.

While, to some extent, the 1986 election outcome was a deviation from the previous "racial" voting pattern, what was clear was that a successful coalition government was possible if groups saw their interest as being represented. Moreover, it was evident that apart from tribal associations, other groups were playing an important role if not "power-broking" in the electioneering process. In the case of this small twin-island republic, apart from the middle and upper classes from both ethnic background, like Guyana, international actors, more particularly the USA also displayed a keen interest in the election outcomes. As soon as the NAR attained victory, however, the fracturing of the groups and group interests emerged. The fight for leadership as well as considerations of which group would be asked to serve as members of the Cabinet began early. Eventually in 1988, this conflict would lead to a breakaway faction, with the Indo-Trinidadian politicians led by the trade union leader, Basdeo Panday, fracturing into a new party, Club 88. The euphoria which accompanied the NAR Government dissipated quickly; first with the fracturing of the party into African-East Indian segments (Club 88) and later with the attempted coup of 1990 when a group of Afro-Muslim supporters led by Abu Bakar attempted to overthrow the government. It was evident that the "dream" of a coalition was to be no more and the PNM regained power in 1991. The PNM won 21 of the seats with 233,550 or 45.1% of the total votes cast while the United National Congress (UNC led by Basdeo Panday of the Club 88 faction of the NAR) won 151,046 or 29.2% of the votes and formed the Opposition with 13 of the seats and the NAR attained 127,335 (24.6%) of the seats with 2 seats (Tobago). Like the 1981 elections, it was more than abundantly clear that while there would no doubt always be tribal moorings and stronghold constituencies representing the two predominant racial groups, yet the increase in the number of "marginal constituencies" along with the nearly forgotten part of the twin-island republic, Tobago would influence the outcome of the elections from 1991 onwards.

Table 6.4   General Elections Results (2000–2010)

Year	Votes and seats attained by the PNM	Votes and seats attained by the UNC	Votes and seats attained by the NAR	Congress of the people
2000	307,791 (51.7%) 19 seats	276,334 (46.5%) 16 seats	7409 (1.2%) 1 seat	
2001[i]	260,075 (46.5%) 18	279,002 (49.9%) 18 seats	5841 (1.0%) 0 seats	
2002	308,762 (50.9%) 20 seats	284,391 (46.9%) 16 seats	6776 (1.1%) 0 seats	
2007[ii]	299,813 (45.85%) 26 seats	194,425 (29.73%) 15 seats	0	148,041 (22.64%) 0 seats
2010	285,354 (39.65%) 12 seats	432,026 (60.3%) 29 seats	0	

Source Author created from Elections and Boundaries Report, Trinidad and Tobago 2000–2010; All the results for the General Elections in Trinidad and Tobago was sourced from: https://en.wikipedia.org/wiki/Elections_in_Trinidad_and_Tobago

Notes

[i] Early general elections were held in Trinidad and Tobago on 10 December 2001 after the ruling United National Congress lost its majority in the House of Representatives following four defections. However, the election results saw the UNC and the People's National Movement both win 18 seats. Although the UNC received the most votes, President A. N. R. Robinson nominated PNM leader Patrick Manning as Prime Minister. Voter turnout was 66.1%

[ii] In 2007 5 new constituencies were added making the total number of constituencies 41

By 1995, it was a neck to neck battle by the two parties, the PNM and the UNC with each party attaining 17 seats. The tie-breaker was the Tobago votes which went to the NAR. Once more a coalition arrangement was brokered but this time Basdeo Panday, the East Indian leader was appointed the Prime Minister and later ANR Robinson would be appointed President of the country. The voter turnout was 63.3%. Over the period 1991–2010, the election results were clearly indicative of the contest for power between the two major parties, each with their embedded ethnic association.

By 2007, however, with an increase in the number of constituencies from 36 to 41, it was abundantly clear that the outcome of the elections would be determined by two major factors namely:

a. The marginal constituencies;
b. The ability of any one of the major political parties to form an affiliation with smaller, independent parties or with the breakaway factions of its opponent.

The election results which followed were indictive of the "new" trends. With, as Table 6.4 indicates, the People's Partnership, a coalition of the United National Congress, the Congress of the People (COP), The National Joint Action Committee Party and some smaller affiliates capturing 29 seats of 60.3% of the votes to the PNM's 12 seats in 2010. The challenge though, in this case, as in the case of the NAR in 1986, was how to keep the coalition together. Like the NAR, the contest for power by the differing alliances, soon resulted in them parting ways with the COP entering the political arena in 2015. The election outcomes were clear. The PNM once again returned to power with 387,447 votes capturing 23 seats, the UNC captured 290,066 votes or 17 seats and the COP captured 43, 991 or 1 seat.

CONCLUDING REMARKS

In the case of Trinidad and Tobago, as in Guyana, both the methods of the first-past-the-post system of voting as well proportional representation have led to the formation and retention of strong two-party systems. Because both countries have strong tribal voting preferences, the political parties in both cases are structured along ethnic lines. In both countries, one party has a predominant support from the Afro-descended population and the other party the Indo-descended population. In both countries, what was evident was the oscillation in government between the two parties. It was obvious, though, in meandering through the various elections over the years, that in the cases where affiliations or coalitions arrangements were brokered then there was a departure from tribal-based voting preference. The major challenge, in both countries, however, was the inability to retain the coalition. The outcomes, where the coalition was fractured, resulted in the return to tribal voting. It can be argued, then, that both models of government have failed to provide a formula to allow for inclusiveness of the various groups. In the case of both Guyana as well as Trinidad and Tobago the various experiments at coalition arrangements and alliances continue to be at the exploratory stages.

REFERENCES

Bart, F. (Ed.). (1969). *Ethnic groups and boundaries.* Boston: Little, Brown.

Bissessar, A. (2017). *Ethnic conflict in developing societies: Trinidad and Tobago, Guyana, Fiji and Suriname.* Cham: Palgrave Macmillan.

Brass, P. R. (1991). *Ethnicity and nationalism: Theory and comparison.* New Delhi: Sage.

Duverger, M. (1963). *Political parties: Their organisation and activity in the modern state.* New York: Wiley.

Fish, S., & Brooks, R. S. (2004). Does diversity hurt democracy? *Journal of Democracy, 15*(1), 153–167.

Geertz, C. (1963). The integrative revolution, primordial sentiments, and civil politics in the new states. In C. Geertz (Ed.), *Old societies and new states: The quest for modernity in Asia and Africa.* New York: Free Press.

Greene, J. E. (1974). *Race vs politics in Guyana: Political cleavages and political mobilisation in the 1968 general election.* Kingston, Jamaica: Institute of Social and Economic Research, University of the West Indies.

Griffith, I. L. (1997). Political change, democracy, and human rights in Guyana. *Third World Quarterly, 18*(2), 267–285.

Hagan, J. (1987). Regimes, political opposition, and the comparative analysis of foreign policy. In C. Hermann, et al. (Eds.), *New directions in the study of foreign policy* (pp. 345–346). Boston: Allen & Unwin.

Horowitz, D. L. (1985). *Ethnic groups in conflict.* Berkeley: University of California Press.

Lijphart, A. (1977). Political theories and the explanation of ethnic conflict in western world: Falsified predictions and plausible postdictions. In M. Esman (Ed.), *Ethnic conflict in thewestern world* (pp. 46–64). Ithaca: Cornell University Press.

Lipset, S. M., & Rokkan, S. (1967). Cleavage structures, party systems, and voter alignments: An introduction. In S. M. Lipset & S. Rokkan (Eds.), *Party systems and voter alignments: Cross-national perspectives* (pp. 1–64). New York: Free Press.

Mozaffar, S., Scarritt, J. R., & Galaich, G. (2003). Electoral institutions, ethnopolitical cleavages, and party systems in Africa's emerging democracies. *The American Political Science Review, 97*(3), 379–390.

Quinn, K. (2015). Introduction: Revisiting Westminster in the Caribbea. *Commonwealth and Comparative Politics, 53*(1), 1–7. https://doi.org/10.10 80/14662043.2014.993146.

Stewart, N. (2004). Race and colour in Trinidad and Tobago. *Trinidad and Tobago News Forum*. http://www.trinidadandtobagonews.com/forum/webs_config.pl?md=read;id=1467.

Torres, A. F. (2007, Spring). *Electoral systems and ethnic identity: A constructivist approach* (Senior Honours Thesis). Department of Politics, New York University.

Woodford, H. *A history of political alliances in Guyana 1953–1977*. http://www.guyanaundersiege.com/Historical/Political%20Alliances.htm.

CHAPTER 7

Equality and the Law: A Caribbean Perspective

INTRODUCTION

International human rights instruments are based on the inherent notion of equality. The Universal Declaration of Human Rights states, "All human beings are born free and equal in dignity and rights" (UN 1948, Art 1). It goes on to note that these rights are to be enjoyed without "distinction of any kind, such as race, colour, sex, language, religion, political or other opinion, national or social origin, property, birth or other status" (UN 1948, Art 2). At the national level, equality before the law is a basic premise of most countries' legal systems. Some 155 countries expressly provide the guarantee of equality before the law to their citizens in their respective constitutional instruments (Persadie 2012). This begs the question as to what degree equality persists beyond constitutional guarantees.

This chapter takes a Caribbean focus and specifically offers an overview of the equality laws that exist in this region. This overview is done primarily on the basis of existing statute that provides for equality in a broad manner as well as statutory provisions that address equality or non-discrimination for employment purposes, but excludes constitutional provisions. These statutory provisions are further examined with respect to their treatment of discrimination at the workplace on the basis of the grounds named in each piece of legislation. Sexual orientation, as a ground of discrimination, does not form part of the focus of this paper for

© The Author(s) 2020   131
J. H. Stephenson et al., *Diversity, Equality,*
and Inclusion in Caribbean Organisations and Society,
https://doi.org/10.1007/978-3-030-47614-4_7

the simple reason that it is not included in the legislation of any Caribbean country, but its exclusion is addressed in the discussion. Case law, for actions taken specifically only under these statutory provisions, is examined as well, as this will highlight the manner in which the laws have been applied by the Courts or relevant Tribunals. This paper does not contemplate a review of constitutional actions taken for discrimination. Where it exists in the enabling statute, the institutional framework for implementing equality laws is reviewed as it relates to specialist courts or tribunals. This is followed by a discussion of the findings and a conclusion.

The data collection method used in the paper is largely qualitative in nature and is premised principally on a documentary review of statutory provisions and case law. A few telephone and email interviews were conducted to determine the status of implementation of the laws in the countries that have enacted equality legislation.

EQUALITY

Equality and Non-discrimination

The notion of equality seems to be a foregone conclusion today, although the year 2020 witnessed serious challenges to its meaning and application. Persons accept it as a natural state of affairs but it is by no means a simple concept. In its most basic form, equality may be viewed as "an ideal of uniformity in treatment or status by those in a position to affect either" (Encyclopaedia Britannica 2019).

A key feature of equality is the notion of non-discrimination; although, there are some legal scholars who argue that they are interchangeable concepts (see MacNaughton 2009) as equality and non-discrimination are positive and negative statements of the same principle. One is treated equally when one is not discriminated against and one is discriminated against when one is not treated equally (Besson 2005). Equality is deemed to be a positive duty on the part of States to promote measures that advance equality, while non-discrimination is a negative duty of restraint designed to suppress acts of unequal treatment of persons by the State (see Fredman 2016; Equality Rights Trust 2014). Generally speaking, "negative" human rights, such as equal rights, are assumed to be those that require State forbearance, while "positive" human rights require active fulfillment by the State (Howard-Hassmann 2013). Non-discrimination is widely understood as a negative restatement of the principle of equality (Sokhi-Bulley 2005) and ensures that no one is denied their rights for any reason (Australian Government, Attorney-General's Department, n.d.).

Equality and non-discrimination recognise difference, otherwise the concepts become irrelevant. Interestingly, discrimination in the form of affirmative action or positive discrimination sometimes becomes necessary to level the playing field, thereby ensuring equality. There are instances in which an individual must be treated differently in order to protect his or her right to equality (Persadie 2012). According to Fredman (2016), affirmative action, or preferential treatment of a disadvantaged group, while apparently breaching the equal treatment principle, is better understood as furthering equality of results, which lies at the heart of equality legislation. Notably, lack of such positive action to overcome past disadvantage and to accelerate progress towards equality of particular groups can constitute a violation of the right to non-discrimination or the right to equality (Equal Rights Trust 2014).

This approach has become necessary since formal equality is premised on an abstract individual, judged on personal merit (Fredman 2016). Born out of the struggles against slavery, racism, classism and sexism, among other prejudices, formal equality insists that such group-based characteristics are irrelevant (Fredman 2016). Such a rigid view of equality, however, denies the existence of difference and the need for the law, and institutions, to cater for this. The many grounds of discrimination covered in various statutory instruments that address equality recognise this need. Phillips (2002) noted, for example, with respect to gender equality, that in the absence of sex-specific legislation to deal with pregnancy and maternity leave, women enter the labour market at a disadvantage. Inherent differences must be accommodated in the application of equal rights, whether as concept or law, in order for it to be useful and result in equality of opportunity. Nevertheless, some authors argue against such a position. Sohrab (1993), for example, articulated quite clearly the fallacy of having to choose one or the other as it relates to gender equality in the law:

The perceived necessity of making a choice between equal or special treatment is a false choice. In some areas equal rights are necessary, while in others it is gender-specific rights that are necessary, for instance, in pregnancy. Neither approach is, nor should be, the exclusive "answer" or strategy or claim, and arguing over substantive equality by opposing equal with special and vice versa is at best redundant and at worst a costly distraction.

As will be seen below, the legal instruments found in the Caribbean take a much more flexible view. The few Caribbean countries which have passed equality legislation recognise the need to protect these differences by ensuring that equal rights are afforded accordingly.

Equality Before the Law

Equality before the law goes one step further and looks at the substance of the law itself (content) and the way in which it is applied to individuals (procedure). Thomsen (2018) noted that equality before the law has at least two fundamentally different meanings. On the one hand, it pertains to the rights and duties contained in positive law, i.e., the content of the law, where there are no distinctions for any reason or category of persons. On the other hand, it pertains to the practices of the institutions responsible for administering such laws, such as courts, police officers, ministries, and so on, i.e., the process of the law, where the law should be applied without distinction and without reference to a person's status. For equality to be said to be true, therefore, there must be no distinction in the application of any law to any individual. Equality requires, then, that courts should treat like cases alike, which creates its own difficulties (see for example Fredman 2016), but which forms the basis of precedent in case law (see Persadie and Ramlogan 2016).

Another way of looking at equality would be to make a distinction between equality of opportunity (*de jure* or formal or abstract equality) and equality of outcome (*de facto* or substantive equality) (Persadie 2012). These are similar to Thomsen's (2018) description above: equality of opportunity looks simply at what exists on the law books while equality of outcome refers to what happens in actual practice. While both are important, there must first be equality of opportunity before there can be any discussion of equality of outcome. As the subsequent sections below illustrate, apart from constitutional provisions guaranteeing equality before the law and equality at work, the existence of law that addresses equality broadly in the Caribbean is not as widespread as one would hope.

Equality and the Law in the Caribbean

There are twelve independent English-speaking Caribbean countries which form the basis of this study: Antigua and Barbuda, The Bahamas, Barbados, Belize, Dominica, Grenada, Guyana, Jamaica,

Table 7.1 English-speaking Caribbean countries with laws addressing equality, equality at work, and equal pay; and constitutional provisions for equality, equality before the law and equal pay

Country	Statutory provisions for equality			Constitutional provisions for equality		
	Equality	Equality at work[a]	Equal pay	Equality	Equality before the law	Equal pay
Antigua and Barbuda	–	–	–	✓	–	–
Barbados	–	–	–	✓	–	–
Belize	–	–	✓	✓	✓	–
Dominica	–	–	✓	✓	–	–
Grenada	–	✓	✓	✓	–	–
Guyana	✓	✓	✓	✓	✓	✓
Jamaica	–	–	✓	✓	–	–
St Kitts and Nevis	–	–	–	✓	✓	–
St Lucia	–	✓	✓	✓	✓	–
St Vincent and the Grenadines	–	–	✓	✓	–	–
The Bahamas	–	✓	✓	✓	–	–
Trinidad and Tobago	✓	✓	✓	✓	✓	–

[a]This addresses non-discrimination
Source Author's creation

St Kitts and Nevis, St Lucia, St Vincent and the Grenadines, and Trinidad and Tobago. As illustrated in Table 7.1, of these twelve, every country provides a constitutional guarantee of equality to all while merely five provide for equality before the law to their citizens (Persadie 2012). Interestingly, only Guyana's constitution guarantees equal pay for equal work to its citizens. In terms of statutory provisions, nine countries have legislated for equal pay for equal work and five for non-discrimination at work, but only two of these Caribbean countries have statutory provisions that provide for equality in general terms outside of the workplace; these are Guyana and Trinidad and Tobago.

STATUTORY PROVISIONS

Statutory provisions that address equality in the Caribbean reflect both the positive duty of states to promote measures that advance equality as well as the negative duty to refrain from treating persons differently based on their status or any named ground of discrimination. They therefore reflect equal enjoyment of rights and the prohibition or elimination of discrimination on various grounds.

Table 7.2 shows the various prohibited grounds of discrimination and status for which persons are not to be treated differently in Caribbean equality legislation. There is a very notable exception: sexual orientation (see also Stephenson and Persadie 2019) which remains incredibly contentious in Caribbean society. Noteworthy is that fact that the Parliament of Barbados only just passed (at the time of proofreading this chapter, which means that it cannot be addressed in detail here) the country's Employment (Prevention of Discrimination) Bill, 2020, in August 2020, and it covers 18 grounds of discrimination, including sexual orientation (The Barbados Parliament 2020). There is also a very interesting inclusion in the statutory provisions of St Lucia and The Bahamas: HIV/AIDS. Nevertheless, while the prohibited grounds of discrimination vary from country to country, the notion of equality in the statutory provisions where they do exist recognises difference and seeks to provide redress.

Table 7.3 provides the names and actual statutory provisions of the relevant pieces of legislation that address equality generally and specifically at the workplace in all nine countries. It is only Guyana and Trinidad and Tobago that have enacted legislation that addresses equality in fields other than just employment; it is the legal and institutional framework established to address equality generally in Guyana and Trinidad and Tobago that is examined further below.

Even where not specifically stated as a ground of discrimination, all employment legislation of the twelve English-speaking Caribbean countries makes provisions for pregnancy and child birth as it relates to maternity leave and/or as not constituting a ground of discrimination between male and female employees.

The provisions of the St Lucia *Labour Code*, in large part, include and repeat the provisions of the *Equality of Opportunity and Treatment in Employment and Occupation Act*, Cap. 16.14; however, under the "Fundamental Principles of Employment", an additional ground is included: HIV/AIDS. This ground is also found in the *Employment Act*, Ch. 321A of The Bahamas.

Table 7.2 Prohibited grounds of discrimination in laws addressing equality generally and at work in English-speaking Caribbean

Country	Law	Prohibited grounds/Status
Belize[a]	*Equal Pay Act*, Chapter 302:01	Sex
Dominica[a]	*Labour Standards Act*, Chap. 89:05	Sex, pregnancy
Grenada	*Employment Act*, Cap. 89	Race, colour, national extraction, social origin, religion, political opinion, sex, marital status, family responsibilities, age or disability
Guyana	*Prevention of Discrimination Act*, Cap. 99:09	Race, sex, religion, colour, ethnic origin, indigenous population, national extraction, social origin, economic status, political opinion, disability, family responsibilities, pregnancy, marital status, age
Jamaica[a]	*The Employment (Equal Pay for Men and Women) Act*, 34 of 1975	Sex
St. Lucia	*Equality of Opportunity and Treatment in Employment and Occupation Act*, Cap. 16:14 *Labour Code*, 2006	Race, sex, religion, colour, ethnic origin, family responsibilities, pregnancy, marital status, or age, social origin, political opinion, disability Race, colour, sex, religion, national extraction, social origin, ethnic origin, political opinion or affiliation, age, disability, serious family responsibility, pregnancy, marital status or HIV\AIDS
The Bahamas	*Employment Act*, Ch. 321A *Persons with Disabilities (Equal Opportunities) Act*, 2014	Race, creed, sex, marital status, political opinion, age or HIV/AIDS Disability
Trinidad and Tobago	*Equal Opportunity Act*, Ch. 22:03 (Revised Laws of Trinidad and Tobago, 2015)	Sex, race, ethnicity, origin, including geographical origin, religion, marital status, or disability

[a]While not specifically set out in the law, this is inferred from the provisions
Source Author's creation

Table 7.3 Laws and relevant provisions addressing equality generally and at work in English-speaking Caribbean countries

Country	Law	Relevant sections/Provisions
Belize	*Equal Pay Act*, Chapter 302:01	3. (1) From and after the appointed day no employer shall, by failing to pay equal pay for equal work, discriminate between male and female employees employed by the employer's establishment
Dominica	*Labour Standards Act*, Chap. 89:05	24. No employer shall establish or maintain differences in wages between male and female employees employed in the same business who are performing, under the same working conditions, the same or similar work or jobs requiring similar skill, effort and responsibility
Grenada	*Employment Act*, Cap. 89	26. (1) No person shall discriminate against any employee on the grounds of race, colour, national extraction, social origin, religion, political opinion, sex, marital status, family responsibilities, age or disability, in respect of recruitment, training, promotion, terms and conditions of employment, termination of employment or other matters arising out of the employment relationship 27. Every employer shall pay male and female employees equal remuneration for work of equal value
Guyana	*Equal Rights Act*, Cap. 38:01[a]	2. (1) Woman and men shall have equal rights and the same legal status in all spheres of political, economic and social life (2) All forms of discrimination against women or men on the basis of their sex or marital status are illegal (3) Women and men shall be paid equal remuneration for the same work or work of the same nature (4) No person shall be ineligible for, or discriminated against in respect of any employment, appointment or promotion in, or to, any office or position on the ground only of sex (6) Without prejudice to the generality of the foregoing provisions of this section it shall be discriminatory against women where in relation to employment (a) in arrangements made for the purpose of determining who should be offered employment; (b) the terms on which employment is offered; (c) by the refusal or deliberate omission to offer employment; (d) in the way access is afforded to opportunities for promotion, transfer or training or to any other benefits, facilities or services, men are afforded more favourable opportunities or conditions than women or preference is given to men

(continued)

Table 7.3 (continued)

Country	Law	Relevant sections/Provisions
	Persons with Disabilities Act, Cap. 36:05[a]	8. (1) An employer shall not deny a person with a disability, on the basis of disability, access to opportunities for employment including open employment
		(2) An employer shall not discriminate against a person with a disability in relation to employment by way of advertisements, recruitment, classification of posts, wages, choice for advancement and provision of facilities
		(3) An employer shall ensure that a qualified person with a disability is subject to the same terms and conditions of employment and the same compensation, privileges, benefits, incentives and allowances as a qualified person who does not have a disability
	Prevention of Discrimination Act, Cap. 99:09[a]	5. (1) It shall be unlawful for any person who is an employer…in relation to recruitment, selection or employment or any other person for purposes of training, apprenticeship or employment, to discriminate against that other person on the grounds listed in section 4(2)—
		(a) in the advertisement of the job;
		(b) in the arrangements made for the purpose of determining who should be offered that employment;
		(c) in determining who should be offered employment;
		(d) in the terms or conditions on which employment is offered;
		(e) the creation, classification or abolition of jobs
		(2) It shall be unlawful for an employer to discriminate against an employee on the grounds listed in section 4(2)
		(a) in terms or conditions of employment afforded to that employee by this employer
		(d) by denying access, or limited opportunities for advancement, promotion, transfer or training, or to any other benefits, facilities or services associated with employment;
		(e) by retrenching or dismissing the employee;
		(f) by subjecting the employee to any other disadvantage
		7. Special measures taken by employers of a temporary nature to promote equality of opportunity in employment based on the grounds set out in section 4(2) shall not be deemed to be unlawful
		9. (1) Every employer…shall be obligated to pay equal remuneration to men and women performing work of equal value for such employer

(continued)

Table 7.3 (continued)

Country	Law	Relevant sections/Provisions
Jamaica	The Employment (Equal Pay for Men and Women) Act, 34 of 1975	3. (1) From and after the 1st day of January 1976, no employer shall, by failing to pay equal pay for equal work, discriminate between male and female employees employed by him in the same establishment in Jamaica
	The Disabilities Act, 2014[a]	25. A person with a disability shall not, by reason of such disability, be subject to any form of discrimination
		29. (1) An employer shall not discriminate against a person with a disability who is otherwise qualified for employment—
		(a) in terms of the employment afforded to that employee;
		(b) in relation to the opportunities afforded to the employee for promotion, transfer, training or the receipt of any other benefit; or
		(c) by dismissing him or subjecting him by virtue of his disability to any other detriment, without reasonable cause
St Lucia	Equality of Opportunity and Treatment in Employment and Occupation Act, Cap. 16.14	4. (2) It is unlawful for any person who is an employer or any person acting or purporting to act on behalf of a person who is an employer, in relation to recruitment, selection or employment of any other person for purposes of training, apprenticeship or employment, to discriminate against that other person on the grounds specified under section 3(2)—
		(a) in the advertisement of the job;
		(b) in the arrangements made for the purpose of determining who should be offered that employment;
		(c) in determining who should be offered employment;
		(d) in the terms or conditions on which employment is offered;
		(e) in the creation, classification or abolition of jobs
		4. (3) It is unlawful for an employer to discriminate against an employee on the grounds specified under section 3(2)—
		(a) in terms or conditions of employment afforded to that employee by the employer;
		(b) in conditions of work or occupational safety and health measures;
		(c) in the provision of facilities related to or connected with employment;
		(d) by denying access, or limiting access to opportunities for advancement, promotion, transfer or training, or to any other benefits, facilities or services associated with employment;

(continued)

Table 7.3 (continued)

Country	Law	Relevant sections/Provisions
		(e) by retrenching or dismissing the employee; (f) by subjecting the employee to any other disadvantage 6. (1) Employers and persons acting on behalf of employers shall pay equal remuneration to men and women performing work of equal value for the employer 7. (1) Subject to subsection 3 special measures of a temporary nature taken by employers to promote equality of opportunity in employment based on the grounds set out in section 3(1) are not considered to be unlawful discrimination within the meaning of section 4
	Labour Code, 2006	7.—(1) Subject to subsection (2), an employer shall not discriminate against any employee on the grounds of race, colour, sex, religion, national extraction, social origin, ethnic origin, political opinion or affiliation, age, disability, serious family responsibility, pregnancy, marital status or **HIV/AIDS**, in respect of recruitment, training, work facilities or service, promotion, terms and conditions of employment or benefit arising out of the employment relationship
St Vincent and the Grenadines	*Equal Pay Act*, No. 3 of 1994	3. (1) From and after the appointed day no employer shall, by failing to pay equal pay for equal work, discriminate between male and female employees employed by the employer's establishment
The Bahamas	*Employment Act*, Ch. 321A	6. No employer or person acting on behalf of an employer shall discriminate against an employee or applicant for employment on the basis of race, creed, sex, marital status, political opinion, age or **HIV/AIDS** by— (a) refusing to offer employment to an applicant for employment or not affording the employee access to opportunities for promotion, training or other benefits, or by dismissing or subjecting the employee to other detriment solely because of his or her race, creed, sex, marital status, political opinion, age or HIV/Aids; (b) paying him at a rate of pay less than the rate of pay of another employee, for substantially the same kind of work or for work of equal value performed in the same establishment, the performance of which requires substantially the same skill, effort and responsibility and which is performed under similar working conditions except where such payment is made pursuant to seniority, merit, earnings by quantity or quality of production or a differential based on any factor other than race, creed, sex, marital status, political opinion, age or HIV/Aids; (c) pre-screening for HIV status

(continued)

Table 7.3 (continued)

Country	Law	Relevant sections /Provisions
	Persons with Disabilities (Equal Opportunities) Act, 2014	14. Employment. (1) No person shall deny a person with a disability equal access to opportunities for suitable employment. (2) A qualified employee with a disability shall be subject to the same terms and conditions of employment and the same compensation, privileges, benefits, fringe benefits, incentives or allowances as qualified able-bodied employees
Trinidad and Tobago	*Equal Opportunity Act,* Chapter 22:03[a]	4. This Act applies to—
		(a) discrimination in relation to employment, education, the provision of goods and services and the provision of accommodation…, if the discrimination is—
		(i) discrimination on the ground of status as defined in section 5; or
		(ii) discrimination by victimisation as defined in section 6;
		(b) offensive behaviour referred to in section 7.
		5. For the purposes of this Act, a person ("the discriminator") discriminates against another person ("the aggrieved person") on the grounds of status if, by reason of—
		(a) the status of the aggrieved person;
		(b) a characteristic that appertains generally to persons of the status of the aggrieved person; or
		(c) a characteristic that is generally imputed to persons of the status of the aggrieved person, the discriminator treats the aggrieved person, in circumstances that are the same or are not materially different, less favourably than the discriminator treats another person of a different status.
		8. An employer or a prospective employer shall not discriminate against a person—
		(a) in the arrangements he makes for the purpose of determining who should be offered employment;
		(b) in the terms or conditions on which employment is offered; or
		(c) by refusing or deliberately omitting to offer employment.
		9. An employer shall not discriminate against a person employed by him—
		(a) in the terms or conditions of employment that the employer affords the person;
		(b) in the way the employer affords the person access to opportunities for promotion, transfer or training or to any other benefit, facility or service associated with employment, or by refusing or deliberately omitting to afford the person access to them; or
		(c) by dismissing the person or subjecting the person to any other detriment.

[a]Covers fields other than employment

Source Author's creation

Antigua and Barbuda has a Disabilities and Equal Opportunity Bill, 2017 which prohibits any form of discrimination against a person with a disability on the basis of disability, but it is not yet law.

CASE LAW

Of the various Caribbean countries under study here, only two have seen actions taken pursuant to equality legislation; these are St Lucia and Trinidad and Tobago. Even though Guyana has equality legislation, no cases have been brought under it to date (George-Wiltshire 2019). As noted in the introduction to this chapter, a review of constitutional actions for discrimination is not part of the scope of this study.

One action was taken in St Lucia, pursuant to the *Equality of Opportunity and Treatment in Employment and Occupation Act*, Cap. 16.14. In the case of *Cecilia Deterville v Foster & Ince Cruise Services (St Lucia) Ltd*, 2009, Deterville claimed that she was dismissed because of her bisexuality, however, since sexual orientation is not a prohibited ground of discrimination in that piece of legislation, the claim was dismissed.

In Trinidad and Tobago, eighteen actions have been heard under the *Equal Opportunity Act*, Ch. 22:03 at the Equal Opportunity Tribunal to date. Table 7.4 summarises the actions based on the parties to the action, the claim made and the specific grounds of discrimination, the decision of the Tribunal and any remedy as relevant.

INSTITUTIONAL FRAMEWORK

The establishment of any institutional framework requires that it be provided for in the enabling statute. Of the countries under review here, only Guyana, St Lucia and Trinidad and Tobago have legislative provisions in their equality laws that allow for the creation of new institutions to hear matters brought under the said equality laws. Guyana's law provides for the establishment of a Rights Commission Tribunal under its *Rights Commissions Tribunal Act*, Cap. 38:02, but this has not been established (George-Wiltshire 2019). St Lucia's law provides for the establishment of a Labour Tribunal under the *Labour Code*, which has been established and is functioning, as well as a Disabilities Rights Tribunal, but this latter has not been established. The Labour Tribunal hears all matters related to employment issues and will hear matters of discrimination as they relate to employment only. Trinidad and Tobago is the only country that has

Table 7.4 Cases and Decisions taken pursuant to the *Equal Opportunity Act*, Ch. 22:03 (Revised Laws of Trinidad and Tobago 2015)

Parties	Claim	Decision	Remedy
Derek Salandy v The Petroleum Company of Trinidad and Tobago, EOT No. 0002 of 2012; 30 June 2016 and 14 September 2017	Discrimination on the basis of origin and the terms or conditions of his employment	Succeeded due to breach of s 9(a) of the Act favouring a Venezuelan national	Compensation: USD $35,852[a] Costs: USD $5378
Anthony Hosein v CARONI (1975) Limited, EOT No. 0001 of 2013; 30 June 2017 and 14 February 2019	Discrimination on the basis of victimisation	Dismissed for breach of procedure and lack of jurisdiction	Costs awarded against him
Wilfred Edwards v Petroleum Company of Trinidad and Tobago (PETROTRIN), EOT No. 0002 of 2013; 30 June 2016	Discrimination on the basis of disability, refusal to offer (re) employment and victimisation	Dismissed as claim was filed outside of statutory time limit	No costs awarded
Giselle Glaude v Quality Security Bodyguard Services Limited, EOT No. 0003 of 2013; 26 July 2016	Discrimination on the basis of her religion – she was not allowed to wear a hijab	Succeeded as she was not accommodated for her religious beliefs while officers of the Seventh Day Adventist faith were. Also, she was summarily dismissed without notice of right to appeal	Compensation: USD $22,222 Costs: USD $3333
Geeta Sahatoo v Ministry of Labour and Small and Micro Enterprises Development, EOT No. 0004 of 2013; 31 July 2017	Discrimination on the basis of race and victimisation	Succeeded partially as she was treated less favourably on the basis of race than three other competitors who all benefited from acting appointments and eventually substantive appointments, despite her holding more and directly relevant qualifications. Victimisation claim failed, however, due to lack of evidence	Compensation: USD $26,667 Costs: USD $4000

(continued)

Table 7.4 (continued)

Parties	Claim	Decision	Remedy
Indra Chankasingh-Budhai v The Ministry of Food Production and The Attorney General of Trinidad and Tobago, EOT No. 0005 of 2013; 11 July 2017	Discrimination at work regarding access to opportunities for promotion on the basis of sex and victimisation	Dismissed as there was no discriminatory practice on the basis of sex or at all given her promotion prior to her male counterpart and her subsequent rescission of it. Neither was she victimised as a result of her action	Costs awarded against her
Dindial Ragoo v Ministry of Food Production, EOT No. 0006 of 2013; 21 July 2017	Discrimination on the basis of race, denial of access to opportunities for promotion and specific discrimination against promotion to the position of diesel mechanic	Succeeded as he was treated less favourably based on his race. Tribunal declared that Ragoo entitled to be given a fair opportunity within a reasonable time to be considered for promotion to the position of diesel mechanic	Compensation: USD $24,793 Costs: USD $3719
Kerwin Simmons v The Water and Sewerage Authority of Trinidad and Tobago, EOT No. 0002 of 2014; 28 July 2016	Discrimination on the basis of race and victimisation	Succeeded as he was treated less favourably on the basis of his race and that he was also victimised as he was encouraged to resign and then be checked for medical fitness for work after lodging his complaint	Compensation: USD $27,556 Costs: USD $4133
Vidya S. Maharaj v Immigration Division, Ministry of National Security, EOT No. 0003 of 2014; 07 April 2017	Discrimination on re-entry into Trinidad on the basis of origin, ethnicity and religion and victimisation	Succeeded as he was discriminated against on the basis of origin, ethnicity and religion and victimisation. He was also unable to take up a job offer due to the stamp in his passport, "employment not permitted"	General damages: USD $34,267 Costs: USD $10,260 Special damages for loss of income from the contract he could not accept: USD $30,133

(continued)

Table 7.4 (continued)

Parties	Claim	Decision	Remedy
Michael Mark Archbald v Trinidad and Tobago Defence Force, EOT No. 0001 of 2016; 13 September 2017	Discrimination of the basis of religion for the Trinidad and Tobago Defence Force's refusal to approve as a full-fledged member of the Defence Force	Succeeded as he was discriminated against on the basis of his religion	Compensation: USD $23,556 Costs: USD $3333
Desmond Noel v The Auditor General of Trinidad and Tobago, EOT No. 0005 of 2016; 15 September 2017	Discrimination on the basis of race and victimisation	Succeeded as he was treated less favourably; discriminated against on the basis of race and was also victimised by not being allowed to act in the next higher position	Compensation: USD $36,296 Costs: USD $5444
Burton Baptiste v The University of Trinidad and Tobago, EOT No. 0008 of 2017; 10 December 2018	Discrimination on the basis of race and the terms or conditions of his employment	Substantive matter not heard due to procedural irregularities	Costs yet to be determined
Andreana Henry v Princess Entertainment Corporation Trinidad and Tobago Limited Owners and Managers of Royal Princess Members Club, EOT 0002 of 2016; 25 September 2019	Discrimination on the basis of victimisation	Substantive matter not heard due to procedural irregularities	Each party to bear own costs
Clarise Jupiter v Petroleum Company of Trinidad and Tobago, EOT No. 0006 of 2017, 15 February 2019; 14 June 2019	Discrimination on the basis of victimisation	EOT found that the allegations made were unclear and was unable to determine the application; the Commission's report was in need of revision for re-filing for Trial	Matter returned to Commission for preparation of all relevant documentation to be filed with Registry of the Tribunal. Trial fixed for 15 October 2019; costs to be determined at trial

(continued)

Table 7.4 (continued)

Parties	Claim	Decision	Remedy
Moriba Baker v The University of Trinidad and Tobago, EOT No. 0004 of 2016, 13 February 2019	Discrimination on the basis of status and victimisation (two matters brought under each category)	Two of the four matters dismissed for want of jurisdiction; the two other matters to be heard on a date to be determined	Costs to be determined at trial
Dr Peter Hanoomansingh v The University of the West Indies, EOT No. 0005 of 2018; 25 September 2019	Discrimination for not being hired by the Respondent	Substantive matter not heard	Costs awarded to Complainant
Dr Raymond Ramcharitar v The University of the West Indies, EOT No. 0001 of 2019; 25 September 2019	Discrimination concerning temporary academic appointment	Substantive matter not heard for want of jurisdiction	Matter referred to the High Court
Rishi Persad Maharaj v Cascadia Hotel Limited, EOT No. 0001 of 2017; 6 November 2019	Discrimination on the basis of sex and/or sexual harassment	On the ground of sex, Complainant failed to show that he was treated less favourably than a non-heterosexual female. The ground of sexual harassment was dismissed as it is not a ground of discrimination under the Act	Costs awarded against the Complainant. To be assessed

[a]Exchange rate of USD-TTD $1.00 = $6.75 used (dollar amounts rounded)
Source Author's creation

established its Equal Opportunity Commission and Equal Opportunity Tribunal pursuant to the *Equal Opportunity Act*, Ch. 22:03 and both are active and treat with discrimination in various fields.

In order to administer the *Equal Opportunity Act*, Ch. 22:03 of Trinidad and Tobago, an Equal Opportunity Commission ("the Commission") and Equal Opportunity Tribunal ("the Tribunal") have been established. The role of the Commission includes, *inter alia*, working towards the elimination of discrimination; promoting equality of opportunity; receiving, investigating and conciliating allegations of discrimination; and, finally, preparing and publishing appropriate guidelines for the avoidance of discrimination (Stephenson and Persadie 2019). Where matters cannot be resolved by conciliation, the Commission may initiate proceedings (with the consent and on behalf of the complainant) to have the matter adjudicated before the Tribunal (Stephenson and Persadie 2019). It is important to note that the Tribunal may not hear a matter unless conciliation at the Commission has failed and the matter has been referred to it by the Commission. These two facts must be true prior to the Tribunal proceeding with any matter. With respect to awards and penalties, these are not outlined in the Act (save for procedural offences) and thus previous decisions provide precedents (Stephenson and Persadie 2019). Interestingly, orders and awards determined by the Tribunal are not open to appeal, as appeals are allowed only on matters of law and mistake of fact.

In the other Caribbean countries, any issue concerning equality at work is heard through the Minister responsible for labour or industrial relations, and escalates to a Labour Commissioner and/or the general magisterial or high court system when there is no resolution at earlier stages. As noted earlier, in St Lucia, such matters are addressed by the Labour Tribunal. Barbados has made provisions for matters to be heard by a previously established Employment Rights Tribunal. Some countries also provide for mediation between the parties. None of these remaining countries have made special institutional provisions to address equality matters in fields other than employment and, even so, only incidentally.

Discussion

Equality legislation has become important as it has expanded the scope of persons against whom action can be taken, namely private entities. Positive duties to promote equality of opportunity are placed on public bodies, not private sector bodies (McCrudden and Prechal 2009). While constitutional equality provisions address behaviours against the State,

Table 7.5 Statistics compiled by the Equal Opportunity Tribunal (Trinidad and Tobago) for the period 2014–2016 for complaints that alleged a status ground

Status	2014	2015	2016
Race/Ethnicity	30	17	22
Sex	23	8	13
Disability	13	12	20
Origin	22	6	8
Religion	11	8	6
Marital Status	2	2	0
Victimisation	18	13	10
Total complaints	126	102	98

[a]Statistics provided via email dated 25 November 2019 from Anne Marie Seenarine-Price, Research Officer II of the Equal Opportunity Commission. The email noted that many persons alleged two or more status grounds, hence the numbers may not easily add up

Source Author's creation

there was previously no recourse for action to be taken against private entities. Equality laws have addressed this gap and now allow for actions against both the State and private entities. In the case of Trinidad and Tobago, Table 7.4 shows that three of the complaints were against private entities, an action that could not have been taken before based on previously existing statute.

The Commission has compiled statistics for the period 2014–2016 for complaints that alleged a status ground as seen in Table 7.5.

The statistics do not further disaggregate the status grounds, such as which race/ethnicity made the claim or what was the sex of the person making the claim. From the cases and status grounds noted in Table 7.4, it can be deduced that ten claims were made on the basis of victimisation, five on race, three on religion, two each on sex and origin and one each on ethnicity and disability. In its decision-making process, the Tribunal appears to be uniform in its approach to addressing claims of unequal or discriminatory treatment. The Tribunal uses an actual or hypothetical comparator to determine whether the complainant has been treated less favourably than someone of a different status in the same position. In the case of Giselle Glaude and her claim of discrimination on the basis of religion, for example, the Tribunal compared the way her employer facilitated members of another faith while she was not and ruled in her favour. Where race is the ground of claimed discrimination, such as in *Desmond Noel v The Auditor General of Trinidad and Tobago*, the complainant was Afro-Trinidadian and his situation was compared to someone of Indo-Trinidadian descent in a similar position. Similarly, with sex, if the complainant is female, such as seen in *Indra Chankasingh-Budhai v The Ministry of Food Production and The Attorney General of Trinidad and Tobago*, her situation will be compared with someone in a similar position who is male.

In two instances, one in St Lucia and one in Trinidad and Tobago, persons attempted to use a status ground that was not part of the country's respective equality law. As noted above in section 7.2.2, an action was taken in St Lucia, pursuant to the *Equality of Opportunity and Treatment in Employment and Occupation Act*, Cap. 16.14, but was dismissed as the complainant attempted to introduce sexual orientation as a prohibited ground of discrimination, which is not a ground included in the law. A somewhat similar approach was taken pursuant to the *Equal Opportunity Act*, Ch. 22:03 in Trinidad and Tobago. Rishi Persad Maharaj attempted to introduce sexual harassment premised on sexual identity as a ground of discrimination under the law. In a 38-page judgement (the longest one delivered by the Tribunal to date), it was determined that "while harassment that is premised on biological sexual identity may be protected, harassment premised on sexual identity caused by sexual preference or orientation is not" (p. 32). The definition of "sex" in the *Equal Opportunity Act*, Ch. 22:03 specifically excludes sexual preference or orientation. Unsurprisingly, his claim also failed. Interestingly, while not directly related to sexual harassment premised on sexual identity specifically, the Chairman of the Commission noted with concern that claims of sexual discrimination in the workplace are not considered as they fall into a category or status where no further action can be taken as the Commission does not have the jurisdiction to entertain such grievances (Christopher 2019).

Table 7.2 shows the various prohibited grounds of discrimination and status for which persons are not to be treated differently in Caribbean equality legislation, with one very notable exception: sexual orientation. Attempts to introduce sexual orientation as a ground through case law have failed. While the Commissioner in the *Persad Case* considered, at some length, whether the law could be interpreted such that the ground of "sex" could include "sexual orientation or preference", she decided that this would go against the stated intention of Parliament as its definition of "sex" specifically excludes this; moreover, the Commissioner noted that it would be outside of the remit of the Tribunal to stretch the definition in such a manner. Caribbean society is still rather conservative in this regard and legally including sexual orientation is not yet on any legislative agenda, with Barbados providing an extremely recent and notable exception. Interestingly, though, while sexual orientation as a ground of discrimination is not generally currently being considered for inclusion in the law, HIV/AIDS has been. St Lucia and The Bahamas have included HIV/AIDS as a ground of discrimination. When one takes into consideration the various means of transmission of the virus, it begs the question as to why sexual orientation is so adamantly excluded. Nevertheless, the fact that Caribbean countries are recognising the need for equality legislation is certainly a step in the right direction. Laws can be, and always are, amended to reflect important emerging trends. There is hope yet.

Even the language used in formulating law needs to be carefully considered. While the term "disability" has become widely accepted in referring to persons with disabilities, the term "handicapped" is no longer acceptable. This statement prefaces the fact that Dominica has a *Labour Standards Act*, Chap. 89:05 which allows for an employer to pay a "handicapped" person a lower wage than any minimum wage set by law. There are two offensive concepts here: the use of the term "handicapped" and the fact that someone so deemed can be paid less than someone without a disability once authorised by the Labour Commissioner. Space does not allow for further consideration of this matter here.

An assessment of the efficacy of the sole existing and operational institutional and legal framework for addressing equality, as found in Trinidad and Tobago, might be premature at this stage, depending on the metric that is used, as so few actions have been heard by the Tribunal and in light of the limited jurisdiction noted by the Commission Chairman. From another perspective, however, when one considers the fact that only unresolved matters from the Commission are brought to the Tribunal to be heard, and in conjunction with the figures in Table 7.5, it would be somewhat safe to surmise that the majority of the cases are addressed at the Commission stage up to the point of conciliation, for matters for which the Commission has jurisdiction, which removes the need for adjudication of the matters. This must mean that the institutional and legal framework established in Trinidad and Tobago to address discrimination has experienced a relatively high success rate. This model can, therefore, be replicated, with appropriate adjustments, in the various other Caribbean islands as it has a proven rate of success in dealing with discrimination matters against the State as well as private entities. Although, the Chairman of the

Commission noted that the majority of complaints received are against the public sector and postulated that this might likely be out of fear of victimisation and job loss (Christopher 2019).

CONCLUSION

This chapter encapsulated an overview of the equality laws that exist in this region, based on existing statute that provides for equality in a broad manner as well as statutory provisions that address equality or non-discrimination for employment purposes. Only two countries have general equality legislation: Guyana and Trinidad and Tobago but just the latter has established an institutional framework to administer the legislation. Apart from constitutional provisions guaranteeing equality before the law and equality at work, the existence of law that addresses equality broadly in the Caribbean is not as widespread as one would hope but tends to focus on equality in the workplace. Nevertheless, legislation addressing equality generally and in the workplace covers numerous grounds of discrimination with the very notable exception of sexual orientation, on the one hand, and the interesting inclusion of HIV/AIDS, on the other. Such legislation reflects both the positive duty of States to promote measures that advance equality as well as the negative duty to refrain from treating persons differently based on their status or any named ground of discrimination. In so doing, the few Caribbean countries which have passed equality legislation have recognised the need to protect personal differences by ensuring that equal rights are afforded accordingly.

Case law has been successfully recorded only in Trinidad and Tobago for actions claiming discrimination on named grounds. Attempts to include omitted grounds of discrimination, such as sexual orientation, in cases have been rejected outright by the various adjudicating bodies of the respective countries where such actions have been brought. Thus far, the approach by the Tribunal has been uniform in its application of the law in addressing claims of discrimination, which in itself is a basic principle of equality. The Tribunal also appears to treat like cases alike, another fundamental tenet of equality. The Commission, which filters matters that go forward to the Tribunal, seems to be performing well in resolving matters that come to it as the number of complaints versus the number of actions filed and heard is quite disparate.

There is still a long road ahead for the establishment of legal and institutional frameworks to address equality and discrimination in the

Caribbean. For countries that have not yet contemplated such a framework, bearing in mind the jurisdictional limitations highlighted by the Chairman of the Commission, as well as any specific national need, the model found in Trinidad and Tobago provides a useful starting point for consideration and adaptation, if not for wholesale replication of the model.

REFERENCES

Australian Government, Attorney-General's Department. (n.d.). *Rights of equality and non-discrimination.* Retrieved 11 November 2019 from https://www.ag.gov.au/RightsAndProtections/HumanRights/Human-rights-scrutny/PublicSectorGuidanceSheets/Pages/Rightsofequalityandnondiscrimination.aspx.

Besson, S. (2005). The principle of non-discrimination in the convention on the rights of the child. *The International Journal of Children's Rights, 13*, 433–461.

Christopher, P. (2019, December 12). EOC chairman: Too many complaints being dismissed. *Trinidad Guardian*, Thursday 10 December 2019, A10.

Encyclopaedia Britannica. (2019). *Equality: Human rights.* Retrieved 8 November 2019 from https://www.britannica.com/.

Equality Rights Trust. (2014). *Economic and social rights in the courtroom: A litigator's guide to using equality and non-discrimination strategies to advance economic and social rights.* London: Equal Rights Trust.

Fredman, S. (2016). Substantive equality revisted. *International Constitutional Law, 14*(3), 712–738. https://doi.org/10.1093/icon/mow043.

George-Wiltshire, R. (2019). Chief Justice of Guyana, 7 November 2019, E-mail communication.

Howard-Hassmann, R. E. (2013). Reconsidering the right to own property. *Journal of Human Rights, 12*(2), 180–197. https://doi.org/10.1080/14754835.2013.784667.

International Labour Organisation. (2014a). *Constitution of Barbados.* Database of national labour, social security and related human rights legislation. Retrieved 5 November 2019 from http://www.ilo.org/dyn/nat-lex/docs/ELECTRONIC/72559/98977/F2125179261/BRB72559.pdf.

International Labour Organisation. (2014b). *Employment Act*, Chapter 89 (No. 14 of 1999) (Grenada). Database of national labour, social security and related human rights legislation. Retrieved 5 November 2019 from http://www.ilo.org/dyn/natlex/docs/WEBTEXT/53925/65176/E99GRD01.htm.

The Barbados Parliament. (2020). History of this Bill: Employment (Prevention of Discrimination) Bill, 2020. Retrieved 18 August 2020 from https://www.barbadosparliament.com/bills/details/477.

The Government of the Bahamas. (2006a). *Employment Act*, Ch. 321A. Retrieved 6 November 2019 from http://laws.bahamas.gov.bs/cms/images/LEGISLATION/PRINCIPAL/2001/2001-0027/EmploymentAct_1.pdf.

The Government of the Bahamas. (2006b). *Persons with Disabilities (Equal Opportunities) Act*, 2014. Retrieved 1 November 2019 from http://laws.bahamas.gov.bs/cms/images/LEGISLATION/PRINCIPAL/2014/2014-0031/PersonswithDisabilitiesEqualOpportunitiesAct2014_1.pdf.

The Government of the Bahamas. (2011). *The Constitution of The Commonwealth of The Bahamas*. Retrieved 5 November 2019 from https://www.bahamas.gov.bs/.

The Government of Dominica. (1978). *The Constitution of the Commonwealth of Dominica*. Retrieved 5 November 2019 from http://www.dominica.gov.dm/laws/chapters/chap1-01-sch1.pdf.

The Government of Grenada. (1973). *The Grenada Constitution Order*. Retrieved 5 November 2019 from https://www.ilo.org/dyn/natlex/docs/ELECTRONIC/16240/95820/F348729948/GRD16240.pdf.

The Government of St Lucia. (1979). *Constitution of Saint Lucia*. Retrieved 5 November 2019 from http://www.govt.lc/media.govt.lc/www/resources/legislation/ConstitutionOfSaintLucia.pdf.

The National Assembly of St Kitts and Nevis. (1983). *The Constitution of St Christopher and Nevis*. Retrieved 5 November 2019 from http://www.parliament.gov.kn/the-constitution/.

Thomsen, F. K. (2018). Concept, principle and norm—Equality before the law reconsidered. *Legal Theory, 24*, 103–134. https://doi.org/10.1017/S1352325218000071.

United Nations. (1948). United Nations declaration of human rights. Adopted 10 December 1948. In I. Brownlie (Ed.), *Basic documents on human rights* (1992). Oxford: Oxford University Press.

CHAPTER 8

Equality Laws Compared: The Caribbean, the UK and the USA

INTRODUCTION

Equality legislation is of recent vintage in the Caribbean region, the earliest notable piece dating to 1990 and having been amended in 2012 (*Equal Rights Act*, 2012 of Guyana). This is likely attributable to the fact that Caribbean countries have only attained the status of independent nations starting from the 1960s, with Jamaica being the first in 1962 and St Kitts and Nevis the most recent in 1983 (The Commonwealth Secretariat 2020). Of the twelve independent Caribbean countries, only three have attained republic status from the 1970s onwards (The Commonwealth Secretariat 2020). In the United States of America (USA), equality became part of the legislative agenda as early as the mid-1860s, shortly after slavery was abolished, in the form of the Fourteenth Amendment to the US Constitution (Library of Congress 2018). In the United Kingdom (UK), interestingly, equality and diversity took on legislative importance only from the mid-1960s, culminating in the enactment of the *Equality Act* 2010, which has consolidated several pieces of legislation (The Diversity Group 2018).

Nationally, some 155 countries expressly guarantee equality to their citizens in their respective constitutional instruments (Persadie 2012). This includes all twelve independent English-speaking Caribbean countries (see Chapter 7). Only two of these countries, Guyana and Trinidad and Tobago, have enacted legislation that provides for equality or the

© The Author(s) 2020   157
J. H. Stephenson et al., *Diversity, Equality,
and Inclusion in Caribbean Organisations and Society,*
https://doi.org/10.1007/978-3-030-47614-4_8

prevention of discrimination in areas other than just employment (see Table 7.3 in Chapter 7). There has been a conspicuous focus in the majority of the other Caribbean jurisdictions to legislate equal pay for equal work and, to a lesser extent, general non-discrimination at work. It would appear that these other Caribbean parliaments' emphasis on equality applies only to employment-related matters for now; although, some governments are discussing anti-discrimination legislation, as is the case, for example, in Belize, where discussions began in mid-January 2020 on an Equal Opportunities Bill which was drafted after twenty years of data collection (Leslie 2020).

The data collection method used in the chapter is largely qualitative in nature and is premised principally on a documentary review of the equality legislation of Guyana, Trinidad and Tobago, the UK and the USA. The legislation reviewed are the *Civil Rights Act* of 1964 and the *Equality Act*, 2019 (USA); the *Equality Act* 2010 (UK); the *Equal Rights Act*, Cap. 38:01 and *Prevention of Discrimination Act*, Cap. 99:09 (Guyana) and the *Equal Opportunity Act*, Ch. 22:03 (Trinidad and Tobago). The chapter begins with a brief history and development of equality legislation in the USA and UK and their key provisions, followed by the key provisions found in the laws of Guyana and Trinidad and Tobago. A selective comparative review of key components of the legislation of the Caribbean territories with that of the two developed countries follows; this can assist in determining what recommendations can be made to improve what currently exists in the Caribbean region, if necessary. This chapter does not contemplate a review of case law or constitutional law (apart from the USA) as it relates to equality but only of statute.

EQUALITY LEGISLATION

Equality legislation is premised on the concepts of equality and non-discrimination (see Chapter 7). Equality places a positive duty on the part of States to promote measures that advance equality, while non-discrimination is a negative duty of restraint designed to suppress acts of unequal treatment of persons by the State (see Fredman 2017; Equality Rights Trust 2014). Generally speaking, "negative" human rights, such as equal rights, are assumed to be those that require State forbearance, while "positive" human rights require active fulfilment by the State (Howard-Hassmann 2013). Non-discrimination is widely understood as a negative restatement of the principle of equality (Sokhi-Bulley 2005) and ensures that no one is denied their rights for any reason (Australian Government, Attorney General's Department, n.d.). The legislation of the four countries under review adhere to these principles of promoting positive measures to ensure equality and suppressing acts of unequal treatment. This section will focus on the historical development of equality legislation in the USA and the UK and their key provisions. A review of the main statutory provisions from Guyana and Trinidad and Tobago then follows.

The United States of America

Equality legislation in the USA has its roots in the Fourteenth Amendment of the US Constitution dating back to 1868 when the amendment was ratified (Library of Congress 2018). Rosenberg (2004) noted that, while the guarantee of equal protection was enshrined in this amendment, it took the three branches of government nearly a full century to meaningfully address it. This came in the form of the *Civil Rights Act* in 1964. In the intervening period, discussions surrounding equality were required to address new and different disadvantaged minorities, ranging from class to gender, as they began to take on social importance. In the era following the abolition of slavery, inequality distinctions arose based on class and geographic/national origin, in New York, for example, as recounted by Nelson (1995), although without any regard for racial prejudices. The issue of race rose to prominence later on, mid-century. During the 1920s–1930s, equality jurisprudence in New York was influenced by concerns over cultural, ethnic and religious discrimination as American immigrant groups, particularly the Jewish and Roman Catholic groups, began to attain significant political power in the 1920s but continued to experience discrimination in the form of "political persecution" on the basis of their "inferiority" (Nelson 1995). Nelson (1995) reported that this discrimination was manifested in the suppression of their freedom of expression as well as their experience of wiretapping, police brutality and searches. This then expanded into discrimination in the areas of education, zoning, taxation and even forced health care.

Towards the end of the 1930s, a new idea of equality began to emerge in New York which required cultural and ethnic discrimination to come to an end. This was coupled with the new social realities surrounding the immediate post-World War II era in which cultural and ethnic discrimination were identified as the new paradigms of inequality (Nelson 1995). At this point, equality required minorities to conform to majority values by shedding their immigrant identities and assimilating into mainstream culture and social practices. Equality meant, therefore, "the gradual assimilation of diverse groups into a pre-existing cultural mainstream" (Nelson 1995) or into what was, at that point, the dominant culture (Fredman 2001). These groups eventually rose above the discrimination they faced, notably without the assistance of any equality or anti-discrimination legislation being passed but, curiously, with the creeping support of the judiciary that began to protect religious freedoms (Nelson 1995). These groups eventually became very socially, politically and economically successful.

Actual anti-discrimination legislation came about as a result of the American civil rights movement, which began in the southern US states, and which had its roots in the century-long efforts of African slaves and their descendants to resist racial oppression and abolish the institution of slavery (Carson 2020). Institutionalised racial discrimination, or racism, came under increasing attack during the 1950s–1960s (Smedley 2017) when the movement assumed national prominence (Carson 2020). Racial inequality faced by African-Americans differed significantly from the other forms of discrimination as state legislatures institutionalised discrimination through statute; moreover, this group was completely excluded from politics and therefore had no political influence (Nelson 1995). The New York judiciary seemed prepared to accept equal protection as a judicially enforceable right in the mid-1960s as it related to numerous social issues affecting this group, such as education, adoption, membership, housing and zoning and employment (Nelson 1995). During this time, the concept of equality continued to slowly evolve, from one that required assimilation of minority groups into the cultural mainstream to accepting and permitting the multicultural practices of such groups (Nelson 1995). This became key to the civil rights movement: a rejection of "assimilationist equality" (Nelson 1995) and a need to simply be allowed to just be, otherwise, African-Americans would continue to be "in a perpetual minority" (Hamilton 1972). It was the unflagging work of the civil rights movements that saw the passage of the *Civil Rights Act* in 1964 as well as the subsequent *Voting Rights Act* of 1965. This latter restored the right to vote guaranteed by the Fourteenth and Fifteenth Amendments (granting citizenship to all and specifically granting African-Americans the right to vote, respectively [Drexler 2019]), deemed "the single most effective piece of civil rights legislation ever passed by Congress" (US Department of Justice 2009).

The *Civil Rights Act* of 1964 banned segregation on the grounds of race, colour, religion or national origin at all places of public accommodation (History.com 2020). Title VII of the *Civil Rights Act* barred race, colour, religion, national origin and gender discrimination by employers and labour unions (History.com 2020). These comprise the five grounds of prohibited discrimination in the law but the ground of sex applies only to employment matters (Ourdocuments.gov, n.d.). The *Civil Rights Act* of 1964 also created a Commission on Civil Rights (Title V) and an Equal Employment Opportunity Commission (Sec 705) with the power to file lawsuits on behalf of aggrieved workers (History.com 2020). The passage of the *Civil Rights Act* of 1964 was hailed a milestone legislative achievement for the civil rights movement as it sought to provide redress for institutionalised discrimination in its many guises. In enacting the *Civil Rights Act* of 1964, Congress validly invoked its powers under the Fourteenth Amendment to provide a full range of remedies in response to persistent, widespread and pervasive discrimination by both private and government actors (Library of Congress 2019). Disability is addressed separately in the *Americans with Disabilities Act* 1990 which is a civil rights law that prohibits discrimination against individuals with disabilities in all areas of public life, including jobs, schools, transportation and all public and private places that are open to the general public (ADA National Network 2020). Despite this undoubted progress pertaining to civil rights, there was one more ground of discrimination that was not fully covered by this particular piece of legislation nor by the constitution: gender.

Gender equality proponents have faced a long and arduous struggle in trying to have this properly reflected in the law. Women as a group have been characterised as the largest, subordinated underclass in American society (Nelson 1995), clearly a categorisation accepted by most feminists, otherwise, there would be no struggle for equality. Nearly 100 years ago, in December 1923, in an attempt to address this situation, an Equal Rights Amendment (ERA) was introduced to Congress with text stating, "Equality of rights under the law shall not be denied or abridged by the United States or by any State on account of sex" (Critchlow and Stechecki 2008). As it was a constitutional amendment, however, it required ratification by 38 out of 50 states (North

2020) before it could become law. It was this numeric requirement that delayed the process. Ratification issues surrounding the ERA as it relates to ratification timelines are well-documented (see, for example, Neale 2019; Held et al. 1997; Critchlow and Stechecki 2008; Suk 2017). Nevertheless, the 38th ratification was received in 2019 but arguments over its validity continue (North 2020). The ERA is meant to come into force two years after the 38th ratification. Opponents of this Amendment argue that the Fourteenth Amendment, or the Equal Protection Clause, sufficiently provides for gender equality. This however, depends on the interpretation and application of "equal protection" (see, for example, Bachman 2019). In this way, the ERA is important as, without it, women are not afforded full federal protection against gender discrimination (Held et al. 1997). The enactment of the ERA would prohibit gender discrimination and, for the first time, would explicitly mandate equal rights for women (Neale 2019). In *Regents of the University of California v. Bakke*, 438 US 265 (1978), Justice Powell wrote that "the Court has never viewed [gender-based] classification as inherently suspect or as comparable to racial or ethnic classifications for the purpose of equal-protection analysis" (Held et al. 1997). This certainly makes a very strong case for its formal inclusion in the law.

While the ERA remains in legislative limbo, the passage of the *Equality Act*, 2019 in the US House of Representatives has been celebrated by its advocates as a major win in the USA in the promotion of equal rights for all. The *Equality Act*, 2019 is meant to address State and local government discrimination on the basis of sexual orientation or gender identity in employment, housing, and public accommodations, and in programmes and activities receiving Federal financial assistance, as this violates the Equal Protection Clause of the Fourteenth Amendment to the Constitution of the United States (Library of Congress 2019). The *Equality Act*, 2019 very specifically seeks to include sexual orientation and gender identity as protected characteristics. "Sex" in the *Civil Rights Act* of 1964, once allowed to come into force, would now be defined as including sexual orientation and gender identity where "sexual orientation" is explicitly defined as "homosexuality, heterosexuality, or bisexuality" and "gender identity" means "the gender-related identity, appearance, mannerisms, or other gender-related characteristics of an individual, regardless of the individual's designated sex at birth" (Library of Congress 2019).

The *Equality Act*, 2019 is most certainly not without its detractors who claim that the Act, if passed in the Senate, would "further *inequality* by penalizing everyday Americans for their beliefs about marriage and biological sex" (The Heritage Foundation 2020) "[u]nder the guise of anti-discrimination protections" (Kearns 2019). This claim is made as "the bill redefines sex to include gender identity, undermines religious freedom, gives males who identify as females the right to women's spaces, and sets a dangerous political precedent for the medicalization of gender-confused youth" (Kearns 2019). The fate of the *Equality Act*, 2019, particularly as it relates to its treatment in the Senate, remains to be seen.

With all this having been noted, the US Supreme Court, in a monumentally landmark ruling on 15 July 2020, has interpreted the definition of "sex" in the *Civil Rights Act* of 1964 to now include sexual orientation and gender identity (de Vogue 2020). Gay, lesbian and transgender workers are now protected by federal civil rights law as it relates to discrimination in employment. In a sharply divided Court, the majority ruled that Title VII of the 1964 *Civil Rights Act*, which prohibits discrimination "because of" sex, extends to people who face job bias arising from their sexual orientation or gender identity (Biskupic 2020). The ruling came about as a decision for three consolidated cases involving two gay men and a transgender woman who were fired from their jobs because of their sexual orientation and gender identity. The first openly gay presidential candidate, Pete Buttigieg (2020), noted that the Supreme Court ruling does not mean that the struggle is over but it is certainly an enormous step forward. This is true as the same arguments that have been made by detractors against the passage of the *Equality Act*, 2019 apply equally to this decision. While certainly a step in a positive direction, the decision is specific to LGBTQ rights in the workplace only, whereas the *Equality Act*, 2019 seeks to be more expansive in its application of the ground of "sex" and not just at the workplace. Therefore, it is still important that advocates continue to lobby for its passage.

The United Kingdom

The development and enactment of equality legislation in the UK have taken a very different trajectory to that of the USA, of course, due to the dissimilar socio-economic and political histories experienced by both countries. In 2010, the *Equality Act* was passed which sought, in part, "to reform and harmonise equality law and restate the greater part of the enactments relating to discrimination and harassment related to certain personal characteristics" (*Equality Act* 2010, Legislation.gov. uk [2020a]). The history of the development of anti-discrimination law in the UK began in the 1960s in a piecemeal fashion when the *Race Relations Act* of 1965, *Equal Pay Act* of 1970 and *Sex Discrimination Act* of 1975 were introduced (Hepple 2010; Feast and Hand 2015). During this era, there was no general equality guarantee but rather a relatively sophisticated set of anti-discrimination statutes operating within a narrow area (Fredman 2001). Anti-discrimination legislation in the UK was partially based on domestic initiatives as well as European Union Directives; there are four main Directives which have helped shape UK anti-discrimination legislation:

- Council Directive 2000/43/EC implementing the principle of equal treatment between persons irrespective of racial or ethnic origin;
- Council Directive 2000/78/EC establishing a general framework for equal treatment in employment and occupation;
- Council Directive 2004/113/EC implementing the principle of equal treatment between men and women in the access to and supply of goods and services;
- European Parliament and Council Directive 2006/54/EC on the implementation of the principle of equal opportunities and equal treatment of men and women in matters of employment and occupation (Legislation.gov.uk 2020b).

After 14 years of campaigning by equality specialists and human rights organisations, the *Equality Act* 2010 came into force (Hepple 2010). According to Hepple (2010), the *Equality Act* 2010 is part of the fifth generation of equality legislation in Britain. The first generation was based on the notion of formal equality where like must be treated as like and led to the enactment of the *Race Relations Act* of 1965 to address discrimination faced by immigrants from the Caribbean and India. The second generation, the *Race Relations Act* 1968, was also a measure of formal equality and was limited to direct racial discrimination but extended coverage to employment, housing, goods and services (Hepple 2010). The third generation started with the extension of legislation to discrimination on grounds of sex (*Equal Pay Act* 1970 and *Sex Discrimination Act* 1975) (Hepple 2010). It was during this particular generation that several Commissions were established to address equal opportunities, racial equality and disability rights (Hepple 2011). The fourth generation resulted from Article 13 of the Treaty of Amsterdam (1997) and the implementing Race Directive and Framework Employment Directive (covering age, disability, religion or belief and sexual orientation) and subsequently the Equal Treatment Directive (covering sex) (Hepple 2010). During this fourth generation, between 2003 and 2007, secondary legislation based on European Union Directives which addressed age, religion/belief and sexual orientation, as it related to employment matters, was passed in the UK and marked the start of comprehensive equality (Hepple 2010). In 2007, a single Equality and Human Rights Commission replaced all the existing commissions to address all forms of discrimination. The fifth, and current, generation marked the start of transformative equality as there was the imposition of public sector positive duties to actively promote equality (Hepple 2010).

The *Equality Act* 2010 is a massive piece of legislation, containing some 218 sections and 28 schedules. It consolidates nine major pieces of legislation and some 100 statutory instruments (Ashtiany 2011) and is hailed as the "new single Equality Act in Britain" (Hepple 2010). Among many of its parts and chapters, it addresses protected characteristics, prohibited conduct, employment, equality of terms, education, enforcement and, importantly, the advancement of equality (*Equality Act* 2010). The application of the law is specific to nine protected characteristics which are covered under the *Equality Act* 2010, section 4: age, disability, gender reassignment, marriage and civil partnership, pregnancy and maternity, race, religion or belief, sex and sexual orientation (*Equality Act* 2010). Major exceptions to the application of the law relate to services and public functions, such as constitutional matters, education, health and care, immigration, insurance, marriage, separate and single services (Schedule 3); equality of terms (Schedule 7); occupational requirements (Schedule 9); single-sex institutions (educational, Schedules 11–12); associations (Schedule 16) and general exceptions (Schedule 23) which can be found in the various schedules to the *Equality Act* 2010.

While, at first glance, the list of protected characteristics seems laudable, the number of relevant protected characteristics frequently varies throughout the *Equality Act* 2010, ranging as it does from nine to four (Hand et al. 2012; extensive and comprehensive critiques of these

Part 11 of the *Equality Act* 2010 is dedicated to the advancement of equality through the imposition of a public sector equality duty to (a) eliminate discrimination, harassment, victimisation and any other conduct that is prohibited by or under this Act; (b) advance equality of opportunity between persons who share a relevant protected characteristic and persons who do not share it; and (c) foster good relations between persons who share a relevant protected characteristic and persons who do not share it (s 149(1)). This stipulation specifically excludes the protected characteristic of marriage/civil partnership. The *Equality Act* 2010 further encourages persons to take positive action to promote equality where they reasonably think that (a) persons who share a protected characteristic suffer a disadvantage connected to the characteristic, (b) persons who share a protected characteristic have needs that are different from the needs of persons who do not share it or (c) participation in an activity by persons who share a protected characteristic is disproportionately low (s 158(1)). This applies to all protected characteristics. Nevertheless, both sections are written with discretionary language, meaning that neither is mandatory to carry out. Critics have also attacked the failing of the law to impose a similar duty on the private sector (Hepple 2011). Positive action seeks to promote disadvantaged and/or underrepresented classes, for example, if one sex is underrepresented in an organisation, once both candidates of either sex are equally qualified for the position, the person of the underrepresented sex would be hired. While this provision can assist in achieving substantive equality, it can have the perverse effect of someone claiming reverse discrimination and should be applied very cautiously (Davies et al. 2016).

Guyana

Guyana is one of two Caribbean countries that has legislated for general equality and not just workplace equality. Apart from its constitutional guarantees of equality, there are two pieces of legislation that ensure equality very broadly: the *Equal Rights Act*, Cap. 38:01 and the *Prevention of Discrimination Act*, Cap. 99:09. The *Equal Rights Act*, Cap. 38:01, section 2, ensures equality on the basis of sex and marital status: (1) Woman and men shall have equal rights and the same legal status in all spheres of political, economic and social life. (2) All forms of discrimination against women or men on the basis of their sex or marital status are illegal. Subsections (3) and (4) ensure equal pay and non-discrimination in employment, respectively. Subsection (5) prohibits discrimination, on the ground of sex only, in the areas of access to training and equal opportunities in social, political or cultural activity. Subsection (7) permits positive action on the part of an employer to make special labour and health protection measures for women or to make provisions for conditions to enable mothers to work.

The *Prevention of Discrimination Act*, Cap. 99:09 provides largely for the elimination of discrimination in employment, training, recruitment and membership of professional bodies as well as in the provision of goods, services and facilities, advertisements and application forms (as it relates to the nature of the information being solicited). This particular piece of legislation contains numerous prohibited grounds of discrimination as it relates to the nullification or impairment of equality of opportunity or treatment in any employment or occupation (s 4): race, sex, religion, colour, ethnic origin, indigenous population, national extraction, social origin, economic status, political opinion, disability, family responsibilities, pregnancy, marital status, age. There is an exception for age related to retirement or the employment of minors as well as genuine occupational qualifications (s 6). Other exceptions relate to charities and religious bodies (ss 19–20). Similar to the *Equal Rights Act*, Cap. 38:01, section 7 of the *Prevention of Discrimination Act*, Cap. 99:09 permits positive action on the part of an employer, though of a temporary nature, to take special measures to promote equality of opportunity in employment. Offences under the *Prevention of Discrimination Act*, Cap. 99:09 include inducing someone to contravene the Act (s 21) or victimising someone for having made a complaint or intending to do so, brought proceedings or intending to do so, provided information or intending to do so, attended an inquiry or made a good faith allegation that an act of discrimination has been committed (s 22). Harassment under the law addresses only sexual harassment and is a form of sex discrimination (s 8) and not harassment related to any other prohibited ground of discrimination.

While the law has not recognised sexual orientation as a ground of discrimination, a recently adopted policy document has. In 2018, the Government of Guyana adopted its National Gender Equality and Social Inclusion (GESI) Policy for Guyana. It is a progressive document that very clearly acknowledges sexual orientation and gender identity as grounds of discrimination. This is due, in large part, to the unwavering work of the advocacy group, Society Against Sexual Orientation

Discrimination (SASOD), which works closely with Guyana Trans United (GTU), to have such status recognised (Ministry of Social Protection 2018). These grounds are yet to be legally reflected in the *Prevention of Discrimination Act*, Cap. 99:09. Policy statements do not always translate into law, but the legislative fate of the additional grounds of discrimination remains to be seen.

Trinidad and Tobago

Trinidad and Tobago is the second of two Caribbean countries to have enacted legislation that provides for equality or the prevention of discrimination in areas other than just employment; this is separate from its constitutional guarantees of equality. The *Equal Opportunity Act*, Ch. 22:03 prohibits certain kinds of discrimination and promotes equality of opportunity between persons of different status. There are seven status protected under the *Equal Opportunity Act*, Ch. 22:03: sex, race, ethnicity, origin, including geographical origin, religion, marital status and disability. The definition of "sex" very specifically excludes sexual preference or orientation (s 3). This Act prohibits discrimination in relation to employment, education, the provision of goods and services and the provision of accommodation as it relates to any named status where a person is treated less favourably than someone of a different status who is similarly circumstanced (s 5) or where a person is victimised for having brought proceedings or intends to do so, given evidence or information in connection with proceedings or intends to do so, or made a good faith allegation that an act of discrimination has been committed (s 6). Also prohibited is offensive behaviour (s 7), which is equivalent to harassment but applies only to five protected status: gender, race, ethnicity, origin or religion (s 7(1)(b)). Interestingly, "gender", rather than "sex", is the term used in this section, but it has not been defined in the interpretation section nor is it a named protected status. Exceptions to the application of the *Equal Opportunity Act*, Ch. 22:03 include genuine occupational exceptions (s 11), religious shops (s 12), domestic services and family businesses (s 13) and unjustifiable risk to employee or hardship to employer in the employment of a person with a disability (s 14). Another exception includes single-sex educational establishments (s 16). The *Equal Opportunity Act*, Ch. 22:03 does not apply to sports (s 19), pregnancy and maternity (s 20), membership (s 21), voluntary bodies (s 22), charities (s 23), insurance (s 24) and religious bodies (s 25). The *Equal Opportunity Act*, Ch. 22:03 also establishes an Equal Opportunity

Commission (s 26) and an Equal Opportunity Tribunal (s 41). The Equal Opportunity Commission plays a key role in working towards the elimination of discrimination; promoting equality of opportunity and good relations between persons of different status generally; and developing, conducting and fostering research and educational programmes and other programmes for the purpose of eliminating discrimination and promoting equality of opportunity and good relations between persons of different status (s 27). This is very similar to the public sector equality duty of the UK *Equality Act* 2010 but resides only with the Equal Opportunity Commission. Curiously, though, the membership of the Commission is meant to reflect only, and as far as possible, a balance of race and gender (s 26(5)).

To highlight the relevance of the definition of "sex" in the *Equal Opportunity Act*, Ch. 22:03, it is necessary to understand the official, government perspective on this. In 2005, in Trinidad and Tobago, a draft Gender Policy document was being circulated but was categorically rejected due to its recommendation to "review all issues (for example legal, medical, religious and/or cultural) relating to the termination of pregnancy" and its recognition of people who subscribe to relationships which "appear antithetical to proscribed rules of religion and culture" (Ministry of Community Development 2005). Notwithstanding the apparent favourable position of the then government on the draft policy, the matter culminated in a major pronouncement by the then Prime Minister as part of his budget presentation in 2005 that effectively dismissed the draft policy (Persadie 2012). "The Government recognises the need to develop a Gender Policy. The draft Gender Policy Document currently being circulated was not issued by the Government and does not reflect Government policy. In fact, *there are certain recommendations in the document to which the Government does not and will not subscribe.* The Government is therefore requesting that the document which purports to be official Government policy be withdrawn from circulation" (Manning 2005; emphasis added). In 2018, the draft policy was followed by a Green Paper on a National Policy on Gender and Development that was issued by the Office of the Prime Minister which continues to firmly hold that "The National Policy on Gender and Development does not provide measures dealing with or relating to the issues of termination of pregnancy, same-sex unions, homosexuality or sexual orientation" (Office of the Prime Minister 2018). This policy position differs starkly to its neighbour's.

Comparison of Equality Legislation

Whereas most countries provide constitutional guarantees of equality, the UK situation is very different (see, for example, O'Cinneide 2011; Fredman et al. 2015) as it has no single, written document representing a constitution. Equality legislation in the USA was borne out of the Fourteenth Amendment to the Constitution, or Equal Protection Clause. In Guyana, this guarantee is found in s 149 of the *Constitution*; in Trinidad and Tobago, it is found in s 4 of the *Constitution*. The UK lacks a constitutional equality guarantee to underpin statutory equality rights and provide background principles to interpret statutes and develop the common law (Fredman et al. 2015). Equality in the UK may be described as an important democratic value that is protected by a complex web of overlapping European and domestic legal standards, but whose scope and content remain very much open to debate (O'Cinneide 2011).

Statutory provisions that address equality in all four countries under study reflect both the positive duty of States to promote measures that advance equality as well as the negative duty to refrain from treating persons differently based on their status or any named ground of discrimination. They, therefore, generally reflect equal enjoyment of rights and the prohibition or elimination of discrimination on various grounds. As it concerns the negative duty, all four countries name varying prohibited grounds of discrimination or protected characteristics—the USA has five, the UK has nine, Guyana has fifteen and Trinidad and Tobago has seven—which are variably addressed in each respective law, except for Guyana. Not all prohibited grounds of discrimination are covered by all provisions. In the USA, for example, sex is only covered in reference to employment in the *Civil Rights Act* of 1964; in the UK, the number of relevant protected characteristics frequently varies throughout the *Equality Act* 2010, ranging from all nine to as few as four; and in Trinidad and Tobago, only five prohibited grounds of discrimination apply to the section dealing with offensive behaviour in the *Equal Opportunity Act*, Ch. 22:03. Guyana is the only country where all prohibited grounds of discrimination apply equally throughout the *Prevention of Discrimination Act*, Cap. 99:09. In addition to being dealt with in this piece of legislation, sex discrimination is also covered in the *Equal Rights Act*, Cap. 38:01.

Each law reflects, in some manner, the positive duty of States to promote measures that advance equality. Such positive duties to promote

need to keep up and ensure inclusivity. This may only happen through constant and unwavering advocacy in the Caribbean. In an interesting postscript, the Supreme Court of Belize ruled that non-discrimination on the grounds of "sex" under sections 3 and 16 of the *Constitution* encompasses sexual orientation, a decision upheld by the Court of Appeal in a judgement delivered on 30 December 2019 (Human Dignity Trust 2020); Belize, however, does not have any equality legislation but is in the consultation stage of a bill which will very specifically not seek to affect the institution of marriage as a union between a man and a woman nor address abortion (Leslie 2020). In an exciting post postscript, in Barbados, there has been a positive development in this regard, as its very recently passed Employment (Prevention of Discrimination) Bill, 2020 has specifically included sexual orientation as one of 18 grounds of discrimination. It must be borne in mind, however, that this is specific only to employment-related matters and not general equality. Still, a positive step. Associative discrimination might be another useful prohibited ground of discrimination that can be included in the laws of Trinidad and Tobago and Guyana. This would ensure the protection of those with family and friends who share the protected characteristics defined in each respective law.

There are two definitions in the Caribbean legislation that should be expanded: these relate to disability and harassment. Very interestingly, the UK definition of "disability" includes certain medical conditions, namely, HIV/AIDS, cancer and multiple sclerosis in the determination of disability (Schedule 1, *Equality Act* 2010). Other definitions are very broad in their approach, looking at a "physical or mental impairment" (ADA National Network 2020; *Prevention of Discrimination Act*, Cap. 99:09) that substantially affects a person's quality of life. Since such medical conditions are part of the lived realities of many Caribbean citizens, it might be useful to consider the expansion of the definition of disability in a similar manner. The employment laws of St Lucia and The Bahamas do include HIV/AIDS as a prohibited ground of discrimination (see Table 7.2) but not as a disability. Without using express language, the ground "medical condition" in the newly-passed Barbados law includes "disease or illness" as well as mental and physical disabilites and can be widely interpreted. This might present one way of including such a definition in the legislation of the other Caribbean countries. The definition of "harassment" should also be expanded as current definitions seem quite restrictive. In Trinidad and Tobago, harassment is treated under "offensive behaviour" in the *Equal Opportunity Act*, Ch. 22:03 which applies only to five protected status. It is not clear why marital status and disability were excluded. Harassment is, however, treated under the *Offences Against the Person Act*, Ch. 11:08, but is not specific to any named grounds. The Chairman of the Equal Opportunity Commission noted, with concern, the Commission's jurisdictional limitations in treating with claims of sexual harassment (see Chapter 7). Conversely, in Guyana, harassment in the *Prevention against Discrimination Act*, Cap. 99:09 addresses only sexual harassment which is deemed a form of sex discrimination and not harassment related to any other prohibited ground of discrimination. There does not appear to be any treatment of harassment in any other law though.

The open-list approach adopted by Canada and the European Union with respect to the prohibited grounds of discrimination is useful in allowing the natural expansion of grounds as they arise, especially through judicial interpretation and application. This is so as the prohibited grounds of discrimination or protected characteristics are most certainly not static. They will continue to evolve based on the different and ever-changing social issues as they arise, which is why the Canadian and European Union open-list approach may be more suitable than what currently obtains in these four jurisdictions. It is therefore suggested that the regional legislation adopt this approach, but given the very dogmatic approach of these governments concerning certain social issues, it will likely not be considered.

Each country under review has legal provisions for the establishment of commissions/tribunals for the purposes of investigating and hearing matters that arise under their respective equality legislation. Three of the four countries have established such. While Guyana's law provides for the establishment of a Rights Commission Tribunal under its *Rights Commissions Tribunal Act*, Cap. 38:02, the Tribunal has not yet been established (George-Wiltshire 2019). This means that there is no right of appeal for any decision made by a Rights Commission (*Rights Commissions Tribunal Act*, Cap. 38:02, s 8). Most actions taken in the other three jurisdictions have been employment related. This seems to be where people experience or are more willing to take action for discriminatory behaviour.

Vicarious liability for the acts of employees and agents is an interesting inclusion in the UK *Equality Act* 2010. While vicarious liability and employer's liability exist in common law, as practised in Guyana and Trinidad and Tobago, the judicial process for making employers and principals liable for the acts of discrimination committed by those in their employ during the execution of their duties would likely be speedier if it were included in the statute. This is an inclusion to be considered by regional lawmakers.

While the law of each country reflects, in some manner, the positive duty of States to promote measures that advance equality, of the four countries under study here, the UK *Equality Act* 2010 contains the strongest statement regarding the positive duty to promote equality. Admittedly, while discretionary, the public sector duty of equality requires public authorities in the UK to consider ways to eliminate discrimination, harassment, victimisation; advance equality of opportunity and foster good relations between persons of different status. This specific duty is absent from the other pieces of legislation and might be something to consider including. Currently, in Trinidad and Tobago, it falls to the Equal Opportunity Commission to perform this function, but not to any other public authority. Employers in Guyana have the discretion to take positive action to accommodate persons as they deem fit. This discretion to take positive action to promote equality is very well set out in the UK but has the potential to lead to legal liability in the form of reverse discrimination actions. In this regard, the inclusion of positive action to promote equality in regional legislation needs to be very carefully considered.

CONCLUSION

This chapter presented a brief history of the development of equality legislation in the USA and the UK and the key principles they cover. In the USA, this saw a century-long struggle evolve over various grounds of discrimination: class, geographic/national origin, culture, ethnicity, religion and race. Disability was also addressed but not as a ground that saw the type of lobbying required for the others. The final ground, gender, is still being hotly debated with respect to its formal inclusion in the law; the Supreme Court's recent decision that sexual orientation and gender identity are prohibited grounds of discrimination in the workplace is certainly noted. In the UK, there was no such similar struggle nor did equality legislation have such a long history. Equality legislation focused, in the early stages, on race, then sex. Other grounds—age, disability, religion or belief and sexual orientation—were eventually addressed and a few more were added to the consolidated Act. Guyana's legislation covers the largest number of prohibited grounds of discrimination of the four countries, with a focus on fifteen, while Trinidad and Tobago's laws

Drexler, K. (2019). 15th Amendment to the U.S. Constitution: Primary documents in American history. *Library of Congress*. Retrieved 22 October 2020, from https://guides.loc.gov/15th-amendment.

Equality Rights Trust. (2014). *Economic and social rights in the courtroom: A Litigator's Guide to using equality and non-discrimination strategies to advance economic and social rights*. London: Equal Rights Trust.

Feast, P., & Hand, J. (2015). Enigmas of the Equality Act 2010—"Three uneasy pieces". *Cogent Social Sciences, 1*, 1–9. https://doi.org/10.1080/23311886.2015.1123085.

Fredman, S. (2001). Equality: A New Generation? *Industrial Law Journal, 30*(2), 145–168.

Fredman, S. (2016). Substantive equality revisited. *International Journal of Constitutional Law, 14*(3), 712–738. https://doi.org/10.1093/icon/mow043.

Fredman, S., Davies, A., Freedland, M., Fudge, J., & Campbell, M. (2015). The potential challenges to equality law in the UK. *Oxford Human Rights Hub*. Retrieved 29 February 2020, from https://ohrh.law.ox.ac.uk/wordpress/wp-content/uploads/2015/08/here.pdf.

George-Wiltshire, R. Chief Justice of Guyana, 7 November 2019, E-mail communication.

Glendon, M. (2004). The rule of law in the universal declaration of human right. *Northwestern Journal of International Human Rights, 2*(1), 1–19.

Gov.uk. (n.d.). *Discrimination: Your rights*. Retrieved 26 February 2020, from https://www.gov.uk/discrimination-your-rights/print.

Government of Canada. (2020). *Canadian Human Rights Act*, RSC 1985, c. H-6. Retrieved 28 February 2020, from https://laws-lois.justice.gc.ca/eng/acts/h-6/fulltext.html.

Griffiths, E. (2015). Would the 'reasonable accommodation' of religious belief in the workplace prevent a hierarchy of protected characteristics from developing? [PowerPoint Slides]. *University of Chester: 'The Equality Act 2010: Five-years on'—Presentation slides*. Retrieved 24 February 2020, from http://www.chester.ac.uk/node/31631.

Hamilton, C. (1972, October 1). The nationalist vs. the integrationist. *The New York Times*. Retrieved 22 February 2020, from https://www.nytimes.com/1972/10/01/archives/the-nationalist-vs-the-integrationist-ideological-foes.html.

Hand, J. (2015). Outside the Equality Act: Non-standard protection from discrimination in British law. *International Journal of Discrimination and the Law, 15*(4), 205–221. https://doi.org/10.1177/1358229115593829.

Hand, J., Davis, B., & Feast, P. (2012). Unification, simplification, amplification? An analysis of aspects of the British Equality Act 2010. *Commonwealth Law Bulletin, 38*(3), 509–528. https://doi.org/10.1080/03050718.2012.695001.

Held, A., Herndon, S., & Stager, D. (1997). The Equal Rights Amendment: Why the ERA remains legally viable and properly before the states. *William & Mary Journal of Race, Gender, and Social Justice, 3*(1), 113–136.

Hepple, B. (2011). Enforcing equality law: Two steps forward and two steps backwards for reflexive regulation. *Industrial Law Journal, 40*(4), 315–335. https://doi.org/10.1093/indlaw/dwr020.

Hepple, B. (2010). The new single Equality Act in Britain. *The Equality Rights Review, 5,* 11–24.

History.com. (2020). Civil Rights Act of 1964. *A&E Television Networks.* Retrieved 24 February 2020, from https://www.history.com/topics/black-history/civil-rights-act.

Howard-Hassmann, R. E. (2013). Reconsidering the Right to Own Property. *Journal of Human Rights, 12*(2), 180–197. https://doi.org/10.1080/14754835.2013.784667.

Human Dignity Trust. (2020). *Belize: A constitutional challenge to the laws criminalising same-sex activity.* Retrieved 20 February 2020, from https://www.humandignitytrust.org/what-we-do/cases/belize-a-constitutional-challenge-to-the-laws-criminalising-homosexuality/.

Kearns, M. (2019, May 20). The Equality Act is a time bomb. *National Review.* Retrieved 21 February 2020, from https://www.nationalreview.com/corner/the-equality-act-is-a-time-bomb/.

Legislation.gov.uk. (2020a). *Equality Act 2010.* Retrieved 14 January 2020, from http://www.legislation.gov.uk/ukpga/2010/15/contents.

Legislation.gov.uk. (2020b). *Equality Act 2010 explanatory notes.* Retrieved 25 February 2020, from https://www.legislation.gov.uk/ukpga/2010/15/notes/division/2?view=plain.

Leslie, K. (2020, January 22). Belize City discusses the Equal Opportunities Bill. *Amandala.* Retrieved 29 February 2020, from https://amandala.com.bz/news/belize-city-discusses-the-equal-opportunities-bill/.

Library of Congress. (2019). *H.R.5—116th Congress (2019-2020): Equality Act.* Retrieved 14 January 2020, from https://www.congress.gov/bill/116th-congress/house-bill/5/text.

Library of Congress. (2018). *Primary documents in American history.* Retrieved 18 February 2020, from https://www.loc.gov/rr//program/bib/our-docs/14thamendment.html.

Manning, P. (2005, September 28). *Budget presentation 2006.*

McCrudden, C., & Prechal, S. (2009). *The concepts of equality and non-discrimination in Europe: A practical approach.* European Commission. Directorate-General for Employment, Social Affairs and Equal Opportunities Unit G.2. Retrieved 11 November 2019, from http://ec.europa.eu/social/BlobServlet?docId=4553.

Ministry of Community Development, Culture and Gender Affairs. (2005). *Draft national gender policy and action plan*. Port of Spain, Trinidad: Ministry of Community Development, Culture and Gender Affairs.

Ministry of Legal Affairs and Attorney General's Chambers. (2019). *Equal Rights Act*, Cap 38:01 (Guyana). Retrieved 6 November 2019, from https://mola.gov.gy/information/laws-of-guyana?limit=20&limitstart=200.

Ministry of Legal Affairs and Attorney General's Chambers. (2019). *Persons with Disabilities Act*, Cap 36:05 (Guyana). Retrieved 6 November 2019, from https://mola.gov.gy/information/laws-of-guyana?limit=20&limitstart=200.

Ministry of Legal Affairs and Attorney General's Chambers. (2019). *Prevention of Discrimination Act*, Cap 99:08 (Guyana). Retrieved 6 November 2019, from https://mola.gov.gy/information/laws-of-guyana?limit=20&limitstart=460.

Ministry of Social Protection, Government of the Cooperative Republic of Guyana. (2018). *National gender equality and social inclusion (GESI) policy for Guyana*. Georgetown: Ministry of Social Protection.

Neale, T. (2019). The proposed Equal Rights Amendment: Contemporary ratification issues. *Congressional Research Service*. Available at https://crsreports.congress.gov.

Nelson, W. E. (1995). The changing meaning of equality in twentieth-century constitutional law. *Washington and Lee Law Review, 52*(1), 3–103.

North, A. (2020). The Drive to pass the Equal Rights Amendment, explained. *Vox*. Retrieved 24 February 2020, from https://www.vox.com/2020/1/8/21054914/era-yes-equal-rights-amendment-virginia-date.

O'Cinneide, C. (2011). Equality: A constitutional principle? *UK Constitutional Law Association*. Retrieved 29 February 2020, from https://ukconstitutionallaw.org/2011/09/14/colm-ocinneide-equality-a-constitutional-principle/.

Office of the Prime Minister of the Republic of Trinidad and Tobago. (2018). *National Policy on Gender and Development of the Republic of Trinidad and Tobago: A Green Paper*. Retrieved 28 February 2020, from http://www.opm-gca.gov.tt/portals/0/Documents/National%20Gender%20Policy/NATIONAL%20POLICY%20ON%20GENDER%20AND%20DEVELOPMENT.pdf?ver=2018-03-08-134857-323.

Ourdocuments.gov. (n.d.). *Transcript of Civil Rights Act (1964)*. Retrieved 24 February 2020, from https://www.ourdocuments.gov/doc.php?flash=false&doc=97&page=transcript.

Parliament of the Co-operative Republic of Guyana. *Constitution of the Co-operative Republic of Guyana*, Cap 1:01. Retrieved 6 November 2019, from http://parliament.gov.gy/constitution.pdf.

Persadie, N. (2012). *A critical analysis of the efficacy of law as a tool to achieve gender equality*. Lanham, MD: University Press of America.

Persadie, N., & Ramlogan, R. (2016). *Commonwealth Caribbean business law*. London: Routledge.

Rosenberg, G. (2004). The 1964 Civil Rights Act: The crucial role of social movements in the enactment and implementation of anti-discrimination law. *St Louis University Law Journal, 49*, 1147–1154.

Smedley, A. (2017). Racism. *Encyclopædia Britannica*. Retrieved 22 February 2020, from https://www.britannica.com/topic/racism.

Sokhi-Bulley, B. (2005). *Non-discrimination and difference: The (non-)essence of human rights law*. Human Rights Law Centre, University of Nottingham. Retrieved 11 November 2019, from https://www.nottingham.ac.uk/hrlc/documents/publications/hrlcommentary2005/nondiscriminationanddifference.pdf.

Stephenson, J., & Persadie, N. (2019). Anti-discrimination legislation in the Caribbean: Is everyone protected? *Equality, Diversity and Inclusion: an International Journal, 38*(7), 779–792. https://doi.org/10.1108/EDI-11-2017-0238.

Suk, J. (2017). An Equal Rights Amendment for the twenty-first century: Bringing global constitutionalism home. *Yale Journal of Law and Feminism, 28*(2), 381–444.

The Commonwealth Secretariat 2020. *Member countries*. Retrieved 5 February 2020, from https://thecommonwealth.org/member-countries.

The Diversity Group. (2018). *Legislation*. Retrieved 18 February 2020, from http://www.diversitygroup.co.uk/resources/legislation/.

The Heritage Foundation. (2020). *The Equality Act: How could sexual orientation and gender identity (SOGI) laws affect you?* Retrieved 21 February 2020, from https://www.heritage.org/gender/heritage-explains/the-equality-act.

University of Cambridge. (2020). *Equality and diversity: Associative discrimination*. Retrieved 26 February 2020, from https://www.equality.admin.cam.ac.uk/training/equalities-law/key-principles/associative-discrimination.

US Department of Justice. (2009). *Introduction to Federal Voting Rights Laws*. Retrieved 22 February 2020, from https://www.justice.gov/crt/introduction-federal-voting-rights-laws-0.

US Equal Employment Opportunity Commission. (n.d.). *The Equal Pay Act of 1963*. Retrieved 24 February 2020, from https://www.eeoc.gov/laws/statutes/epa.cfm.

CHAPTER 9

Liberalisation of Higher Education in the Caribbean: Situating Matters of Access, Diversity and Equity

INTRODUCTION

Across the globe, the rise of the global higher education market and the ensuing liberalisation of higher education institutions (HEIs) continue to attract the attention of researchers, policy makers, and university officials (Altbach and Knight 2007; Hyde et al. 2013). While often couched as borderless, transnational or cross border or global education, an inherent ethos within the higher education literature has been on the processes through which market-based reforms continue to alter the internal workings/practices, governance structures and relative positioning of HEIs within and beyond specific contexts (Olssen and Peters 2005; Slaughter and Rhoades 2004). At the heart of this neoliberal thrust is a logic of the market that ushers in new public management principles and approaches to running public organisations; with high premiums on matters of performance, accountability, efficiency and effectiveness within higher education (Olssen and Peters 2005). More specific functional shifts and points for empirical interrogation have also been on growing patterns of privatisation, commercialisation, internationalisation; with some attention to the implications on how we define the nature of academic work in relation to the market, and, how we think of the sustainability of HEIs within this matrix (Slaughter and Leslie 2001; Levin 2006; Hyde et al. 2013).

Such globalising trends continue to shift the higher education landscape with the Caribbean (Hickling-Hudson 2000; Howe 2003; Jules

© The Author(s) 2020
J. H. Stephenson et al., *Diversity, Equality,
and Inclusion in Caribbean Organisations and Society*,
https://doi.org/10.1007/978-3-030-47614-4_9

2008; Coates 2012). A growing point of examination has been that of the globalisation of the higher education within the region; particularly, on widening levels of access to post-secondary or high school education, on the growing levels of diversity within that sector, on the permeability between different types of programmes, and, on the subtle forms of enmity that surface between transnational institutions across historical periods. Related points of contention therefore have centered mainly on trepidations over the relevance and quality of the offerings/programmes (Leo-Rhynie 2005; Gift et al. 2006), the market-like behaviours that ensues between sellers/institutions (Bacchus 2008; Bernal 2019) and the implications for governance structures, institutional innovations and international cooperation within that market (Howe 2003; Austin 2009). In *Globalization and Comparative Education,* Louisy (2001, 2004) also directs attention to growing patterns of institutional differentiation amidst deepening social inequalities, and, advocates for action on the part of HEIs in the Caribbean.

However, while socio-political agendas around access remain core aspects of these conversations on how HEIs respond to changes within the market, fewer interrogations of and connection to equity issues within that sector unfold. I would argue in this case that questions of equity (applied here to refer to principles of fairness and inclusion within the engagement of key stakeholders) must be situated as integral to how we make sense of the relevance and sustainability of institutions in the region; both in terms of the scope and impact within and perhaps beyond that sector. This is particularly important given growing possibilities for democratising higher education, but also for how we promote equitable opportunities, how to secure the meaningful engagement of diverse populations across the region, and, how we work through competing players and agendas within the market. Understanding the magnitude of these considerations however requires that we contextualise and problematise emerging patterns of liberalisation of higher education, and, the nuanced ways in which these complicate calls for equity and diversity within the region.

Higher Education in the Caribbean: Liberalising Trends

The advancement of higher education within the Caribbean region represents a complex interplay of structural and ideological milieus that continue to define and refine that sector; albeit in more qualitative ways.

Historically, we see this murkiness in the fact that just after World War II, the growing concerns for the social inequalities, and/or, systemic structural limitations within the region at the time provided important impetuses, not just for the expansion of higher education, but also for the adoption of British educational frameworks to do so (see Cobley 2000; Peters 2001). Such is evident in the establishment of many college-type institutions modelled after traditional British educational systems (such as Codrington Grammar School, now Codrington College in Barbados and the University College of the West Indies, now the University of the West Indies). In both cases, these institutions emerged as part of a socio-political response to increase demands for access to higher education institutions across the Anglophone Caribbean (Cobley 2000; Sylvester 2008), but, in the shadow of British colonialism (Blair 2013).

While by the mid-twentieth century, this sense of British imperialism within higher education systems of the Caribbean did not go uncontested, it remained unchanged. As such, despite the push for Caribbean leaders to make relevant, the educational agendas and structures of HEIs, initial apprehension remained over the capacity of regional governments to advance higher education within the post-independence era. Of note within that critical historical period, was the call for Caribbean leaders to serve as champions of freedom/self-determination, while improving the socio-cultural and economic realities for Caribbean peoples. The onset of political and racial consciousness through the emergence of nationalist, communist and Pan-Africanist ferments in this immediate period, also served as critical ideological forces, that influenced the intellectual ferment within institutions of higher education within the region, albeit before the onset of the economic crisis. What we see therefore by the mid-1950s was an inherent focus on the widening of access and participation driven by the nationalists and regional agendas, but, which remained couched within imperial models of educational provision.

Towards the end of the twentieth century however (late 1970s and beyond), growing contradictions unfolded. In fact, the penetration of neoliberal ideology into the region ushered in structural adjusted programmes/measures that collectively affected not just the socio-political and economic realities of the region, but more fundamentally, the privatisation of the higher education within the region. In fact, it is against the understanding of these contextual factors, and in particular deregulation of the market, that the rise of higher education institutions across the Caribbean, is often perceived or framed as a direct response to the fiscal and resource development challenges of that period. As such, researchers often underscore the link between the decade of development (with growing demands of the market and the increasing liberalisation policies of World Trade Organization) and that of the growth in the number of tertiary institutions between 1996 and 2006 (Beckles et al. 2002; Brandon 2003; Roberts et al. 2007).

By the late 1970s into the early 1980s, the region saw an increased liberalisation of that sector with the rapid expansion of many United States-US based medical colleges and institutes, across the Anglophone Caribbean (namely; St. Lucia, Grenada, St. Kitts, Guyana, and Barbados)- (Browne and Shen 2017). The increasing liberalisation of this sector also prompted the establishment of other non-medical entities, such as the University of Technology in Jamaica (1994), the Northern Caribbean University in Jamaica (1999) and, the growth of existing ones; particularly with that of the many franchise arrangements between non-campus Caribbean countries and those within UWI campus territories. Whether foreign or locally based, such expansionist trends raised greater interest in and attention to alternative institutional offerings/ programmes, and, to the growing patterns of commodification within higher education landscape. At some level, it is important to recognise that such shifts also provided a platform to address the challenges associated with providing access for a wider catchment of Caribbean students and engagement of diverse educational providers (Cobley 2000; Howe 2005; Miller 2000; Roberts 2003; Woodall 2011). However, such matters of access and equity must be qualified.

An analysis of higher education patterns within the twenty-first century captures deepening patterns of liberalisation and fragmentation, albeit with some qualitative differences in the manifestations and impressions within this sector. On one level therefore, growing patterns of internationalisation and marketisation within higher education systems (Bastick 2004; Jules 2008) resulted in the continued surge of private institutions of higher education across the region (Knight 2008; Stromquist 2007). By 2008 therefore, there were over 150 higher education institutions; of which 30% are privately owned, 10% receiving government support and of which 60% remain public entities (Tewarie 2010). In immediate effect of these liberalising patterns was that of a noticeable increase in the enrolment and participation levels of peoples across the region (Roberts 2003; Segrera 2010). On the other hand, many of these institutions operated as national (e.g. in Guyana, Belize,

Jamaica and Trinidad and Tobago), regional (for instance, the University of the West Indies and University of the South Pacific), international or affiliated entities (e.g. privately owned institutes, colleges and off-shore medical schools), but with growing fragmentation in the identities, visions and/or orientations of the programmes being offered (see Brandon 2003; Howe 2003, 2005).

Here, the infiltration of such transnational institutions and players presented a compounded challenge of coping with the dynamics of market mechanisms and the external influences on Caribbean citizens and societies (Howe 2003), while forming monitoring institutions like that of the Caribbean Tertiary Institutions (ACTI) to guard against the growing differentiation and fragmentation of the sector (Nettleford 2005). On a broad level therefore, such liberalising trends represent a complex interplay of widening access with growing patterns of inequity within the higher education market; particularly in this case, between existing and emerging educational providers, and, in the respective positioning of the brand and the visions that they promote within that market. Such structural configurations and apprehensions also introduce many questions related to the possibilities and/or constrains for (i) rationalising this sector, (ii) assessing the quality of these programmes therein, and, (iii) understanding how these institutions contribute to or impact on the advancement of the wider societies that they serve. As a premier institution across the Caribbean,[1] the University of the West Indies (UWI) presents an interesting case of the intricacies embedded within contending local and global factors. This will be examined within the following subsection.

THE CASE OF THE UNIVERSITY OF THE WEST INDIES (UWI)

While the developmental role of the UWI within the postcolonial era provides key points of reference within the advancement of higher learning and research in the Caribbean (Cobley 2000; Sherlock and

---

[1] Today however, the university has evolved into a premier regional university with four physical campuses; Mona (Jamaica), St. Augustine (Trinidad and Tobago), Cave Hill (Barbados), most recent addition (Antigua & Barbuda), and Open campus, which operates as a virtual university. There are also many satellites programs across several Caribbean countries (as in the cases of, Anguilla, The Bahamas, Belize, Bermuda, British Virgin Islands, Cayman Islands, Dominica, Grenada, Montserrat, St. Kitts and Nevis, St. Lucia, St. Vincent and the Grenadines, and Turks and the Caicos Islands).

questions of how these collaborations advance the capacities of or transformative agendas of the institution, and, by extension, of the region are yet to be examined.

While the UWI's climb in the rankings from 37th to 32nd among 150 universities across Latin America and the Caribbean in the last year marks a significant milestone in that process, and, can be used as an initial yardstick to evaluate the relatively positioning within the higher education market (but specifically for the global south), the trials going forward remain those of securing global reputation, regional accountability, financial sustainability and market permeability. Related questions are also of how can the university leverage its resources and brand to expand internationally, while expanding access, equity and diversity. These are addressed subsequently at a broader level.

Access, Diversity and Equity

There is no doubt that the liberalisation of higher education in the Caribbean has increased access to, or the participation of diverse populations across the region. Access here is situated within the matrix of enrolment or admissions; as inherent measures for participation. If we use this as a benchmark for measuring and/or speaking to access within the region, then surely, the expansion of higher education sector has certainly impact on this achievement. The prospect for transnational or cross border higher education has also expanded both the scope and impact of expanding access. Knight (2015) notes for instance that these expanded opportunities (both through local opportunities and for scholarships to be trained abroad) advance the mobility and status of different racial and class groupings across the Caribbean. In Jamaica, Coates (2012) points to the importance of flexible programme structures to that of the increased engagement of previously excluded or marginalised populations such as working persons and others from rural areas. In Trinidad and Tobago, Herbert and Lochan (2014) draws on the significance of the Government Assisted Tuition Expenses (GATE) and the growth in over 70 locally accredited HEIs for participation rates; namely from 6% in 2001 to 65.23% in 2013.

Access however does not necessarily translate into equity. In treating with this issues of equity within higher education, it is important that we also consider questions of fairness within that participation of underrepresented groups, rather than merely on the use of academic merit

(OECD 2008). If we extend such considerations, then important questions become those of how do we address the social or personal circumstances that affect the participation of such groups within higher education across the region. In speaking to such concerns, Roberts et al. (2007, p. 8) for instance contend that while there is "some relationship between improved access and increased enrolment, the latter is necessary but not a sufficient condition for widening access". Of note are "geographical, financial, informational, attitudinal, technological, and physical disability barriers [that] also impact on the access formula" (ibid., p. 8). The main issue here is that of equity of opportunity or in the condition and/or criteria necessary for acceptance into higher education institutions.

The key challenges here remain those of narrow conceptualisations and operationalisations of *access* within the higher education market. Under the logic of the market, access is limited to objective measures that count enrolment as related indicator of expanding opportunity, rather a more expanded or integrated approach that also takes into consideration the need for other measures, such as cultural and social investments, within the advancement of that sector (Giroux 2002, 2010). In the case of the latter, access emerges as a social investment with growing concerns for issues of equity and diversity in the educational structures and processes that value the needs and potential contributions of all stakeholders involved. Deepening one's understanding of the connection between access, equity, and diversity call for more critical examinations of how social and economic structures of difference on macro and micro levels affect not just access to or increased institutions of higher education, but also, to that of retention of those who are admitted within these institutions across the region. These factors are addressed in the following subsections.

Class Differences

Class differences must be conceived as central to addressing issues of equity and diversity within HEIs. The seminal work of Fanon (1963) is notably important here to appreciate how Eurocentrism and elitism were grounded within the structural and ideological realities that obtained for the region. Here, we begin to appreciate that a central aspect of that historical experience was the intermingling of racialised and classed differences and the relative importance of these stratifying factors on the social status, positioning, and opportunities of social groups across various Caribbean societies. While these historical markers of social differences are beyond the scope of the chapter, the significance of the realities for how we begin to contextualise and treat with systemic issues within the higher education systems for the region within the contemporary period cannot be treated discreetly.

Even with change and progress therefore, a contention is that some of these elitist threads still obtain for the region. In their review of the region's response to change patterns prior to the 1990s, Sherlock and Nettleford (1990), for instance, underscore the development of a new group of academic elites within the region. In the specific case of the UWI, Walker (2000) contends that while there were noted efforts to democratise higher education in the region, that rates of access to the UWI over various periods of time, were still far below that of other regions of the developing world. Key concerns remained that of the limited resources of the institution, the limits associated with the regional thrust of the institution, and, of persistent levels of elitism within the requirements for entry and structure of existing programmes. Similarly, Hickling-Hudson (2000) asserts that the size of the HEI sector substantively restricts access and possibilities for ensuring equity; particularly within a highly stratified educational system such as what exists across the Caribbean. For Leo-Rhynie (2005), these structural and stratified systems within HEIs strengthen ongoing calls for rethinking educational policies and practices across the region.

Such rethinking and re-envisioning are particularly important where inklings of classism, closely tied to subtle or not so subtle expressions of colourism and inadvertently racism, create tensions between the need for expansion and that of maintaining the standards and status quo of higher educational institutions. An important recognition here is that while university systems are increasingly promoting social mobility based on academic merit, it is particularly important for educational policy makers and administrators to address some of the uncomfortable questions related to socially constituted axes of difference and of power in the planning and operations of university systems. These concerns also raise more pointed questions related to how HEIs in the region are both sensitive and responsive to the specific needs and challenges for economically and socially disadvantaged students; both in terms of access to higher education and in the provisions/accommodations of equity programmes and inclusive academic environments that are designed to support them while they are registered into specific programmes.

Gender Disparities

While largely examined within the context of high/secondary school education (see Bailey 2009; Chevannes 1999; Figueroa 2004; Parry 2004), the question of gender equity within higher education has occupied the scholarly agendas of many researchers within the Caribbean (see Miller 1991; Reddock 2010; UWI 2017b). Using regional statistics from the United Nations, Reddock (2010) notes that while female participation in higher education has significantly improved across the Anglophone Caribbean region that gender differences continue to exist, with notable impact on the educational performance within higher education. Of note here are the many concerns of participation that obtain for women within science, technology, engineering and mathematics (STEM) fields (Martin-DeLeon 2010; Whiteley 2002a), and, as members of faculty within the higher echelons of university systems (Hamilton 2015; Kassim et al. 2015; Leo-Rhynie and Hamilton 1996). In fact, Esnard et al. (2017, p. 125) contended that a "major deficiency [within higher education research for the region] remains the lack/absence of scholarship that questions the structures and practices of HEIs...and its implications for institutional contexts, culture, and for young or emerging academics". While such disquiets with the representation and/or participation of women in the STEM fields and within positions of leadership remain relatively underexplored within the region, they remain central to how we situate issues of gender equity and justice within institutions of higher education in the region.

Market Hegemony, Inequity and the Global Higher Education Market

Given unfolding hegemonic patterns and growing lines of inequity within the global education market (Altbach 2001; Carnoy 1999), it is also critical that we treat with the marginalising effects of these for HEIs within the Caribbean (Jules 2008; Louisy 2001). In this chapter, this is addressed through issues of market equity and quality; with specific attention to brand and relevance.

Market Equity

The internationalisation of higher education in the region can produce many possibilities and constraints for Caribbean HEIs. Issues of market equity are also important for how we respond to the liberalisation of higher education. Thus, with the increasing liberalisation of the higher education market, related questions emerge as to how can we both nego-tiate market barriers, while also safeguarding the national and regional goals of the governments across the region. Concerns here are for mar-ket equity; specifically, how we think of the economic and I would argue social and political values that are attached to higher education within the global education market.

On one end, this degree of internationalisation promotes international standardisations or homogenisation patterns that run the risk of silencing institutions with lack the resources and share within the market to do otherwise. The challenge for Caribbean territories remain that of how do they "transcend insularity and expand its horizons" (Roberts 2003, p. 27). Here, related contentions are for how HEIs (re)negotiate market equity within the corporatisation of scholarly activities; namely research priorities and/or curricular development within HEIs (Ali 2010; Beck 2012; Gacel-Avila 2007). Interrelated questions are for the clashing agendas within the design, execution and value of curricula, pedagogy, as well as, policies and management strategies of HEIs in the region. Dallas and Virgo (2015) point to a-contextual lenses through which techno-logical innovations and certification of Caribbean persons are executed within the arts and social sciences. Knight (2015) for instance questions the relevance and meaningfulness associated with the use of international practices as best practices that run the risk of being wholesomely adopted in the design of student programmes, curricula, research streams and service options, without attention to the local and regional relevance of these. Here, noted points of contention are those of how do these per-formance measures treat with the relative importance of more qualitative engagements among key stakeholders within and outside the university.

A related question that emerges is also those of whether international comparisons are robust indicators of quality or as a measure of the lev-els of internationality associated with a given institution. Of note here is the argument against the use of international standards as a proxy for measuring and determining the quality of a university sets false com-parisons and evaluations, which are deemed counterproductive to the development of institutional branding. Similar questions also surface around the benefits of international agreements/collaborations for institutional ranking and/or for the quality of pedagogical approaches within the broader spectrum of education and training programmes within the higher education sector. In his examination of the five myths of internationalisation, Knight (2015) cautions about the myths of foreign students on the campus. Roberts (2003) spoke of the erosion of national boundary with international student mobility. Here, ongoing threats are for the transcending of international experiences on persons within the region. However, the questions then are those of what are the experiences of our regional students, and, how have the curricula and experiences across disciplines catered to the cultural and local realities of these students? While the intercultural experience and exposure can surely offer useful points of development for these students, one can justifiably ask also, of how their own experiences are reflected within the broader orientations associated with these programmes. While one cannot dismiss the symbiotic value of these partnerships, the call is for deeper interrogations of the potential benefits and risk of globalising trends within HEIs (Jibeen and Khan 2015).

An interrelated but central issue is that of how we begin to define higher education; that is, whether it can be commodified to fully work within the confines of a market logic, a private good, or to be expanded in ways that accommodate notions of higher education as a public good, with some of the social responsibilities of HEIs. While the engagement in the market requires the commodification of knowledge production, teaching and learning, the social and cultural mandates of higher education are also essential to how we situate the developmental role of these institutions. Alleyne (2005), for instance, raises the concern for the public mandate of universities within the region. Central issues here are those of defining/articulating its social responsibility, while paying attention to the instrumental value of the education it provides to Caribbean citizens. Where the supply factor remains central to this process, Alleyne speaks to the role of the state and of the initiatives that are required to sustain this developmental role. However, the reduction of state funding for higher education in recent times, raises fundamental questions/issues of sustainability emerge. The central question therefore becomes that of whether academics can emerge as public intellectuals, as academic entrepreneurs, and/or as intellectuals who scholarly work reflects diverse deliberations on the complex landscapes of their times.

Brand Equity and Relevance

On the other hand, these patterns of internationalisation problematise contextual sensitivities, regional thrusts, cooperation and the extent to which these unique brands and the relevance of these for its citizenry, are relatively positioned within the market. Deeper questions also unfold as it related to the impact of these globalising trends on issues of identity and sovereignty (Grieco and Holmes 1999). In situating this issue here, I think of the work of Marginson (2004) for instance who advances the notion of the global education market as a competition for status and social positioning. I am reminded of Edward Said's (1994) work of *Orientalism* and more specifically on the scepticism around the role of an intellectual, and by extension, of how institutions of higher learning respond to institutional dogmatism in the quest to become advocates of social and political forms of change. As an advocate for self-determination and knowledge, Best (1997, p. 21) too reiterates that the:

> Atomisation of teaching endeavour, and the commercialization of research, the social sciences [remain] hostile to the required reconceptualization of internal relations... The needed structural adjustment, it seems to me, would entail an investment pause increasingly more costly as it continues to be postponed. The same problem of imperial education which [C.L.R.] James had discerned at QRC before 1932 was as prevalent and as virulent among the validating elites in 1962....is the problem today not as instrument as it was then with some of our economists claiming that there is no such thing as the Caribbean economy and what with leaders pursuing almost blindly-marketization, liberalization, divestiture and facilitation, in much the same way as we pursued nationalization and centralization 25–40 years upstream?

Inherent contentions here are for the ideological orientations and responsibilities of Caribbean institutions of higher education. We see for instance that an immediate consequence of this neoliberal script within higher education is that of how it influences the adoption of efficiency driven financial models to support academic teaching, research and service (Giroux 2014; Levin 2006; Slaughter and Rhoades 2004). We can also appreciate an understanding of how the infiltration of market-based principles increasingly sways the engagement of HEIs (Levin 2006; Olssen and Peters 2005). An immediate concern therefore is that of how do institutions in the region negotiate their brand and the relevance of these for the broader communities that they serve.

In his seminal work, Best (1997) calls for researchers/scholars in the region to address the epistemological and ontological questions related to independent thought and Caribbean freedoms. Within that treatise are questions related to the self-hood where there is the "crisis of self-knowledge...self-confidence, one in which we have been precipitated latterly on account of the approaches we have carried-perhaps necessarily-to the rendezvous with popular and therefore subversive democracy, via the stances we adopted during the transition to independence and beyond" (Best 1997, p. 21). While such considerations have been comprehensively examined by development scholars in the region, this epistemological and ideological problem within the education system still obtains (Best 2000; Cobley 2000; Louisy 2004). This is particularly the case where dominant narratives of higher education and scholarly activities feed into comparative critiques of educational structures and processes that render invisible subaltern form of knowledge and/or socio-cultural realities (Mignolo 2003). These draw on concerns for how we begin to recognise the potential for culturally affirming methodologies and indigenous ways of knowing within the region (Smith 1999; Nakhid et al. 2019). These contestations also introduce an important discussion around the politics of knowledge or on the *coloniality of power*, specifically related to how dominant knowledge systems are (re)constituted or (re)produced through global higher education (Delgado and Romero 2000; Mignolo 2000, 2003).

Question of internalisation also clash with historical concerns for questions related to that of how does a "system generate its own fertility" (Best 1997, p. 24). At an institutional level, such concerns are echoed by Cobley (2000) who speaks of the university's struggle to keep its regional character and mandate and to maintain its reputation in the process. Jules (2008) for instance calls for the centring of educational reform that decolonises knowledge systems and that explores the possibilities for small states to exercise some measure of autonomy and regional identity despite the onslaught of hemispheric changes taking place. Thus two unexplored consequences of institutionalised partitioning are those of the "low group entitativity... [and]...understanding of what local educational identity might be" (Blair 2013, p. 4) and that of how plantation like structures also "engenders an ethos of dependence and patronage and so deprives people of dignity, security and self-respect [that] impedes the material, social and spiritual advance of the majority of people" (Best 2000, pp. 247–248). Jules (2008, p. 204) also contends that "education reform efforts within Caribbean states have not lived up to expectations and that in the current conjuncture, educational reform can no longer be incremental". The problem is further intensified with the pursuit of educational agendas and models based on Eurocentric and Anglocentric development paradigms that structure the policies and practices within HEIs of the region (Esnard 2014; Hickling-Hudson 2003; Howe 2005; Jules 2008). While there is a history of cooperation or regionalism used to combat the external forces of globalisation within the region (Cobley 2000; Jules 2015; Sylvester 2008), the challenges of cooperation among educational providers remain comprised by the widening gap between inter-regional (EU & Latin America) and intra-regional (Latin America) partners (Gacel-Avila 2011), the lack of political will and faculty professionalisation within the region (Gacel-Avila and Marmolejo 2016).

Moving beyond the uncertainty of globalised era requires that we carefully consider the opportunities and challenges that global educational trends create. Knight et al. (2014) call for explorations of multilateralism as a gateway to regional cooperation and exchange. There, the need for resource rationalisation (World Bank 1993), increased funding or changes in the finance models for higher education in the region (Browne and Shen 2017; Gacel-Avila and Marmolejo 2016; Nkrumah-Young et al. 2013), and for the legislative structures that ensure regional cooperation and effective governance across these institutions remain of critical importance (Roberts et al. 2007). An overriding concern going forward is that of the need for "development of national and regional institutions to ensure the levels of relevance, responsiveness, innovation, quality, and accountability necessary to meet the needs of students, employers, and developing societies" (Leo-Rhynie 2005, p. 282).

While conversations on the way forward for Caribbean institutions of higher education remain ad hoc, there are some useful starting points. Alleyne (2005, p. xxv) for instance calls for a "detailed analysis of the tertiary educational institutions and to develop a taxonomy that allows for the definition of their various roles". Other scholars advocate for the development of what can tantamount to the formation of a *quasi* or *pseudo* market with greater degrees of regulation and coordination to affect market equity and relevance for key stakeholders in the process. Jules (2008, p. 206) for instance starts with the absence of a "harmonized agenda for education across the region..." that allows for more profound developmental impacts across the region. Tewarie (2011) calls for the rationalisation of HEIs with particular considerations for the roles of coordination and accreditation bodies that regulate the cooperation across and operations within these given institutions.

Given that governmental support and policies emerged as the main driver of internationalisation for Latin America and the Caribbean (Gacel-Avila 2014; Gacel-Avila and Marmolejo 2016), then critical points of departure here are for critical interrogations of the process that allow for analyses of collaborative exchange, cooperation, governance and transformation of higher education institutions in the Caribbean. Perhaps, it is necessary here to interrogate the possibilities for such collaboration against that of the competitive thrust that obtains within the market. These considerations or deliberations however do not emerge as a structured or regional response to the marketisation of higher education within the Caribbean. Therein lies the conundrum.

CONCLUSION

While the post-independence agenda of creating accessible and quality based systems of higher education, fundamental questions now become social, political and economic. Socially, the question is that of how do we address the challenges that confront our communities and societies at large, while systematically tackling the social inequalities and injustices that exist. Roberts (2003, p. 80) notes that "mass or tertiary education must accommodate heterogeneity of innate abilities, educational achievement, interests, aspirations, and socio-economic background". This level of heterogeneity however calls for "tertiary education ...to produce graduates who, by virtue of their criticality, are adaptable, creative, and productive in a global environment of uncertainty and change" (Roberts 2003, p. 88). Economically, the challenge is also that of how do HEIs in the region leverage knowledge and training to drive a competitive engagement in the global market (Bacchus 2008), while securing market permeability and relevance as important aspects of market equity. Politically, the litmus test is also that of how do we adhere to the national and regional responsibilities of HEIs and to ground these within the developmental needs of the peoples and economies of the region.

Where globalisation presents both peril and promise, there is a growing need for more pointed policy frameworks and intervention/

implementation strategies that specifically address issues of representation and inclusion. In producing a counter-narrative that challenges deepening patterns of internationalisation, the push is for greater regulation of and cooperation within this sector and for fiscal measures that support diverse forms of learning, teaching and research. A critical aspect of that process is that of defining, carving and measuring the institutional mandates and outcomes for the region, while also being mindful of the power structures within the market and broader societies that continue to reproduce the injustices that exist. We must in this critical exercise address concerns for how we make sense of, value, and position of our reference points within that process creating access, equity and promoting diversity within Caribbean institutions of higher education. Such deliberations must extend to social, economic and political subjectivities for the region, and, inadvertently, of how issues of access, diversity and equity are situated within that matrix. Certainly, these concerns echo the need to reflect and discuss some of the fundamental processes associated with globalisation, and possibly the search for more hybridised, socially just and authentic ways of being and becoming institutions of higher learning in the Caribbean.

REFERENCES

Ali, E. (2010). Decolonizing educational policy in the Caribbean: Shifting our practice from an internationally dependent policy consumption model to a contextually relevant policy research model. *Caribbean Education Research Journal, 2*(1), 75–86.

Alleyne, G. (2005). Keynote address: Public good and personal gain in higher education. In R. Holding & O. Burke (Eds.), *Revisiting tertiary education policy in Jamaica: Towards personal gain or public good* (pp. xiv–xxxiii). Kingston: Ian Randle Publishers.

Altbach, P. G. (2001). Academic freedom: International realities and challenges. *Higher Education, 41*(1–2), 205–219.

Altbach, P., & Knight, J. (2007). The internationalization of higher education: Motivations and realities. *Journal of Studies in International Education, 11*(3/4), 290–305.

Austin, I. O'B. (2009). *Understanding higher education governance restructuring: The case of the University of the West Indies* (Publication No. 14353) [Doctoral dissertation, Virginia Polytechnic Institute and State University]. Virginia Tech Doctoral Dissertations.

Bacchus, M. K. (2008). The education challenges facing small nation states in the increasingly competitive global economy of the twenty-first century. *Comparative Education, 44*(2), 127–145.

Bailey, B. (2009). Needed! *A paradigm shift in addressing boys' underachievement in education.* Paper presented at 18th Meeting of Council of Social and Human Development (COHSOD) Montego Bay, Jamaica.

Bastick, T. (2004). Commonwealth degrees from class to equivalence: Changing to grade point averages in the Caribbean. *Journal of Studies in International Education, 8*(1), 86–104.

Beck, K. (2012). Globalization/s: Reproduction and resistance in the internationalization of higher education. *Canadian Journal of Education, 35*(3), 133–148.

Beckles, H., Perry, A., & Whiteley, P. (2002). *The brain train: Higher education quality and caribbean development.* Kingston: The University of the West Indies Press.

Bernal, R. (2019). The globalization of higher education: The imperative for a Caribbean regional cluster. *Caribbean Journal of Education, 41*(1), 1–52.

Best, L. (1997). Independent thought and Caribbean freedom thirty years later-The plenaries: Conference on Caribbean culture in honour of Professor Rex Nettleford. *Caribbean Quarterly, 43*(1/2), 16–24.

Best, L. (2000). Institutional foundations of resource underdevelopment in the Caribbean. In G. Beckford & K. Levitt (Eds.), *The George Beckford papers* (pp. 242–259). Mona: Canoe Press.

Blair, E. (2013). Higher education practice in Trinidad and Tobago and the shadow of colonialism. *Journal of Eastern Caribbean Studies, 38*(3), 85–92.

Brandon, E. P. (2003). *New external providers of tertiary education in the Caribbean.* International Institute for Higher Education in Latin America and the Caribbean (IESALC). https://go.aws/3cYwchP.

Browne, R. A., & Shen, H. (2017). Challenges and solutions of higher education in the Eastern Caribbean states. *International Journal of Higher Education, 6*(1), 169–179. https://files.eric.ed.gov/fulltext/EJ1126023.pdf.

Carnoy, M. (1999). *Globalization and education: What planners need to know.* Fundamental of Educational Planning Series. Paris: United Nations Educational, Scientific and Cultural Organization.

Chevannes, B. (1999). *What we sow and what we reap: Problems in the cultivation of male identity in Jamaica.* Kingston: Grace Kennedy Foundation.

Coates, C. O. (2012). The rise of private higher education in Jamaica: neo-liberalism at work? In N. Popov, C. Wolhuter, B. Leutwyler, G. Hilton, J. Ogunleye, & P. Almeida (Eds.), *International perspectives on education* (pp. 341–346). Sofia: Bulgarian Comparative Education Society.

Cobley, G. A. (2000). The historical development of higher education in the Anglophone Caribbean. In G. D. Howe (Ed.), *Higher education in the*

Caribbean: Past, present and future directions (pp. 1–23). Kingston: The University of the West Indies Press.

Dallas, S. P., & Virgo, J. G. (2015). Science, technology, and innovation: Entrepreneurial universities for Caribbean development. In A. K. Perkins (Ed.), *Quality in higher education in the Caribbean* (pp. 67–81). Kingston: The University of the West Indies Press.

Delgado, E., & Romero. 2000. Local histories and global designs: An interview with Walter Mignolo. *Discourse, 22*(3), 7–33.

Esnard, T. (2014). Historical and contemporary issues-developmentalist approaches. In E. Thomas (Ed.), *Education in the commonwealth Caribbean and Netherland Antilles* (pp. 323–342). London: Bloomsbury.

Esnard, T., Descartes, C., Evans, S., & Joseph, K. (2017). Framing our professional identity: Experiences of early Caribbean academics. *Social and Economic Studies, 66*(3–4), 123–150.

Fanon, F. (1963). *The wretched of the earth*. New York: Grove Press.

Figueroa, M. (2004). Male privileging and male 'academic underperformance' in Jamaica. In R. Reddock (Ed.), *Interrogating Caribbean masculinities: Theoretical and empirical analyses* (pp. 137–166). Kingston: The University of the West Indies Press.

Gacel-Avila, J. (2007). The process of internationalization of Latin American higher education. *Journal of Studies in International Education, 11*(3/4), 400–409.

Gacel-Avila, J. (2011). The impact of the Bologna process on higher education in Latin America. *Revista de Universidad y Sociedad del Conocimiento (RUSC), 18*(2), 285–296. http://rusc.uoc.edu/ojs/index.php/rusc/article/view/v8n2-gacel/v8n2-gacel-eng.

Gacel-Avila, J. (2014). New directions for internationalization of tertiary education in Latin America and the Caribbean. *International Higher Education, 78*, 16–17.

Gacel-Avila, J., & Marmolejo, F. (2016). Internationalization of tertiary education in Latin America and the Caribbean: Latest progress and challenges ahead. In E. Jones, R. Coelen, J. Beelen, & de Wit, H. (Eds.), *Global and local internationalization* (pp. 141–148). Rotterdam: Sense Publishers.

Gift, S., Leo-Rhynie, E., & Moniquette, J. (2006). Quality assurance of transnational education in the English-speaking Caribbean. *Quality in Higher Education, 12*(2), 125–133.

Giroux, H. A. (2002). Neoliberalism, corporate culture, and the promise of higher education: The university as a democratic sphere. *Harvard Educational Review, 72*(4), 425–464.

Giroux, H. A. (2010). Bare pedagogy and the scourge of neoliberalism: Rethinking higher education as a democratic public sphere. *The Educational Forum, 74*(3), 184–190.

Giroux, H. (2014). *Neoliberalism's war on higher education*. Chicago: Haymarket Books.

Grieco, M., & Holmes, L. (1999). Tele options for community business: An opportunity for economic growth in Africa. *Africa Notes, 38*(1), 1–3.

Hamilton, M. (2015). Women and higher education in the commonwealth Caribbean: UWI: A progressive institution for women? *Caribbean Review of Gender Studies, 9*, 245–286.

Herbert, S., & Lochan, S. (2014). An analysis of recent developments in tertiary, technical and vocational education and training (TVET), and post-secondary sector in Trinidad and Tobago (2000–2010). In E. Thomas (Ed.), *Education in the commonwealth Caribbean and Netherland Antilles* (pp. 398–416). London: Bloomsbury.

Hickling-Hudson, A. (2000). Globalization and universities in the commonwealth Caribbean. In, N. P. Stromquist & K. Monkman (Eds.), *Globalization and education: Integration and contestations across cultures* (pp. 219–236). New York: Rowman & Littlefield.

Hickling-Hudson, A. (2003). Multicultural education and post-colonial turn. *Policy Futures in Education, 1*(2), 381–401.

Howe, G. (2003). *Contending with change: Reviewing tertiary education in the English-speaking Caribbean*. Venezuela: The International Institute for Higher Education in Latin America and the Caribbean (IESALC), UNESCO. https://unesdoc.unesco.org/ark:/48223/pf0000131593.

Howe, G. (2005). ICR and the expansion of tertiary education providers. In G. Howe (Ed.), *Tending with change: Reviewing tertiary education in the English-speaking Caribbean* (pp. 88–115). Venezuela: International Institute for Higher Education in Latin America and the Caribbean (IESALC-UNESCO).

Hyde, A., Clarke, M., & Drennan, J. (2013). The changing role of academics and the rise of managerialism. In B. M. Kehm & U. Teichler (Eds.), *The academic profession in Europe: New tasks and new challenge* (pp. 39–52). Dordrecht: Springer.

Jibeen, T., & Khan, M. A. (2015). Internationalization of higher education: Potential benefits and costs. *International Journal of Evaluation and Research in Education (IJERE), 4*(4), 196–199. https://files.eric.ed.gov/fulltext/EJ1091722.pdf.

Jules, T. D. (2008). Rethinking education for the Caribbean: A radical approach. *Comparative Education, 44*(2), 203–2014.

Jules, T. D. (2015). "Educational regionalization" and the gated global: The construction of the Caribbean educational policy space. *Comparative Education Review, 59*(4). http://www.jstor.org/stable/10.1086/683025.

Kassim, H.-S., Dass, A., & Best, B. (2015). *Higher education and statistical review: Issues and trends in higher education*. Office of Planning and

Development, The University of the West Indies. http://www.uwi.edu/ sf-docs/default-source/uopd—general/hesr2013–sues-and-trends-in-higher-education-march2015-for-univer-council.pdf?sfvrsn=2.

Knight, J. (2008). *Higher education in turmoil: The changing world of internationalization.* Rotterdam: Sense Publishers.

Knight, J. (2015). Five myths about internationalization. *International Higher Education, 62,* 14–15.

Knight, W. A., Castro-Rea, J., & Ghany, H. (2014). Backdrop- re-mapping the Americas. In W. A. Knight, J. Castro-Rea, & H. Ghany (Eds.), *Re-mapping the Americas: Trends in region-making* (pp. 3–37). Farnham: Ashgate.

Leo-Rhynie, E. (2005). Diversity, liberalization and competition in tertiary and higher education: Implications for quality assurance. In R. B. Holding (Ed.), *Revisiting tertiary education policy in Jamaica: Towards personal gain or public good* (pp. 269–283). Kingston: Ian Randle Publishers.

Leo-Rhynie, E., & Hamilton, M. (1996). Women in higher education—A Caribbean perspective. In D. R. Craig (Ed.), *Education in the West Indies: Developments and perspectives* (pp. 75–86). Kingston: UWI Institute for Social and Economic Studies.

Levin, J. S. (2006). Faculty work: Tensions between educational and economic values. *The Journal of Higher Education, 77*(1), 62–88.

Louisy, P. (2001). Globalization and comparative education: A Caribbean perspective. *Comparative Education for the 21st century: An International Response, 37*(4), 425–438.

Louisy, P. (2004). Whose context for what quality? Informing education strategies for the Caribbean. *Compare, 34*(3), 285–292.

Marginson, S. (2004). Competition and markets in higher education: A 'glonacal' analysis. *Policy Futures in Education, 2*(2), 175–244.

Martin-DeLeon, P. (2010). *Increasing the Caribbean's human capital in the STEM (Science, Technology, Engineering, and Mathematics) fields: The pivotal role of mentoring.* http://www.caribank.org/uploads/publications-reports/lecture-series/DeLeon_WGDemas.pdf.

Martin, M., & Bray, M. (2012). Higher education in small states. In B. Adamson, J. Nixon, & F. Su (Eds.), *The orientation of higher education: Challenging the east-west dichotomy* (pp. 50–75). Dordrecht: Comparative Education Research Centre, The University of Hong Kong, and Springer.

Mignolo, W. (2000). *Local histories/global designs: Coloniality, subaltern knowledges and border thinking.* Princeton, NJ: Princeton University Press.

Mignolo, W. (2003). Globalization and the geopolitics of knowledge: The role of the humanities in the corporate university. *Nepantla: Views from South, 4*(1), 97–119.

Miller, E. (1991). *Men at risk.* Kingston: Jamaica Publishing House.

Miller, E. (2000). Access to tertiary education in the commonwealth Caribbean in the 1990s. In G. D. Howe (Ed.), *Higher education in the Caribbean: Past, present, and future directions* (pp. 117–141). Kingston: The University of the West Indies Press.

Nakhid, C., Mosca, J., & Nakhid-Schuster, S. (2019). Liming as research methodology, ole talk as research method—A Caribbean methodology. *Journal of Education and Development in the Caribbean, 18*(2), 1–18.

Nettleford, R. (2005). Tertiary education and engagement with the society. In R. B. Holding (Ed.), *Diversity, liberalization and competition in tertiary and higher education: Implications for quality assurance* (pp. 358–373). Kingston: Ian Randle Publishers.

Nkrumah-Young, K. K., Huisman, J., & Powell, P. (2013). The impact of funding policies on higher education in Jamaica. In P. Mayo (Ed.), *Education in small states: Global imperatives, regional initiatives and local dilemas* (pp. 91–103). London: Routledge.

Olssen, M., & Peters, M. A. (2005). Neoliberalism, higher education and the knowledge economy: From the free market to knowledge capitalism. *Journal of Education Policy, 20*(3), 313–345.

Organization for Economic Cooperation and Development, OECD. (2008). *Tertiary education for the knowledge society, volume 2*. Paris: OECD.

Parry, O. (2004). Masculinities, myths and educational underachievement: Jamaica, Barbados, St. Vincent and the Grenadines. In R. Reddock (Ed.), *Interrogating Caribbean masculinities: Theoretical and empirical analyses* (pp. 167–184). Kingston: The University of the West Indies Press.

Peters, B. (2001). Tertiary education development in small states: Constraints and future prospects. *Caribbean Quarterly, 47*(2 & 3), 44–57.

Reddock, R. (2010). Gender and achievement in higher education. *Journal of Education and Development in the Caribbean, 12*(1), 1–21. https://www.researchgate.net/profile/Rhoda_Reddock/publication/235500045_Gender_and_Achievement_in_Higher_Education/links/0fcfd51354c3802303000000.pdf.

Roberts, V. (2003). *The shaping of tertiary education in the Anglophone Caribbean: Forces, forms and functions*. London: Commonwealth Secretariat.

Roberts, V., Long, J., & Estwick, S. (2007). *Caribbean tertiary education development (1996–2006)*. Kingston: The University of the West Indies.

Said, E. W. (1994). *Representations of the intellectual: The 1993 Reith lectures*. New York: Random House.

Segrera, F. L. (2010). *Trends and innovations in higher education reform: Worldwide, Latin America and in the Caribbean*. University of California, Berkeley. https://escholarship.org/content/qt5505n8m3/qt5505n8m3.pdf.

Sherlock, P., & Nettleford, R. (1990). *The University of the West Indies—A Caribbean response to the challenge of change*. London: Macmillan Publishers.

Slaughter, S., & Leslie, L. L. (2001). Expanding and elaborating the concept of academic Capitalism. *Organization, 8*(2), 154–161.

Slaughter, S., & Rhoades, G. (2004). *Academic capitalism and the new economy: Markets, state and higher education.* Baltimore: The John Hopkins University Press.

Smith, L. (1999). *Decolonizing methodologies: Research and indigenous peoples.* London: Zed Books.

Stromquist, N. (2007). Internationalization as a response to globalization: Radical shifts in university environments. *Higher Education, 18*(3), 81–105.

Sylvester, M. (2008). The globalization of higher education: Assessing the response of the University of the West Indies. In R. Hopson, C. Camp Yeakey, & F. Musa Boakari (Eds.), *Power, voice and the public good: Schooling and education in global societies* (pp. 261–284). Bingley: Emerald Group Publishing.

Tewarie, B. (2010). *Concept paper: For the development of a CARICOM strategic plan for tertiary education services in the CARICOM Single Market and Economy (CSME).* http://www.caricom.org/jsp/single_market/services_regime/concept_paper_tertiary_education.pdf.

Tewarie, B. (2011). Thinking through sustainable funding. In M. Martin & M. Bary (Eds.), *Tertiary education in small states. Planning in the context of globalization.* UNESCO Publishing and IEP Policy Forum, 2011. http://www.iiep.unesco.org/fileadmin/user_upload/Info_Services_Publications/pdf/2011/MartinBray_Small_states.pdf.

The University of the West Indies. (2017a). The UWI Triple *A* strategy 2017–2022: Revitalizing Caribbean development. Kingston: The University of the West Indies.

The University of the West Indies. (2017b). *Student statistical digest 2011/2012–2015/2016.* Kingston: The University of the West Indies.

Walker, G. (2000). *The democratization of higher education in Jamaica: The role of the University of the West Indies* (Publication No. AAI9991055) [Doctoral dissertation, Florida International University]. ProQuest ETD Collection for FIU.

Whiteley, P. (2002a). Gender issues in science education. In P. Mohammed (Ed.), *Gendered realities: Essays in Caribbean feminist thought* (pp. 183–200). Kingston: The University of the West Indies Press.

Whiteley, P. (2002b). Quality assurance in selected Caribbean universities. In I. Austin & C. Marrett (Eds.), *Adult education in Caribbean universities* (pp. 249–271). UNESCO.

Woodall, L. C. (2011). *Transitioning to online education in the Caribbean: The UWI Open Campus.* Toronto: University of Toronto.

World Bank. (1993). *Caribbean region: Access, quality, and efficiency in Education.* Washington: The World Bank.

CHAPTER 10

The Challenge of Equity, Diversity and Inclusion Within Educational Reform: The Case of Trinidad and Tobago

INTRODUCTION

On a broad level, educators and policy makers shoulder the hope that inclusive education agendas remain responsive to the diverse needs of all learners, cultures and communities (Ainscow et al. 2006; Booth 1996). With increasing attention to issues of equity and equality of opportunity for diverse groups, a central strategy in inclusive education policies has been that of creating and sustaining institutional contexts that leverage the unique skills, cultural experiences and forms of knowledge to ensure maximum participation of and potential for diverse groups. On a more specific level, operationalisations of inclusivity within educational systems, push for policy frameworks that promote non-discriminatory practices and parity within its' visualisations and configurations. We see for instance that as part of the Brussels Declaration, the United Nations Educational, Scientific, and Cultural Organization (UNESCO 2018, p. 2), accentuated the "right to safe, quality education and learning throughout life...that requires particular attention to be given to those in vulnerable situations, persons with disabilities, indigenous peoples, those in remote rural areas, ethnic minorities, the poor, women and girls, migrants, refugees, and displaced persons..." These guidelines have and continue to influence public policy agendas within the Caribbean.

Often times however, this laudable goal is not without conflict and systemic barriers to change. This is particularly the case where inclusive

J. H. Stephenson et al., *Diversity, Equality, and Inclusion in Caribbean Organisations and Society,* https://doi.org/10.1007/978-3-030-47614-4_10

policy frameworks are utilised to affect change or to democratise access and participation within highly stratified and contentious socio-political contexts. In such circumstances, Armstrong and Barton (2008, p. 16) remind us that the struggle for inclusion "involves a critical analysis of [the fundamental basis for] discrimination and exclusion, and that this entails a developing appreciation of the multi-layered, contradictory, deeply rooted nature of these barriers to inclusion". In many cases, these stumbling blocks are rooted in systemic structural issues that (in)directly confront a given citizenry. Fully delving into these strata of social inequalities requires considerations of the historical, social, cultural and political landscapes and/or perspectives that frame particular policies, the underlying philosophies, and, the practical dimensions that capture strategic policy goals. Whether through the prisms of macro and micro isms of power (such as neoliberalism, colonialism, racism, sexism or classism), these types of analyses become particularly important for how we both understand and treat with designing and implementing policy to move forward the goal of social transformation.

It is here that educational policy agendas within multicultural and racial societies like Trinidad and Tobago, present instructive cases that can both promote conscientisation about complexities of inclusive agendas within highly structured contexts, and, advocate for public policies that potentially disrupt tacit power relationships that are (re)produced and sustained within such contexts. The chapter presents a consideration of these possibilities and constraints. I start therefore with the recognition that despite decades of educational reform in Trinidad and Tobago, the education system remains stratified; with persistent forms of inequality and power-riddled tensions that continue to affect educational experiences and outcomes (De Lisle 2012; Deosaran 2016). I also acknowledge that educational reform in the context of Trinidad and Tobago represented a muddled mix of political urgency and shifting agendas across different political administrators and periods of time (Conrad and Brown 2008; Mohammed 2019).

Whether these forms of inequalities have emerged out of the vestiges of the colonial past, or, from the remnants of more contemporary socio-political reforms by changing governments, an underlying argument of this chapter is that these structures and relations of power have, and, continue to function, as a major impediment to inclusive education in Trinidad and Tobago. Understanding the dynamics and complexities of that shortcoming (that is, the lack of direct confrontation on the structural forms of power and inequality in the broader society), call for critical reflections on the social, economic, political and cultural constituencies that have affected the achievements and gaps in educational policy reforms overtime.

The chapter therefore provides a critical discussion on how Caribbean scholars have attempted to theorise the structural inequalities and systems of power in Trinidad and Tobago, of how these have affected the patterns, process and outcomes of educational reforms, and, of the inherent gaps that obtain for securing inclusive educational agendas in the contemporary period. The chapter also offers a socio-historical assessment of inclusive education agendas with educational policy at the primary (elementary) and secondary (high school) levels of the education system. These are presented as an important aspect of closing the gap between the peculiarities of context and the goals of inclusive education systems.

THEORISING DIFFERENCE: THE CASE OF TRINIDAD AND TOBAGO

Trinidad and Tobago is a twin-island democratic Republic with a multicultural and racial population where two dominant ethnic groups coexist; namely, those of East Indian (35.4%) and African descent, with 34.2% of the population (CSO 2011). While a sizeable percentage of this population are of mixed racial backgrounds (that being, 22.8%), one observes within the most recent population census that the African/East Indian combination only accounts for 7.7% and from diverse religious backgrounds (ibid.). In terms of for the religious composition within this population, one notes that Roman Catholics make up the largest group with 21.5%, followed closely by Hindus (18.07%), Pentecost (11.97%), Seventh-Day Adventists (8.67%) and Baptists (6.84%)-(ibid.). While ethnic distribution in this chapter is not disaggregated by religion to show the nuances within and between groups, we begin to discern intriguing demographic patterns that strengthen the need for theorising difference in the context of Trinidad and Tobago.

The rich history of Caribbean scholarship offers some insightful points of reference for the scholarly understanding of social structures and relations. An important consideration here is for the early work of Caribbean theorists who speak to the historical importance of racism, classism, and colourism as idiomatic frameworks for establishing rigid social strata within former plantation societies such as Trinidad and Tobago (see for instance the early work of Beckford 1972; Braithwaite 1975). What unfolds within this type of sociological theorising is an attention to the significance of these socially constituted markers of difference, to *inter alia*, the subjugation, oppression and assimilation to the cultural idio-syncrasies of Eurocentric systems for the ex-slave population (Braithwaite 1960; Alleyne 1995). A major contention within this body of work therefore is for the dehumanising effects of colonialism on the peoples and countries of the region. A key position here is that the slavery and by extension, colonialism operated as totalising systems, which through rigid social hierarchies and relations of engagement, created deeply rooted values, practices and identities that continue to affect Caribbean civilisations and expressions of freedom.

In the case of Trinidad and Tobago, one notes that through the sys-tem of forced slavery and indentureship that peoples of Africans and East Indian descents entered into colonialised space, which remained highly racialised through pervading notions of White supremacy. One discerns through the *Parsonian* analysis of Lloyd Braithwaite and Raymond T. Smith for instance that Eurocentricism served to dis-privilege both African and East Indian groups; albeit with different patterns of ethnic affiliations and assimilations (Braithwaite 1960; Smith 1955). In par-ticular, these scholars contended that European cultures and identities became grounded within a shared value system that inadvertently fos-tered a certain degree of consensus and level of cordial ethnic relations within Trinidad and Tobago. Within this premise of normative consen-sus, the understanding was one where ethnic affiliation was noticeably evident between Blacks[1] and Whites, but with a perceived superiority of the White culture and the denigration of the Black.[2] Within this perspec-tive, Blackness unfolded as a construction and lived experience that was defined in relation to whiteness and white supremacy. Here, the cultural constructions of race, far removed from its phenotypical constructions, emerged as a symbolic marker of difference that intensifies where it inter-sects with class divisions (Watson 2001; Wilder 2015). From this body of

---

[1] Black is used here interchangeably to refer to people of African descent.

[2] This argument is also reflected in the work of Kamau Braithwaite, who distinguishes between the big 'C'-representing idealized European culture and that of the little 'c' cap-turing the relative positionality of African culture in relation to that of the former.

work, we begin to appreciate the discursive constructions inherent within racial ideology, logic and practice and its collective impact on colonial and neocolonial forms of subjugation and interactions between ethnic groupings (Escayg and Kinkead-Clark 2019).

Despite these functionalist theorisations, it is the plural society thesis, which has received much intellectual scrutiny and empirical application to the context of Trinidad and Tobago. Much of that scholarship remains grounded in the early work of Michael G. Smith, who fundamentally rejected the *Parsonian* consensual model and advanced a more pluralistic perspective that draws on the importance and challenge of diverse ethnic fractions/segments for multiracial societies. Smith (1960, p. 10) contended for instance that multiracial societies display cultural "features that manifest their differing occupations, education, wealth, rank or social class, although they share such basic institutions such as language, education, economy...so lack the institutional differences that constitute pluralism". The thinking here is that these cultural differences have the potential to create socially identifiable clusters/divisions/cleavages that can be sustained by political and social conditions inherent within the society. In fact, by the 1980s, M. G. Smith (1984, p. 28) described the Caribbean as having a "composite nature and artificial combinations of elements from differing regions and traditions, brought about by the forcible domination of one racial and ethnic group with the resources, organization and will to rule the rest". Plurality in such contexts emerges as a more complex structural and cultural reality; where notions of race and ethnicity functioned to affect weak ethnic relations, social ties and mobility across the two main segments of the population. As an analytical category and theoretical perspective, the value of this work is in the assessments and interrogations of the inherent conflicts (subtle or otherwise) that undergird patterns of racialised identities, ethnic relations/ethnopolitics and the imbalances that these create within multicultural and racial contexts. Although in no way consistent in their analyses and conceptualisations, this conflict model advances a critical perspective through which researchers can contextualise the possibilities and implications for social and cultural pluralism.

While theorisations on the socio-cultural and political dimensions of Trinidad and Tobago have significantly declined since the 1990s, there are many lessons and points of reference that remain worthy of social interrogation. As a starting point, such theorisations have centred the importance of Caribbean subjectivities, with a deeper appreciation for the ideological and cultural landscapes that continue to affect how these subjectivities develop (Adams 2005). Thus, whether we apply the consensus or conflict perspective to the understanding of the social structure for Trinidad and Tobago, we begin to situate the importance of racialised, gendered, classed, and ethnicised identities, relations of power that unfold from these and possibilities or constraints for fostering inclusivity contexts. In fact, critical historical events such as that of the Black power movement illuminate the problem of racialised and classed consciousness, identities, and, by extension of enhancing race relations, ethnic assimilation and social mobility in multiracial and ethnic contexts such as Trinidad and Tobago. It is against similar assessment and more contemporary developments that Premdas (2002) stressed on the ethnically bifurcated nature of Trinidad and Tobago, and, the relative impact of such contradictory omens, which differently shape identity formation and relations of power across racial groups. It is through this type of social investigations and theorisations that we become sensitive to the tensions and social divisions that ethnic cleavages create and sustain within various institutional spheres. The following subsection speaks to this challenge.

INCLUSIVE EDUCATIONAL REFORMS? A CRITICAL REVIEW

From the standpoint of a critical policy approach, any evaluation of existing policies calls for a triadic approach that questions the ideological, philosophical and contextual underpinnings of public design and implementation. Here, the core benefit of this triadic approach is that of the multiple lenses through which public and social policies are assessed. Such an approach is particularly important for how we make sense of the intended and unintended consequences (both materially and symbolically), as well as, the achievements and gaps within inherent policy agendas (Taylor et al. 1997). From this perspective, delving deeper into these trifold facets of inclusive education policies for multicultural and racial societies like Trinidad and Tobago command an analytical and multidimensional gaze into the design and implement of existing policy with the goal of uncovering the value laden or ideological aspect of such processes. Within the review of educational policies, I argue here that interrogations of systemic issues within this context, or, of the socio-political aspects of the social structure, also offer valuable insights into the complexities of inclusive educational reforms within the pre and post-independence experiences of Trinidad and Tobago.

Pre-independence

While educational reforms within pre-independence Trinidad and Tobago advanced access to educational opportunities, the structures and practices within the school system reflected the racialised and divisive contexts of the colonial period, albeit with some qualitative differences. One can take note for instance, of the persistence of rigid educational structures and practices (around school placements), which were marred by racist and classist criteria of selection and inclusion. Thus, contradictory patterns emerged. On one hand therefore, analyses of this period point to an increased focus on access; as an underlying philosophical element of educational policy during that period. Here, assessments of strategic interventions show improved educational provision and participation for persons of different classes and ethnicities. On the other hand, we also become cognisant of growing observations that such reforms did not remove the relative significance of race and class, as defining lines of demarcation and ideological frameworks, which determined the type of access and quality of education afforded to different groups during that period (Bacchus 1994; Campbell 1996). For Campbell (1996), this was particularly the case where schooling was reserved for white upper-class boys, who generally held privileged access to exclusive professional development, and, who are exposed to Eurocentric models of education and knowledge dissemination. In this case, the imposition of school fees imposed restrictions on the socio-economic profiles of persons who were able to access educational opportunities and social mobility in Trinidad and Tobago. Such restrictive educational structures also served to reinforce Eurocentric values and models of education that became grounded within British influenced curricula and assessments. In many cases, these racialised and classist determinants of educational opportunities also masked a historical gendering of the curriculum, while deepening patriarchal structures via the mechanism of gender role socialisations across the sexes (Browne and Chevannes 1998). What we see therefore is the advancement of educational opportunity that was conditioned upon the reproduction of a Eurocentric ideology; characterised in this period, by the establishment of classist and racialised criteria for social inclusion, and, by hegemonic notions and forms of masculinity.

While the involvement of religious entities[3] played a key role in diversifying educational provisions and opportunities in Trinidad and Tobago,

---

[3] Such is the case of the Roman Catholic and Presbyterian churches, just to name a few.

this did not remove the weight associated with socially constituted markers of difference within pre-independence Trinidad and Tobago. In fact, Campbell (1996) contended that the involvement of religious entities added another layer in the hierarchy and criteria for inclusion within the educational system of Trinidad and Tobago; that being, religious affiliation. Such is evident in the rise of church schools; with clear imbalances in the sex, race, class, and religious backgrounds of enrolled students. For Campbell (1996) these patterns of representation within religious/ church schools (as they are often referred to), functioned to create a growing perception of prestige,[4] and a reputational divide between government and religious schools. What emerges therefore in that period is an increasing tension between the church and the state, and growing questions over the legitimacy and authority of either stakeholder in the design and implementation of educational reform. Inadvertently, one can also argue that this both reflected and extended to concerns over the relative influence of the church and the state over (re)engineering of social issues within Trinidad and Tobago.

While the signing of the Concordat in 1960[5] elevated much of these tensions between the church and the state, it did not remove the divisive tendencies that unfolded within the education system. In fact, one perception is that, through their opposition, these religious or denominational schools continued to exert great influence on government policy, and, in the perpetuation of the elitist educational structures (Mohammed 2019). It is against this thinking that Mohammed (2019, p. 175) contended that the "root of the failure of education reform today can be traced to the events that fashioned this dual system [particularly where] the prestige sector influences how state schools are regarded, because the ideologies in the society about education continue to prize denominational schools, and a classical curriculum". What we see therefore is a politics of educational provision that to some extent increased the possibilities for inclusive education in Trinidad and Tobago, but, which failed to disrupt the systemic/structural and ideological underpinnings that affected the democratisation and diversification of that system.

[4] This emerged from the examination of the existing trends within the background of enrolled students and performance of these schools.

[5] The Concordat represented an agreement between the state and denominational school bodies. The agreement allowed for church schools to maintain control and ownership of their schools with a say or choice in the selection of 20 per cent of their intake, and with the responsibilities for the maintenance and payment of salaries assigned to the state.

Such illogicalities around expanding access with restrictions also extended to the secondary levels of education. In fact, on one hand we see that the five-year developmental plan of (1958–1962) introduced free secondary education as a strategic way of widening the secondary school curriculum and that of access to secondary education in Trinidad and Tobago (MOE 1957). On the other hand, analyses of this particular period suggest that this broadening of access did not succeed in weakening or shattering the pervading status quo. This is captured in the early work of Cross and Schwartzbaum (1969, p. 206) who during this critical time posited that the "overall picture which emerges with respect to secondary school selection in Trinidad and Tobago is one where, although considerable inequalities of educational opportunity exist". We also see an inherent argument that students attending the prestige schools, like Queen's Royal College (QRC) and CIC at that time, tended to hold monopolies on the university scholarships (Alleyne 1995; Campbell 1996). In this regard, Nakhid, Barrow, and Broomes (2014) noted that while academic performance served as a legitimate criterion for entry into secondary schools, and, gave the appearance of a socially just processes for inclusion, the enrollment of White students into these perceived prestigious schools, festered growing tensions around issues of equality of opportunity. Examinations of secondary school placements during this period also point to limited opportunities for college and university scholarships, and for accessing alternative pipelines for upward social mobility by the mass majority of the population. In essence therefore, the problem of a rigid social structure remained. Whether this social rigidity unfolded as a consequence of these structural inequalities or inherent distinctions of the cultural capital or social networks of persons who attend these institutions, the outcome remains one that we cannot continue to dismiss. In this sense, inclusivity as a philosophical goal is fundamentally hampered.

Post-independence

With the advent of independence in 1962, the state/government became the major agent of educational change in Trinidad and Tobago. However, an important consideration within the evaluation of educational policy reform during this period is that of the challenge of responding to the imperatives of nationalism and democracy against those of colonialism and elitism that perpetuated therein. It is with an appreciation of the multifarious nature of the independence question that Newton and Braithwaite (1975, pp. 245–246) suggested that:

> The looming of independence…its actual arrival presented formidable challenges. There was no integrated system of education and relatively little secondary or higher education; the population comprised of many races and many religions with no manifest national spirit; unemployment was high and resources low; political independence had to face economic dependence on developed countries and transnational companies; the social attitudes born of slavery, indentured labor and colonialism were well entrenched.

While Newton and Braithwaite (1975) acknowledged that education alone could not address the totality of the independence conundrum, they conceded to the critical role that educational reforms of the post-independence period played in the fractional shift of the educational and national landscape of Trinidad and Tobago. Thus, from a policy perspective, the strategic plans that followed (namely, 1964–1968) represented a real attempt to advance inclusive educational structures and systems; with noted foci on key areas of access, quality, and efficiency (Jules 2008; London 1997a). A significant legislative intervention here was that of the signing of the Education Act of 1966, which granted the state, administrative and managerial authority over pre-primary, primary, secondary and tertiary schools in Trinidad and Tobago. In fact, this 1964–1968 developmental plan served in many ways to legitimise the role and involvement of the state (MOE 1963), and, to activate significant changes (such as those of needed expansion, modification and regularisation, etc.) in the education system (Campbell 1996). Scholars also underscore that this period represented a distinct period of educational expansion; with many achievements in the way of significant expansions in the number of secondary schools,[6] of enrolled students at that level, and, in the number of students who were granted national scholarships, *inter alia* (Alleyne 1995; London 1997a).

However, from the perspective of the state, a fundamental test of that period was that of the ability of the government to balance such goals of equity with that of national sovereignty (London 1997b). In fact, during

---

[6]This period allowed for the development of a two tied system; with the introduction of a number of five year and junior secondary schools.

this period, one observes that Dr. Eric Williams[7] attempted to advance a nationalist education system that allowed for increased control over educational developments in Trinidad and Tobago, the use of a standard or common examination to replace a system of selective entry secondary school, and, a related opening of educational opportunities across racial and ethnic social groups. The latter became evident both in the number and diverse orientations of the schools established. This change process however was obscured by many forms of dualisms. As such, the adoption of the 11+ British examination to that of then named common entrance examination (CEE),[8] and, the assignment of students to government or denominational schools also presented a complex case of equalitarianism, elitism and imperialism. London (1997b) for instance contended that despite the de-Anglocentrification of the curriculum (specifically in areas of history, geography and social studies for instance) and the participatory approach to decision-making around the strategic plan, the language of the policy at the time reflected an acceptance and adoption of modernising principles which pervaded at that time. MacKenzie (1991) also suggested that on a broader scale, an unintended consequence of this move was that of heightening the attention and status of the prestige schools. Such is the case where religious schools placed increasing attention to levels of performance as a criterion for entry. This creates a related problem of access, where limited school spaces existed. Thus, while the Peoples National Movement (PNM) at the time increased the number of government schools, they were generally unsuccessful in creating comparative respect and reputation for these schools in relation to what had already been established for religious schools. In this sense, the marginalisation of the mass majority remained.

This dichotomy also deepened the social divides that obtained and competition for these prestige schools; a challenge which directly influenced the 1968–1983 educational development plan. On a philosophical level, this strategic plan promoted the development of a moral, emotional and intellectual citizenry, ready to engage the challenges associated with a multiracial and developing society like Trinidad and Tobago

---

[7]Dr. Eric Williams served as the Chief Minister of the country (1956–1959), as Premier (1959–1962) and as the 1st Prime Minister from 1956 until his death in 1981. He was also the leader of the Peoples National Movement (PNM).

[8]In more recent times, the examination has been renamed the Secondary Entrance Examination (SEA).

(MOE 1967). This policy pushed for the introduction and development of technical/vocation studies, and, of the establishment of Junior and Secondary Schools; as a noticeable deviation away from an academic orientation which predated the school system before that move. On a practical level however, some of the noticeably inconvenient truths during this period (at least for state officials and policy administrators), were those of poor management of the shift system, the less than complete absorption of junior high students into higher levels of the secondary school system, and with the negativity towards and stereotypes associated with technical and vocational education. While alluding to a drop in the academic performance of students during that period, Campbell (1992) questioned the criteria used to evaluate the relative outcomes of such an initiative, and, the lack of research during that particular period to inform policy evaluations and agendas moving forward. If anything, these tribulations underscored the need for empirically driven educational policy and reforms, which through its very strategic thrusts, attempt to debunked elitist notions of education and schooling. This is particularly important here where dominant ideologies of education continue to privilege academically driven curriculum, assessment types and conceptualisations of educational outcomes; leaving little room for alternative models and outputs. A fundamental failure of such policy reform however was the absence of psychological and sociological aspects of this change process that directly addressed intersectional structuralisms such as socio-economic background of students, gender socialisation, and systems of support available to sustain positive educational outcomes. The debt crisis of the 1980s, and the increasing conditionalities and ideological agendas of international financial institutions (IFIs), who funded these projects further complicated the freedom to determine the ins and outs of this process (Alleyne 1995; Lavia 2007; Jules 2008).

The 1990s however is defined by a stronger effort towards inclusive policy. In fact, ongoing concerns for the structural inequalities and inefficiencies also prompted public policy interventions on local and international fronts. At the local level, we see the appointment of the 1993 National Task Force on Education, or, with a broader call for the revision of educational provision within the context of Trinidad and Tobago (MOE 1994). In fact, this White Paper report which followed, highlighted the many inefficiencies of the education system, and, renewed calls for addressing fundamental issues of equity and inclusion for educational success of all (MOE 1993). In this sense, the issues and processes related to promoting inclusivity are prioritised within educational policy reform. Framed within the vocabulary of democratic and meaningful participation, the policy paper advanced educational initiatives grounded in building interpersonal and intergroup relationships that at a collective level has the potential to address the complexities and challenges of a multicultural, racial and religious society. The participatory style heralded in the policy paper therefore presented a framework from which attention to broader issues of nationhood, sustainability, community emerged.

While not specifying or operationalising the workings of these noble intentions, the policy paper delved into many initiatives associated with improvement of school management, governance, and learning. An inherent failure however was that the policy lacked needed specifications on how these strategic goals would be converted into tangible outcomes for creating an integrated society, or, in the particular role of key stakeholders in the process. This lack of specificity within the policy eventually became a problem of implementation and execution. At the international level, such concerns for structural inequities also prompted the Salamanca Statement (UNESCO 1994), the introduction of the "Education for all" (EFA) policy; both in terms of access and in the mechanisms that were introduced to maximise participation and inclusion. Collectively, these two policy interventions worked in parallel ways to advance a wave of educational projects, initiatives, and practices that attempted to foster inclusive schooling/environments, albeit with growing concerns for the quality of that experience and the relevance of the outcomes.

At the turn of the twenty-first century, Trinidad and Tobago, like many other Caribbean countries, found itself at a peculiar crossroad with many possible endings and turning points. A defining aspect of this period however was that deepening of global interaction and relations with increasing penetration of governing ideologies within the design and implementation of educational policy at a national level. These developments also created a challenge of navigating the mandates of nationalism and that of globalism. While increasing the scope and reach of educational reform, such developments also deepened the complexities of that process. For Jules (2008), Caribbean countries were perched at the centre of multiple paradoxes; where the state was faced with many educational deficits that persisted as legacies of colonialism and in the wake of liberalists reforms that ushered in as many opportunities and challenges, both locally and globally. This changing landscape was certainly reflected in the 2002–2006 Strategic Plan. In fact, the vision of the Ministry of Education (MOE 2002, p. 7) at that time was that of becoming "a pacesetter in the holistic development of an individual through an education system which enables meaningful contributions within the global context". These goals are implicit within the strategic objectives of that period and which aimed to improve issues of quality and equity across all levels. The expectation here is for the sustainable policy development in the education sector fosters a culture of lifelong learning. Here, we see that the attention to the goals of integrity, trust and customer service emerge as key values in the modernisation of the education system, and to the promotion of technological and skills-based learning within that system. No doubt, these strategic goals capture the increasing penetration of neoliberal ideals into the re-envisioning and reform education system in Trinidad and Tobago for the development of a knowledge-based economy. These developments also deepened concerns for the autonomy of the state and for the advancement of strategic goals that are rooted in the understanding of and appreciation for the local dynamics and social fabric of a given society. It is here that we can begin to question whether, [even with some of the commendable prioritizations associated with Early Childhood Care and Education (ECCE), curriculum and assessment reforms, teacher training, and the Secondary Education Modernization Program (SEMP)], these agendas remained responsive to the rich cultural and social heritage that define the peoples of Trinidad and Tobago. This unease is certainly one that warrants further interrogations.

As we respond to global education trends therefore, it is important that we foster and sustain some degree of contextual relativity in the design and implementation of educational policy. For Louisy (2004) this is particularly important given external conceptualisation of quality within educational reform, and, the lack of attention to the cultural difference and richness in the traditions/practices of Caribbean people. It is against such concerns that Jules (2008) however reminds us that while this measure certainly ensures increased access to marginalised or disadvantaged groups within the population, it also holds the threat of hegemonic governance of the planning and development that remains dependent on the funding of International Financial Institutions. The challenge here is that of striking a balance between (if possible), or of taking a position on, the concerns for the provision of access and that of celebrating the multiple capabilities/competencies and intelligences that define multicultural nature of the society. This adds a deeper question of the purpose of education system, and, the process through which the education system responds to diverse interpretations and requirements of the system. This discussion introduces a broader question of how can the education system balance the concerns for the individual (cognitive, emotional, behavioural, characteristics), the community (family, neighbourhood, nation) and national resources (fiscal, professional expertise), with those of the fundamental goals of the education system (dissemination knowledge, fostering skill-based learning and competencies). A related question is that of whether governments within small island states such as Trinidad and Tobago have a collective battery of resources, will power and/or vision to both plan and execute a policy that can radically remove the inequalities that exist within the system. Perhaps bigger questions are those of whether these inequalities can be structurally addressed at a local level, and, relatedly, of what are the global ties that both complicate and reproduce the challenge of creating inclusive educational environments that encourage institutional diversity. The answers to these questions are neither simple nor obvious. However, early theorisations on the social structure of Trinidad and Tobago (as earlier discussed in the chapter), and, evaluations of educational reforms in this context, provide critical starting points.

If we use the work of Ainscow and Miles (2009), then the key areas of interest going forward would be those of removing structural barriers for diverse groups, increasing representation and participation, as well as, enhancing the experiences of and outcomes for diverse learners. These combined foci directly hit at the core of inclusion. Some of these points of reference are evident in the subsequent 2007, Draft National Model for Education in Trinidad and Tobago (MOE 2007). What is evident in the examination of this draft national education model is the direct attention to some of the challenges of inclusion and diversity; whether in the enrolment of students, the measurement of quality, or in the management of these processes. What we also observe within this model is the promotion of key matters; namely, national unity, national culture and the notion of schools as centres of excellence. Conceptually, these key areas within the model connect the dots between learners, teachers, communities and schools; therefore, strengthening the prospects for securing inclusive contexts. One obvious and often neglected caveat in this national model however was that of ongoing research/feasibility studies that can advance knowledge on the role of these connectors within the process of creating inclusive contexts. In the absence of this research at the local level, the MOE underlined in the National Report on the Development of Education in Trinidad and Tobago, the importance of strategic planning and implementation for the education system. Of the many initiatives mentioned within this document, a critical one is that of plans inherent within the promotion of Vision 2020. With attention to seamless education, decentralisation, curriculum and assessment reform, quality management and overhaul of the secondary school system, the strategic interventions seemed more operational than structural. Some of the major achievements of that time however are the introduction of the Universal Secondary School (USE) in 2000 and the establishment of a support services unit within the MOE in 2004 with direct responsibilities for disadvantaged, troubled, marginalised students with emotional, behavioural and learning difficulties. However persistent challenges remained that of the readiness of teachers and other school stakeholders to address the needs of struggling students, while promoting the advancement/achievement of the performing ones.

This task of creating access with quality became the main aspect of the Inclusive Education Policy of 2008. I recognise here that while there was some attention to inclusive systems in the MOE 1993 and 2002 strategic plans, it was the draft policy on Inclusive Education in Trinidad (MOE 2008) which outlined a plan for promoting diversity, equality, participation and partnership among its key stakeholders. In keeping with this inclusive policy and legislative thrust of the Dakar agreement of Education for All, the MOE (2008) also drafted an inclusive policy framework that centred issues of diversity and equity. At the heart of this change was that of the attention to poverty, social barriers to participation and the introduction of school nutrition programme, book loans/rental, transportation programme). While strategising around the expansion of educational opportunities in Trinidad and Tobago, the 2017–2022 Education strategic plan, stressed on the advancement of early childhood education, protocol for placement of students with special needs, teacher training, private–public collaborations to advance these agendas, quality mechanisms to monitor, regulate and evaluate these developments (MOE 2017). While not an exhaustive list, these initiatives capture strategic interventions that can possibly shatter the status quo within the education system. On more specific levels, we see the possibility for reducing the discriminatory practices that exist within the placement of students at the primary level, promoting a well-balanced academic and non-academic curriculum across all levels, and, pushing for more equitable norms and practices of learning for underprivileged and underserved populations in Trinidad and Tobago. Despite these changes, some unrelenting challenges remained. Some of the key areas are discussed below.

Persistent Issues

While we cannot dismiss the many gains within the education systems of the Caribbean,[9] we cannot ignore the many inequalities that obtain within the education system. Miller (2002) for instance noted that despite the many advances of the post-independence era, the focus on nationalism during that era, masked the social divides that were built upon the history of oppression and marginalisation within the region. Miller (2002, p. 5) also called attention to the unfinished agendas of educational reform in the region, where "notwithstanding the impressive gains, the goals of equity and equality of opportunity remain distant for the majority of the Caribbean people...[and]while the barriers of ethnicity, race, and class have been lowered, they have not been removed". The need is therefore for more complex analyses that can potentially close the gaps and reduce the psychological and social effects of race, class, gender inequalities on students from diverse backgrounds.

One pervasive issue within the educational system is that of the under-performance of males. In fact, there is a growing body of research in Trinidad and Tobago that underscores the differences in educational performance; with girls outperforming their male counterparts (De Lisle and Smith 2004; Kutnick et al. 1997; Worrell and Noguera 2011). Such findings have raised more pointed questions about the underlying factors that affect the observed differences between males and female students. Using the lenses of Critical Race Theory, Rampersad (2012) examined the intersection of race and class for the achievement levels of primary school Afro-Trinidadian boys to underscore the disparities in educational

---

[9]Regional scholars for instance continue to recognize the high levels of literacy, steady advanced in early childhood education, enrolment at the primary and secondary levels, stellar performances across a range of examinations and levels, renowned scholars (like C. L. R. James, Eric Williams, George Beckford) and Nobel Laureates (Derek Walcott, Sir Arthur Lewis, Saint-John Perse, and V. S. Naipaul), and educational opportunities up to the highest level of certification, that is doctorate.

outcomes based on race, gender and class. Here, the author argued that race and colour (with reference to whiteness and lightness) provided different access to resources (school type, status, expertise and reputation of teachers and quality of the curriculum) and achievement patterns (where working-class boys more likely to underachieve). Thus, while the right to exclude as obtained under the period of colonialism may not be perceived as an aspect of the contemporary experiences within the education system, the question here is of whether this form of exclusion takes on new manifestations and expressions (in this case, streaming of classes based on learning abilities or cognitive competencies) that continue to disadvantage certain segments of the population along racial, classist and sexist lines. Similarly, Nakhid et al. (2014) contended that the underperformance of Afro-Trinidadian male students underscores the problems related to the legacies of colonialism, racism and elitism within the educational system of Trinidad and Tobago. As a way of counteracting these identities, Escayg and Kinkead-Clark (2019) spoke on the importance of anti-colonial analysis that questions the level of racial awareness, attitudes and identity among school aged children. In their work, the authors call for decolonised praxes that underscore the relational and contextual dynamics that shape children's social and psychological tendencies within the classroom. An important case is being made here for decolonising both space and place; how we practice and live through racial messaging, socialising, symbolic representations and reproductions of these. Even within their work is a call to diverse methodologies and pedagogies that celebrate cultural diversity; such as Afro-centric and Pan-Africanist teaching that (re)names and (re)frames issues of structure, identity and action. These can include anti-colonial lesson plans and activities that offer critical points of intervention and circumvention of these colonialised ideologies and lived realities. Such ideas offer critical praxes for altering the educational system.

The participation of persons who are differently abled also surface as an ongoing concern in Trinidad and Tobago. For Blackman and Conrad (2017), interpersonal conflicts with teachers or peers, teacher preparedness and ineffective methods of engaging students in class remain key areas that are in need of intervention. Similarly, in her examination of special education in the English and Dutch speaking territories of the Caribbean, Lavia (2008) contended the rhetoric of "integration" and "modernisation" did not resolve the historical circumstances of disabled people and/or persons who were perceived to have some degree of learning disability. The argument here being that the region's focus on aptitude as an objective measure of performance and excellence in education, presents a serious dilemma for special education. Lavia (2007) also cautioned against the simultaneous inclusion of children with special needs within mainstream education, but segregation into special classes within that system. The underlining argument here is that the language of "inclusion" and "mainstreaming" reinforce stereotypes, ignorance and suspicion. Thus while universal education initiatives have significantly expanded special needs education and educational provisions for differently-abled children, the physiological and sociological aspects of the experiences that are afforded within the classroom continue to remain unaddressed. The narrow view or reference to inclusion as special education also presents useful points for departure.

CONCLUSION

While enhancement of access to and improvement in educational opportunities remain highly state driven, it sits at the centre of personal, social, cultural and national change. In carving policy agendas for the twenty-first century and beyond, then questions of inclusion and diversity must be nested within considerations of the socio-cultural, structural and political facts of educational reform. In so doing, the push is for celebrating difference; both in terms of how it is sustained and supported to be fully recognised, but also, of how the celebration can begin to (re)define the underlying purpose(s) and goal(s) of our education system. In so doing, Smith (1999) reminds us of the need for: (i) deconstruction and reconstruction, (ii) self-determination within social justice agendas, (iii) historicisation of oppressive practice, and, (iv) ethical considerations. The move forward therefore can no longer be incremental but rather radically to address the systemic deficiencies of the legacies and vestiges of servitude, indifference, self-hate that continues to inflict pain and tension within and between groups in multicultural and racial societies, such as Trinidad and Tobago. The call is also for a postcolonial turn where the rich cultural traditions of the region are embedded within inclusive agendas (Hickling-Hudson 2003) and where new ontologies, epistemologies and methodologies that are grounded in that policy framework (Conrad ans Brown 2008; Louisy 2004). It is here that Lavia's (2006, 2012) writings on "the practice of post-coloniality" and "resisting the inner plantation" become particularly relevant for how we begin to decolonise and re-envision educational policy and practices in Trinidad and Tobago. These present important starting points where we can begin to create socially just measures of inclusion and diversification that are reflective of, and relevant to, the multicultural and complex structures that define our societies.

REFERENCES

Adams, C. J. (2005). Subjectivity, difference and commonalities in the context of gender in the Caribbean. *Caribbean Quarterly: A Journal of Caribbean Culture, 51*(2), 1–13.

Ainscow, M., Booth, T., & Dyson, A. (2006). *Improving schools, developing inclusion*. London and New York: Routledge.

Ainscow, M., & Miles, S. (2009). *Developing inclusive education systems: How can we move policies forward?* Chapter prepared for a book in Spanish to be edited by Climent Gine et al., 2009. Retrieved from http://www.ibe.unesco. org/fileadmin/user_upload/COPs/News_documents/2009/0907Beirut/ DevelopingInclusive_Education_Systems.pdf.

Alleyne, M. (1995). *Nationhood from the schoolbag: A historical analysis of the development of secondary education in Trinidad and Tobago*. Washington: Organization of American States.

Armstrong, F., & Barton, L. (2008). Policy, experience and change and the challenge of inclusive education: The case of England. In L. Barton & F. Armstong (Eds.), *Policy, experience and change: Cross-cultural reflections on inclusive* (pp. 6–18). Dordrecht, Netherlands: Springer.

Bacchus, M. K. (1994). *Education as and for Legitimacy: Developments in West Indian education between 1846 and 1895*. Waterloo, ON: Wilfrid Laurier University Press.

Beckford, G. L. (1972). Institutional foundations of resource underdevelopment in the Caribbean. *The Review of Black Political Economy, 2*(3), 81–101.

Blackman, S., & Conrad, D. A. (2017). The pre-university experiences of students with disabilities in Barbados and Trinidad. *International Journal of Special Education, 32*(2), 238–270. https://files.eric.ed.gov/fulltext/ EJ1184058.pdf.

Booth, T. (1996). Stories of exclusion: Natural and unatural selection. In E. Blyth & J. Miller (Eds.), *Exclusion from school inter-professional issues for policy and practice* (pp. 21–36). London: Routledge.

Braithwaite, L. (1960). Social stratification and cultural pluralism. *Annals of the New York Academy of Sciences, 83*(5), 816–831.

Braithwaite, L. (1975). Problems of race and colour in the Caribbean. *Caribbean Issues: A Journal of Caribbean Affairs, 1*(1), 1–14.

Brown, J., & Chevannes, B. (1998). *Why man stay so: An examination of gender socialization in the Caribbean*. Mona, Jamaica: Caribbean Child Development Center, School of Continuing Studies, The University of the West Indies.

Campbell, C. C. (1996). Society, education and educational expansion 1834–1939: A summary. In C. C. Campbell (Ed.), *The young colonials: A social history of education in Trinidad and Tobago 1834–1939* (pp. 266–282). Kingston: The Press University of the West Indies.

Campbell, C. C. (1992). *A short history of education in Trinidad and Tobago*. Kingston: Ian Randle.

Conrad, D. A., & Brown, L. I. (2008). Dared men leading: Lessons on leadership. In K. Mutua & C. S. Sunal (Eds.), *Undertaking educational challenges in the 21st Century* (pp. 109–129). Charlotte, NC: Information Age.

Central Statistical Office (CSO). (2011). *Population and housing census-demographic report*. Ministry of Planning and Sustainable Development, Government of the Republic of Trinidad and Tobago.

Cross, M., & Schwartzbaum, M. A. (1969). Social mobility and secondary school selection in Trinidad and Tobago. *Social and Economic Studies, 18*(2), 189–207.

De Lisle, J. (2012). Secondary school entrance examination in the Caribbean: Legacy, policy, and evidence within an era of seamless education. *Caribbean Curriculum, 19,* 109–143.

De Lisle, J., & Smith, P. (2004). Secondary school entrance examination in the Caribbean: Legacy, policy, and evidence within an era of seamless education. *Caribbean Curriculum, 11,* 23–55.

Deosaran, R. (2016). *Inequality crime & education in Trinidad and Tobago: Removing the masks*. Trinidad: Ian Randle Publishers.

Escayg, K.-A., & Kinkead-Clark, Z. (2019). Promoting a positive racial identity in young African Caribbean children: An anti-colonial approach. *Journal of Curriculum, Teaching, Learning and Leadership in Education, 4*(2), 29–36.

Hickling-Hudson, A. (2003). Multicultural education and a post-colonial turn. *Policy Futures in Education, 1*(2), 381–401.

Jules, D. (2008). Rethinking education for the Caribbean: A radical approach. *Comparative Education, 44*(2), 202–214.

Kutnick, P., Jules, V., & Layne, A. (1997). *Gender and school achievement in the Caribbean*. London: Department for International Development.

Lavia, J. (2006). The practice of postcoloniality: A pedagogy of hope. *Pedagogy, Culture & Society, 14*(3), 279–293.

Lavia, J. (2007). Girls and special education in the Caribbean. *Support for Learning, 22*(4), 189–196.

Lavia, J. (2008). Inclusive education in Trinidad and Tobago. In L. Barton & F. Armstrong (Eds.), *Policy, experience and change: Cross-cultural reflections on inclusive education* (pp. 107–122). Dordrecht, Netherlands: Springer.

Lavia, J. (2012). Resisting the inner plantation: Decolonisation and the practice of education in the work of Eric Williams. *Postcolonial Directions in Education, 1*(1), 9–30.

London, N. (1997a). Educational planning and its implementation in Trinidad and Tobago. *Comparative Education Review, 41*(3), 314–330.

London, N. (1997b). Sociopolitics in effective curriculum change in a less developed country. *Curriculum Inquiry, 27*(1), 63–80.

Louisy, P. (2004). Whose context for what quality? Informing education strategies for the Caribbean. *Compare, 34*(3), 285–292.

MacKenzie, G. C. (1991). Denominational primary schooling: The case of Trinidad and Tobago. *International Review of Education, 37*(2), 211–226.

Miller, E. (2002). *Education reform in the commonwealth Caribbean.* http://www.iacd.oas.org/Interamer/miller.htm.

Ministry of Education (MOE). (1957). *Five year development program 1958–1962.* MOE, Government of the Republic of Trinidad and Tobago.

Ministry of Education (MOE). (1963). *Second five year development program, 1964–1968.* MOE, Government of the Republic of Trinidad and Tobago.

Ministry of Education (MOE). (1967). *Draft plan for educational development in Trinidad and Tobago 1968–1983.* MOE, Government of the Republic of Trinidad and Tobago.

Ministry of Education (MOE). (1993). *Education policy paper-1993–2003.* MOE, Government of the Republic of Trinidad and Tobago.

Ministry of Education (MOE). (1994). *Report of the National Task Force of education.* MOE, Government of the Republic of Trinidad and Tobago.

Ministry of Education (MOE). (2002). *Strategic plan 2002–2006.* MOE, Government of the Republic of Trinidad and Tobago.

Ministry of Education (MOE). (2007). *Draft-the national model for education in Trinidad and Tobago (Early Childhood, Primary and Secondary).* MOE, Government of the Republic of Trinidad and Tobago.

Ministry of Education (MOE). (2008). *Forty-eighth session of the International Conference on Education (ICE): National report on the development of education in Trinidad and Tobago.* MOE, Government of the Republic of Trinidad and Tobago.

Ministry of Education (MOE). (2017). *Draft of the education policy paper for 2017 to 2022.* The MOE, Government of the Republic of Trinidad and Tobago. https://www.moe.gov.tt/education-policy-paper-2017–2022/.

Mohammed, J. (2019). *Education reform in Trinidad and Tobago through the lens of complexity theory.* https://pdfs.semanticscholar.org/ab11/1a4b90207bd17d65615890dbc35a378f8c5e.pdf.

Nakhid, C., Barrow, D., & Broomes, O. (2014). Situating the education of African Trinidadians within the social and historical context of Trinidad and Tobago: Implications for social justice. *Education, Citizenship and Social Justice, 9*(2), 171–187.

Newton, E., & Braithwaite, H. E. (1975). New directions in education in Trinidad and Tobago: Challenge and response. *Comparative Education, 11*(3), 237–246.

Premdas, R. R. (2002). Identity in an ethnically bifurcated state: Trinidad and Tobago. In S. Fenton & S. May (Eds.), *Ethnonational identities* (pp. 176–197). Basingstoke: Palgrave.

Rampersad, R. (2012). Interrogating pigmentocracy: The intersections of race and social class in the primary education of Afro-Trinidadian boys. In K. Bhopal & J. Preston (Eds.), *Intersectionality and race in education* (pp. 57–75). New York: Routledge.

Smith, L. (1999). *Decolonising methodologies: Research and indigenous peoples*. London: Zed Books.

Smith, M. G. (1955). *A framework for Caribbean studies: Caribbean affairs.* Extra-Mural Department, University College of the West Indies.

Smith, M. G. (1960). Social and cultural pluralism. *Annals of the New York Academy of Sciences, 83*(5), 763–777.

Smith, M. G. (1984). *Culture, race and class in the commonwealth Caribbean.* Department of Extra Mural Studies, The University of the West Indies.

Taylor, S., Rizvi, F., Lingard, B., & Henry, M. (1997). *Educational policy and the politics of change.* London: Routledge.

UNESCO. (1994). *Final report: World conference on special needs education: Access and quality.* Paris: UNESCO.

UNESCO. (2018). *Global education meeting, Brussels declaration.* https://unesdoc.unesco.org/ark:/48223/pf0000366394?posInSet=1&queryId=f00b-beb5-caf0-495d-9782-e4caad1e9e0f.

Watson, H. (2001). Theorizing the racialization of global politics and the Caribbean experience. *Alternatives: Global, Local, Political, 26*(4), 449–483.

Wilder, J. A. (2015). *Color stories: Black women and colorism in the 21st century.* Santa Barbara, CA: Praeger.

Worrell, F., & Noguera, P. (2011). Educational attainment of Black males: Views of male secondary school students in Trinidad and Tobago. *The Caribbean Journal of Teacher Education and Pedagogy, 2,* 7–23.

CHAPTER 11

Conclusion

Diversity, equality and inclusion are emerging areas of research in the English-speaking Caribbean. This collection sought to explore these areas as they relate to politics, employment and education, as well as social and legal systems in this region. Threaded throughout this collection, therefore, are the concepts of equality and non-discrimination, which are understood as positive and negative statements of the same principle, key to promoting diversity and inclusion. The authors adopt the position, therefore, that one is treated equally when one is not discriminated against and one is discriminated against when one is not treated equally (Besson 2005). Equality, in this sense, is deemed to be a positive duty on the part of States to promote measures that advance equality, while non-discrimination is a negative duty of restraint designed to suppress acts of unequal treatment of persons by the State (see Fredman 2016; Equality Rights Trust 2014). Importantly, equality and non-discrimination must recognise difference, otherwise the concepts become irrelevant. In such cases, these raise questions of equity, reinforcing the appreciation of instances in which an individual must be treated differently in order to protect his or her right to equality (Persadie 2012). This would also be recognition of diversity. Once diversity is acknowledged and appreciated, it can be harnessed to the benefit of an organisation, which would lead to inclusion.

This volume, therefore, presents some useful starting points for thinking through current landscapes and complexities related to inclusion,

© The Author(s) 2020   233

J. H. Stephenson et al., *Diversity, Equality,*
and Inclusion in Caribbean Organisations and Society,
https://doi.org/10.1007/978-3-030-47614-4_11

equality and diversity. To do so, the authors attempted to situate these notions within an analysis of institutional contexts (e.g. education, labour market, government and legal systems), their histories, structures and relational dynamics that are (re)produced therein. By taking this evaluative stance, the authors affirm the need for critical reflections and actions that fundamentally address the gaps and deficiencies within broader inclusivity agendas, while advancing noted achievements, possibilities and potential threats that obtain within institutional frameworks. What unfolds throughout these chapters, then, are multiple perspectives and treatments of equality, diversity and inclusion that both contextualise and problematise the strategies for promoting inclusive societies within the Caribbean. While not exhausting institutional frames of analysis related to inclusion, the volume offers a useful starting point for more pointed theorisation and advancement of policy and advocacy that challenge discriminatory practices, whether on the basis of sex, gender, sexual orientation, disability, race, ethnicity or class. The extent of these contributions is captured within the chapters of the volume.

In Chapter 2, Bissessar speaks to the "challenges of ethnic assimilation in an ex-colonial society of Trinidad and Tobago". An important aspect of this chapter is that of dispelling some of the myths of common value and consensus that undergird notions of representative bureaucracy. In fact, through her examination of the mechanisms by which ethnic groups are accommodated in the context of Trinidad and Tobago, Bissessar interrogates notions of public sector representation and assimilation for major ethnic groups. This is done as a way of centring the persistent problems of inclusivity within multicultural societies, where two dominant ethnic groups reside. By delving into historical allegations of discrimination and ethnic polarisation within the political sphere and public service, the chapter provides an insightful gaze into the mechanisms for and outcomes of ethnic accommodation. Part of this interrogation involves a discussion on the relational and constitutional challenges associated with multicultural or plural societies and the peculiar considerations that these present for public policy formation and public or civil engagement. When such tensions are examined through institutional dynamics, such as the ethnic leanings of, or affiliations within, the public sector, then one begins to appreciate the importance of legislative and ideological considerations within the workings and dynamics of representative bureaucracies. It is through such pointed discussions on the socio-cultural dynamics of Trinidad and Tobago that Bissessar underscores some of the inherent failures of these legislative mechanisms that were established to promote ethnic assimilation. These deliberations raise more pointed questions on how public sector institutions address claims of ethnic imbalances or disparities in the context of multicultural societies and racial cleavages. These discussions also underscore the need for deeper considerations of how these legislative or constitutional mechanisms both aid and/or hinder ethnic assimilation and social inclusion in such multicultural contexts. Collectively, these are employed as a strategic way of drawing on persistent forms of inequalities and claims of discrimination that continue in the contemporary period to trouble ethnic assimilation in Trinidad and Tobago.

Chapter 3 provides a theoretical review of equality and discrimination at the workplace. The inherent focus of the chapter is on the extent to which sexes are equitably perceived, how gender stereotyping and identities affect interaction within the workplace, and how these affect patterns of workforce integration across the Caribbean. An important contribution of this chapter, therefore, is in the centring of workplace practice, perspectives and (in)action. It is through the focus on sex, gender and organisations that Stephenson speaks to the gendered divisions of labour that exist and the extent to which gender expectations, if unchecked, can lead to divergent opportunities available to men and women in relation to remuneration, leadership, control and promotional opportunities (Acker 1990, 2006). This is particularly true of management positions, which the literature shows is largely related to family obligations. It is noted, too, that this is compounded by the fact that organisations may deem women a liability and not invest in development opportunities for them, which in turn negatively affects the possibility of promotion (ILO 2018). It is through a review of the organisational perspective or "business case argument" that Stephenson also discusses practices related to anti-discrimination in the workplace that underlie the many benefits for organisations. Such benefits include profitability, diverse workforce, widened customer base, competitive advantage, positive employer image, improved organisational performance, enhanced creativity and innovation, international awareness, better decision-making and problem-solving, flexibility, better work environment and employee satisfaction (Allard 2002; Cornelius et al. 2001; Robinson and Dechant 1997; Singh et al. 2002). While Stephenson recognises that such benefits are not easily measurable, particularly given considerations for the profit motive on which organisations are founded, she underlines the strengths and possibilities within anti-discriminatory practices for mitigating against gender stereotyping and prejudicing within the development of human resources and, particularly, the advancement of women within the organisation. These however, are certainly not without their challenges (see Chapter 8).

Chapter 4 focusses on discrimination on the basis of sexual orientation. This remains an inherently controversial social and legal issue in the Caribbean due to very conservative religious and social mores. Here, Stephenson presents a useful overview of the statutory provisions of ten Caribbean countries that criminalise buggery which carry varying penalties (Table 4.1), relics of the colonial era. Interestingly, "buggery" is not always defined in the respective law nor does it always refer only to sexual activity in same-sex relationships. Stephenson notes, in this sense, that criminal prosecution is unlikely where sexual preferences and behaviours are kept private. Nevertheless, one notes that there is a real fear of victimisation and discrimination faced by members of this group. In this chapter, Stephenson notes that while three Caribbean countries have developed anti-discrimination legislation (namely, Guyana, St Lucia, and Trinidad and Tobago), each of these notably omits sexual orientation as a ground of discrimination, on the basis of the laws criminalising certain intimate behaviours. This is certainly evident in the case of court actions or lawsuits taken by advocacy groups to change the law, albeit with varying degrees of success. Undoubtedly, these prejudices carry over to the workplace. Stephenson remarks, in this case, that the absence of anti-discrimination legislation on the grounds of sexual orientation means that employers can legitimately discriminate against job applicants and employees on the grounds of their sexual orientation without fear of prosecution, though, not all employers are inclined to behave in this way. The strength of this chapter, therefore, is in the way in which Stephenson begins to unsettle persistent acts of discrimination, resistance to the decriminalisation of homosexuality in the Caribbean, and an appreciation of the ripple effects of these for workplace incivility and employee engagement. It is here that the typology of workplace change, which she offers in this chapter, presents a critical response to the advocacy for non-discrimination on the grounds of sexual orientation. The usefulness of this model is in how it advances non-discrimination on the grounds of sexual orientation, and workplace policies that promote fair procedures, namely, bureaucratisation of decision-making processes, and implementation of non-discriminatory practices (Jewson and Mason 1986, 1993). The push here is also for categories of change that are reflected in agenda-setting by workplaces in the areas of non-discrimination considered important; the establishment of equal opportunity policies; and data collection and monitoring of the workforce (Dickens et al. 2005). The spectrum of anticipated change ranges from no change; minimal change; change of selected aspects of practice; to comprehensive workplace change (Goss and Adam-Smith 2001; Kirton and Greene 2006; Laughlin 1991). This model is largely informed by legislation that is enacted to prohibit discrimination on the basis of sexual orientation and its implementation would vary depending on the workplace. A salient point of this chapter is that the existence of legislation will not necessarily effect immediate societal change and that any such change required by law is likely to be incremental.

In Chapter 5, Stephenson presents a review of discrimination as it relates to the employment of persons with disabilities. This chapter is grounded within concerns for the high prevalence of disability based on sight and mobility (Table 5.4), the levels of employment rates for persons with disabilities in the Caribbean (see Table 5.4) and the attribution of disabilities in this region to the availability and standard of health care, lifestyle choices, accidents, dietary options and safety standards (Jones and Serieux-Lubin 2018; Schmid et al. 2008). It is against such concerns that she also acknowledges that, while there are five Caribbean countries that have enacted legislation that deals with disability either as part of general equality legislation or separately, these remain limited by the use of a medial model to think through notions of disability. However, it is the treatment of the discrimination against persons with disabilities that allows for critical assessments of the accommodations that have been designed to encourage both representation and participation within the workplace. She notes here that, while Caribbean legislation, where enacted, does require employers to make reasonable accommodations for persons with disabilities, this is not meant to impose hardship on the employer. Such accommodations may include, but are not limited to, sign language or other interpreters; environmental or assistive devices; assistive technology or equipment; job restructuring; or personal assistance, all of which may influence whether and the extent to which persons with disabilities are able to actively participate in the labour market (Colella and Bruyere 2011; Ren et al. 2008; Vornholt et al. 2018). While such accommodations must be specific to the individual impairment experienced, they are not usually costly; nevertheless, there remains an unwillingness by employers to hire persons with disabilities. She notes in this chapter that this is compounded by weak equality legislation and governmental policies; attitudinal barriers; lack of government support; and infrastructural barriers, including accessibility of buildings and public transport. Stephenson remarks, therefore, that there needs to be a systematic and multipronged stakeholder approach to addressing the difficulties experienced by persons with disabilities within legal, social, political and economic spheres.

In Chapter 6, Bissessar engages in a comparative analysis of the experiences of inclusivity within the political histories and experiences of two plural societies within the Caribbean region, namely, Guyana and Trinidad and Tobago. In presenting this work, a major contention is that of the significance of the political structures and systems of these two Commonwealth Caribbean countries to the observed failures within inclusive political agendas. Of note in this discussion were the particular challenges of working through two-party systems (albeit under different models of government) and politics of representation and segmentation that resulted within such constitutional and structural frameworks. Within this discussion is a treatment of the social categories of difference (race, class and ethnicity) and the implications of these for the political structures, dynamics and tensions that obtain over the questions of resources, power and authority. From this perspective, Bissessar takes issue with the notion of democratic structures and reflects on the appearance of an ethnic consensus within the voting patterns and representations that follow. By so doing, the chapter repositions structural issues of race and ethnicity within the political landscape of these two countries. In this case, the examination of general elections in these two countries presents an opportunity, not just to rethink ethnic relations within multicultural societies, but also to underscore the contentious ways in which such contexts (re)produce ethnic tribalism, which ultimately influences major political outcomes and prospects for governing such societies. A major contention within this chapter, therefore, is that ethnic boundaries and distinctions served to delineate social, occupational and political affiliations, a reality which, for this author, equated to the politics of divide and rule. Using declassified files, reviews of legal dispatch letters during particular voting periods, constitutional amendments for Guyana and voting patterns across both countries, Bissessar offers a critical review of the race, ethnicity and politics nexus, and the complications that arise. One notes, therefore, that whether under the auspices of a hybridised model of representation or that of the traditional Westminster Whitehall model, ethnic tribalism presents strong social and political realities that continue to disrupt inclusive agendas within these contexts.

In Chapter 7, Persadie provides an overview of the equality laws that exist in the Caribbean region, based on current statute that provides for equality or non-discrimination in a broad manner and, more specifically, for employment purposes. A useful starting point, therefore, is in the reiteration that equality serves as a positive duty on the part of States to promote measures that advance equality, while non-discrimination is a negative duty of restraint designed to suppress acts of unequal treatment of persons by the State (see Fredman 2016; Equality Rights Trust 2014). As a way of deliberating on this, Persadie reviews the relevant legislation of the twelve independent English-speaking Caribbean countries to evaluate the strategies that have been used to address issues of equality and non-discrimination. She notes that, of these twelve, just two countries have general equality legislation: Guyana and Trinidad and Tobago, but only the latter has established an institutional framework to administer the legislation, the efficacy of which is very briefly considered. Apart from constitutional provisions guaranteeing equality before the law in all twelve countries and equality at work in five (Persadie 2012), the existence of law that addresses equality broadly in the Caribbean is not as widespread as one would hope but tends rather to focus on equality in the workplace. She shows, nevertheless, that legislation addressing equality generally and in the workplace covers numerous grounds of discrimination with the very notable exception of sexual orientation (except in the case of Barbados, which is only very recently included this in its prevention of discrimination in employment legislation), on the one hand, and the interesting inclusion of HIV/AIDS, on the other. She remarks also that Caribbean legislation reflects both the positive duty of states to promote measures that advance equality, to varying degrees, as well as the negative duty to refrain from treating persons differently based on their status or any named ground of discrimination. These assessments are used to argue that there is still a long road ahead for the establishment of legal and institutional frameworks to address equality and non-discrimination in the Caribbean. In fact, Persadie suggests that for countries that have not yet contemplated such a framework, bearing in mind certain jurisdictional limitations and specific national needs, the model found in Trinidad and Tobago can provide a useful starting point for consideration and adaptation, if not for wholesale replication.

Given current global discussions on diversity and inclusion, Persadie offers in Chapter 8 a review of the equality legislation of Guyana,

Trinidad and Tobago, the United Kingdom and the United States of America to compare the Caribbean legislative approach to that of the selected developed countries. The focus here is on law that is not specific to the workplace only, but to society generally. Whereas the equality legislation in each country tended to originally focus on employment issues, it later expanded to cover various civil rights. Persadie notes, in this case, that the evolution of anti-discrimination law differed significantly between the UK and the USA. In the USA, for example, this saw a century-long struggle evolve over various grounds of discrimination: class, geographic/national origin, culture, ethnicity, religion and race. Disability was also addressed but not as a ground that saw the type of lobbying required for the others. She contends that, in the final round, gender is still being hotly debated with respect to its formal inclusion in the law, but the Supreme Court's recent ruling that sexual orientation and gender identity are prohibited grounds of discrimination in the workplace is certainly noted. In the UK, she suggests that there was no such similar struggle nor did equality legislation have such a long history. Anti-discrimination legislation in the UK was partially based on domestic initiatives as well as European Union Directives. Equality legislation focused, in the early stages, on race, then sex. Other grounds—age, disability, religion or belief, and sexual orientation—were eventually addressed and a few more were added to the consolidated *Equality Act* 2010. She shows that Guyana's legislation covers the largest number of prohibited grounds of discrimination of the four countries, with a focus on fifteen, while Trinidad and Tobago's law addresses seven grounds. Through this critical comparative analysis of legislative frameworks, Persadie makes a credible case for contextualising legislation, both in terms of what they attempted to address and the effectiveness of the strategies used to do so. Moreover, she makes several recommendations for what Caribbean equality legislation could include to be more comprehensive and effective. In the Caribbean legislation (with the notable exception of Barbados), and to some extent that of the USA too, sexual orientation and gender identity have been very consciously omitted, due to prevailing conservative social mores (see also Chapter 7). Persadie comments here that the exclusion of sexual orientation and gender identity from their respective equality laws is tantamount to a denial of the rights of persons in these groups. The law needs to be flexible enough to address ever-changing social issues as they arise, otherwise it cannot be said that true equality is legally available to all, nor are diversity and inclusion properly addressed. Although the prohibited grounds of discrimination vary from country to country, the notion of equality in the statutory provisions where they do exist recognises difference and seeks to provide redress, all the while balancing conservative interests. Any shortcomings of the Caribbean legislation aside, the fact that the countries chose to address equality legislatively should be viewed as a positive step. These discussions are used to show that, with advocacy, the laws can eventually be amended to reflect current social realities.

In Chapter 9, Esnard examines the liberalising contexts of higher education to situate the challenge of diversity and inclusion for higher education institutions in the Caribbean. This she frames within broader patterns of global education, the logic of the market, and of neoliberal regimes that continue to restructure both the landscape and the processes within the delivery and governance of higher education in the region. A key contribution of this chapter is in its attention to the challenges of privatisation for the recognition and celebration of diversity, both in terms of the particularities within the curriculum, and the philosophies that underlie the visions and/or missions of these institutions. These present critical discussions of how to mitigate against broader patterns of homogenisation and marketisation that sweep through the corridors of higher education. In so doing, this chapter therefore presents a critical analysis of the structural and ideological thrusts of higher educational reform, the opportunities and constraints that these create, and the responsiveness of Caribbean institutions of higher education within that matrix. What has been learnt, therefore, is how these connections between structural forms of inequalities problematise the dual goals of diversity and inclusion within the context of higher education. As a way of moving beyond the challenge of systemic inequalities within higher education, whether on the micro or macro scale, Esnard pushes for deeper interrogations and interventions that confront the marginalising effects of class, gender and race divides, at one level, and those of the philosophical mooring that undergird knowledge exchange and dissemination on the other. On one level, these bring to the fore the many clashes between the ideologies, epistemologies and ontologies that govern international collaboration within the academic market. On another level, these also raise deeper concerns for the subjective realities of Caribbean institutions of higher education, the extent to which globalising trends challenge fundamental issues, diversity in how identities are being revered and preserved, in the level of autonomy that is present to do so, and in the extent to which national and regional goals remain central to the underlying orientations and projections of these institutions.

In Chapter 10, Esnard presents a critical treatise on inclusive education policy agendas in a multicultural and racial society like Trinidad and Tobago. Taking a critical policy approach, Esnard delves into an evaluation of educational policy agendas to show the inherent weaknesses within inclusive educational reforms. While Esnard acknowledges the significance of exogenous (e.g. Eurocentric models of education, ideological conditions of the international funding) and endogenous factors for educational reform (e.g. the political priorities and expediencies of ruling governments), she argues that a fundamental failure of educational reform for Trinidad and Tobago is in the inability to address systemic structural issues that continue to affect desires for more equitable distribution of resources and creation of opportunities for all. A major push within this chapter, therefore, is that of building inclusive or socially just educational systems, supported by policy framework and legislative structures that directly confront systemic forms of inequalities. This call raises more pointed questions of how to rethink and rebuild the education system to accommodate the multiple voices and realities of those which it is built to serve, and also to maximise the potential for all in that process. The push is also needed for reflection on pertinent issues of conscientisation and resistance as a critical aspect of de-colonialising existing social and educational systems that continue to oppress and marginalise vulnerable groups within the population. These are presented as important ways of (re)naming, (re)framing and (re)building social and cultural capital that expand beyond racialised presentations and classist ideological frameworks that permeate the current education system.

IMPLICATIONS FOR POLICY, RESEARCH AND PRACTICE

The chapters in this volume stress on the multiple challenges that persist in advancing inclusive agendas in the Caribbean. In moving beyond the current state of affairs on matters of inclusion and diversity in the Caribbean, it is important to advance relevant understandings and interventions that remain structurally relevant. Given such, a call is made for deeper interrogations of diversity and inclusion in the Caribbean that treat with the following issues:

i. Policy design, implementation and inclusive agendas
ii. The politics of identity and inclusivity
iii. Race, ethnicity and democracy in multicultural societies
iv. Racialised identities and social mobility
v. Social and legal inequalities and equity
vi. Culturally relevant notions of inclusion
vii. Celebration of diversity in sexual orientation and disability, across gender, age, race, ethnicity, marital status, place of origin and class
viii. Relevance and effects of affirmative action for institutional change
ix. Democratisation, inclusion and self-determination
x. Internationalisation, cultural imperialism and institutional fragmentation.

As scholars in diverse disciplines (management, politics, law and sociology), we all recognise the many challenges that affect the promotion of inclusive societies. While we remain cognisant of the nuances across institutional contexts and disciplinary perspectives, we see much value in underscoring the complexities and multiplicities within notions of inclusivity and diversity for our Caribbean societies. This volume, therefore, represents both a check on how much we have advanced these agendas in the Caribbean, and of the need for greater theorisation and actualisation of policy initiatives that remain responsive to the contextual realities of our societies. While addressing some of these issues may awaken systemic deficiencies of institutions, and deepen our concerns for equity and social justice, we also see these interrogations and recommendations as an important part of envisioning policy, legal, institutional and, by extension, societal change. Our hope is also that such scholarship will raise greater levels of awareness around issues that affect social inequality, and encourage others to push back against discriminatory practices that curtail the possibilities for authenticity, liberty and integrity at the micro and macro levels.

REFERENCES

Acker, J. (1990). Hierarchies, jobs, bodies: A theory of gendered organizations. *Gender and Society, 4*(2), 139–158.

Acker, J. (2006). Inequality regimes: Gender, class, and race in organizations. *Gender and Society, 20*(4), 441–464.

Allard, M. (2002). Theoretical underpinnings of diversity. In C. Harvey & M. Allard (Eds.), *Understanding and managing diversity*. Upper Saddle River, NJ: Prentice-Hall.

Besson, S. (2005). The principle of non-discrimination in the convention on the rights of the child. *The International Journal of Children's Rights, 13*, 433–461.

Colella, A. J., & Bruyère, S. M. (2011). Disability and employment: New directions for industrial and organizational psychology. In *APA handbook of industrial and organizational psychology, Vol 1: Building and developing the organization* (pp. 473–503). Washington, DC: American Psychological Association.

Cornelius, N., Gooch, L., & Todd, S. (2001). Managing difference fairly: An integrated 'partnership' approach. In M. Noon & E. Ogbonna (Eds.), *Equality, diversity and disadvantage in employment*. Palgrave: Basingstoke.

Dickens, L., Hall, M., & Wood, S. (2005). *Review of research into the impact of employment relations legislation*. Employment Relations Research Series No. 45. London: Department of Trade and Industry (DTI).

Equality Rights Trust. (2014). *Economic and social rights in the courtroom: A litigator's guide to using equality and non-discrimination strategies to advance economic and social rights*. London: Equal Rights Trust.

Fredman, S. (2016). Substantive equality revisited. *International Journal of Constitutional Law, 14*(3), 712–738. https://doi.org/10.1093/icon/mow043.

Goss, D., & Adam-Smith, D. (2001). Pragmatism and compliance: Employer responses to the working time regulations. *Industrial Relations Journal, 32*(3), 195–209.

International Labour Organization. (2018). *Gender at work in the Caribbean—Synthesis report for five countries*. Geneva, Switzerland: International Labour Organization.

Jewson, N., & Mason, D. (1986). The theory and practice of equal opportunities policies: Liberal and radical approaches. *The Sociological Review, 34*(2), 307–334.

Jewson, N., & Mason, D. (1993). *Equal employment opportunities in the 1990s: A policy principle come of age?* University of Leicester, Department of Sociology.

Jones, F., & Serieux-Lubin, L. (2018). *Disability, human rights and public policy in the Caribbean: A situation analysis (No. 64)*. Naciones Unidas Comisión Económica para América Latina y el Caribe (CEPAL).

Kirton, G., & Greene, A. (2006). *The dynamics of managing diversity* (2nd ed.). Oxford: Elsevier Butterworth Heinemann.

Laughlin, R. (1991). Environmental disturbances and organizational transitions and transformations—Some alternative models. *Organization Studies, 12*(2), 209–232.

Persadie, N. (2012). *A critical analysis of the efficacy of law as a tool to achieve gender equality.* Lanham, MD: University Press of America.

Ren, L. R., Paetzold, R. L., & Colella, A. (2008). A meta-analysis of experimental studies on the effects of disability on human resource judgments. *Human Resource Management Review, 18*(3), 191–203.

Robinson, G., & Dechant, K. (1997). Building a business case for diversity. *The Academy of Management Executive, 11*(3), 21–31.

Schmid, K., Vézina, S., & Ebbeson, L. (2008). *Disability in the Caribbean. A study of four countries: A Socio-demographic analysis of the disabled (Vol. 7).* United Nations Publications.

Singh, V., Kumra, S., & Vinnicombe, S. (2002). Gender and impression management: Playing the promotion game. *Journal of Business Ethics, 37*(1), 77–89.

Vornholt, K., Villotti, P., Muschalla, B., Bauer, J., Colella, A., Zijlstra, F., et al. (2018). Disability and employment—Overview and highlights. *European Journal of Work and Organizational Psychology, 27*(1), 40–55.

INDEX

CPI Antony Rowe
Eastbourne, UK
September 23, 2020